Regent's St
General Editor:

C000061277

# A Cry in the Darkness

*The Forsakenness of Jesus in Scripture,*
*Theology and Experience*

Regent's Study Guides

# A Cry in the Darkness
## The Forsakenness of Jesus in Scripture, Theology and Experience

Anthony J. Clarke

Regent's Park College, Oxford
*with*
Smyth & Helwys Publishing, Inc.
Macon, Georgia

*A Cry in the Darkness: The Forsakenness of Jesus in Scripture, Theology and Experience*

Anthony J. Clarke

© 2002
Published by Regent's Park College, Oxford OX1 2LB, UK
in association with Smyth & Helwys Publishing, 6316 Peake Road,
Macon, GA 31210, USA

A Cry in the Darkness: The Forsakenness of Jesus in Scripture, Theology and Experience / Anthony
J. Clarke
    p. cm. — (Regent's study guides; 10)
       Includes bibliographical references and index.

    ISBN (UK)0-9518104-9-9 (pbk.)
    ISBN (USA)1-57312-402-8 (pbk.)

    1. Jesus Christ—Seven last words. 2. Suffering—Religious aspects—Christianity. 3. Bible. N.T.
Mark XV, 34—Criticism, interpretation, etc.—Germany—History—20th century. I. Title. II. Series.

    BT457 .C57 2002
    232.96'35—dc21

                                                                                    2002006634

# Contents

**To Amanda**

---

Strange way to hang around for hours
Strange way to imitate a kite
Strange way to get a view of Auschwitz
Strange way to represent the light

Strange dissident of meekness
And nurse of tangled souls
And so unlike the holy
To end up full of holes
Strange way

'Strange Way'
from Martyn Joseph's album *Tangled Souls*

# Acknowledgements

This book began life as a thesis for a research degree at the University of Oxford. My supervisor was the Rev. Dr. Paul S. Fiddes, Principal of Regent's Park College, who has since edited the rewritten manuscript for this publication. I am deeply grateful to Paul for all his gracious support, for without his time, encouragement, and critical debate over ten years the thesis and the book would never have been written. Having become very familiar with this work during this time, I am grateful too for his faith that it would be a suitable book to be included in the *Regent's Study Guide* series. Two people in particular read and re-read chapters, checking for mistakes and suggesting how the English could be improved, and so my thanks go to my Father, Jim Clarke, and to Chris Holmwood. My wife, Amanda, has endured my long evenings at the computer to meet publication deadlines as well as providing support in all manner of ways through the years. The dedication of this book to her expresses my profound thanks.

The lyrics of the song, 'Strange Way,' by Martyn Joseph, copyright ©1998 The Grapevine Label Ltd., are reproduced by kind permission of Grapevine Music and Waif Music.

# Foreword

On Sunday 15 September 1963, in the midst of the civil rights movement in the United States of America, a bomb exploded in 16th Street Baptist Church, Birmingham, Alabama. It had been planted by white extremists. Four girls, Denise McNair, Carole Robertson, Addie Mae Collins, and Cynthia Wesley, were killed by the blast, which badly damaged the church. A major stained glass window, which depicted a very pastoral image of Jesus, largely escaped damage – it was only the face of Jesus that was blown out. One year after the bombing, the 16th Street Baptist Church received a gift from the people of Wales, a new stained glass window, this time portraying Jesus as he hung on the cross. This window, which encapsulates solidarity in the midst of suffering, is now mounted above the main entrance of the church.

In South Oxford Baptist Church, where I am currently the minister, a number of visual symbols have been placed to make the building of the church a more inspiring place to worship. My predecessor at South Oxford visited the church in Birmingham, Alabama, and, struck by what she saw, produced a copy of this window, which now hangs on the front wall of the church. I have frequently both preached in front of it and sat and looked it. The window is reproduced on the front cover of the book, by kind permission.

# 1
# Introduction: Seeing Salvation Strangely

## 1. The cross

There is a town in Nepal, to the south-west of Kathmandu, in which stands a church. It is small and simple, with an unpainted mud front and one narrow door. There are no decorations and no notice-boards, nothing to signify that this is a church building rather than just another house. For in Nepal the freedom of worship was severely curtailed in the late 1980s, and the open preaching of Christianity was forbidden. There is no sign to indicate a church, except that on the apex of the roof two pieces of wood hold the electricity wire that comes from a neighbouring building, goes into the church and then on to the house next door. One piece of wood is about three feet high and the other piece, about two feet wide, is nailed across it. To a government official it is simply a practical device to hold the cables. But the small group of Christians, as they come to worship, see the unmistakable shape of the cross. If there is any imaginative power in signs, then the cross must be one of the most powerful. Through the centuries it has called the Christian church to prayer, overshadowed the church's worship and critiqued its theology. The cross has always been the most potent of symbols.

Now if we were able to somehow step outside our own familiarity with the cross, and the fashionable gloss with which the bare wood is so often covered, we might consider its importance to be something strange. On the one hand, our irrepressible desire for some kind of natural theology that celebrates power and glory and fame has always struggled with understanding the God who is revealed in the depths of the cross. Humanly speaking it *is* strange that those who claim to worship the one God, creator of all, should meet around a cross. On the other hand, governments which have rejoiced in their own all-embracing authority have banished the lowly cross from public view. Humanly speaking it *is* strange that those with such power have feared the weakness of the cross.

But it is a cross, in its imaginative construction, that is the pinnacle of that small church in Nepal. It is also, now, an image of Jesus dying on the cross which greets the worshippers at the restored 16th Street Baptist Church, Birmingham, Alabama, whose story is told in the Foreword above. For the church, in all its historical, geographical and theological breadth, has always understood salvation to be focused on the death of Jesus on the cross. Even in our own familiarity, we recognize that the cross speaks of depths in God's relationship with the world which we find hard to fathom.

One aspect of the death of Jesus that resonates with our general understanding is that of sacrifice, far removed though we are from the Jewish sacrificial system, for many a good story tells of the sacrifice of one for the sake of another. For example, in the recent popular film *Titanic*, Jack, the happy-go lucky hero, does all that is in his power to ensure that Rose, his new found love, survives the sinking of the unsinkable ship, even though he himself dies in the water. There is the sense in the film that Jack not only physically saves Rose from the water, but as a result of their whole relationship, Rose is freed to live a new life. We may, therefore, not be surprised that Jesus refused to back down in the face of opposition, but continued to defend the poor and vulnerable and preach the kingdom of God, accepting the consequences. That such a cruel means of torture and execution becomes so potent a symbol for those who followed is equally understandable, for it signified the great love and commitment at the heart of Jesus' ministry.

What is significant, but also somewhat strange, is that Christian theology has understood the cross to be the most crucial act of God. The whole of salvation, with all its implications for a suffering-free eternal life with God, characterized by peace, harmony and worship, and whether it has been understood mainly in terms of the salvation of soul or the creation of a new heaven and earth, rests upon the execution of this Jewish teacher. In the exodus of the people of Israel from Egypt, the great salvation story of the Old Testament, the first-born of the Egyptians are slain and Pharaoh's armies are drowned in the Red Sea. God's people are saved by a mighty act of God which is described in military terms. Christian theologians have also spoken of the cross as no less of a victory, but one in which the *weakness* of the cross both reveals the love of God, and also effects our salvation. In Barth's well known phrase, that so well describes the shocking reality of the cross, 'God wills to lose, in order that man may gain'.[1] Faced with the cosmic significance of an event that inverts so many of our natural assumptions, there is a real sense that when we enter the vast majority of church buildings, with a cross on the wall, we see salvation strangely.

## 2. The darkness

There is a book called *Night*, by Holocaust survivor Eli Wiesel, which is a narrative reflection on suffering against the personal background of fervent Jewish faith. In it there is the now famous account of the boy on the gallows hanging between life and death.

> The three victims mounted together on to the chairs.
> The three necks were placed at the same moment within the nooses.
> "Long live liberty!" cried the two adults.
> But the child was silent.
> "Where is God? Where is He?" Someone behind me asked.
> At a sign from the head of the camp, the three chairs tipped over.
> Total silence throughout the camp. On the horizon, the sun was setting.
> "Bare your heads!" yelled the head of the camp. His voice was raucous.
> We were weeping.
> "Cover your heads!"
> Then the march past began. The two adults were no longer alive. Their tongues hung swollen, blue-tinged. But the third rope was still moving; being so light, the child was still alive . . .
> For more than half an hour he stayed there, struggling between life and death, dying in slow anger under our eyes.
> Behind me I heard the same man asking:
> "Where is God now?"
> And I heard a voice within me answer him:
> "Where is he? Here He is – He is hanging here on this gallows . . ."
> That night the soup tasted of corpses.[2]

Over the last thirty-five years this story has challenged and provoked many theologians, to the point that the very legitimacy of reading

Wiesel's Jewish story in a Christian context, where the gallows and the cross are placed side by side, has itself been questioned.[3] Although it is certainly true that this account is deeply ambiguous, something which Wiesel himself has recently recognized,[4] essentially when the boy hangs on the gallows Wiesel loses God; for him God has died. Yet looking with Christian eyes, it is at this very point that Jürgen Moltmann, for example, finds God, alive in the midst of death.[5] But central to both Wiesel's original intention and Moltmann's later reflections is the issue of God's relationship to suffering. The 'where?' cried out in Auschwitz certainly resonates with the 'why?' cried out by Jesus in the darkness of the cross: 'My God, my God, why have you forsaken me?' How can God and suffering be spoken of together, and how can we make sense of the strange Christian account of the cross, that it is through suffering that salvation is brought?

For the majority of the Christian period, the prevailing view in responding to this dilemma has been firmly that, whatever else we might say, at least God cannot suffer and change.[6] During the past century this has been challenged on a number of fronts, galvanized by a greater realisation that the early Church Fathers drew some of their thinking from their Platonic background and education and so merged Hebrew and Greek conceptions of God. But it is also important to realize that this was not an uncritical merging of ideas with an entirely negative result.[7] The notion of divine impassibility, which emerged from Platonic ontology, positively distinguished the Christian God from the mythologies of pagan religion and, once established, had an important function within the developing soteriology, as the ground for hope in a suffering-free heaven. Irenaeus' famous dictum that 'Christ became what we are, that he might bring us to be even what He is Himself'[8] exemplifies the patristic explanation of salvation as divinisation. The Christian belief in eternal life is understood as *theosis*, or as involving a sharing in God's own divine life, and thus the exact nature of divinity has ramifications for our future hope. Athanasius expresses this understanding by explicitly drawing on the key concept of impassibility:

> And while He [The Word] Himself, being impassible in nature, remains
> as He is, not harmed by these affections, but rather obliterating and

destroying them, men, their passions as if changed and abolished in the Impassible, henceforth become themselves impassible and free from them for ever.[9]

These early theologians were acutely aware of the suffering in the world around them, and no doubt it frequently seemed to them to be both unnecessary and excessive, but it was precisely such suffering that confirmed their belief in God's impassibility. In a world of flux and change, this distinction between God and the world offered the hope that believers, in becoming like God, would share in a suffering-free future. The present suffering was to be endured because God had promised a better future.

Most modern writers have approached their experiences of suffering from an altogether different perspective. It would be both unhelpful and futile to make comparisons as to the degree and depth of suffering between different generations. We must resist the temptation to pretend that this is a modern problem, for it has been a concern expressed since the beginning of literature, but there is a distinctly modern response to suffering. It is no longer justifiable simply to accept our present sufferings – an attitude which locates God too much in the future; we need also to talk about God and suffering together in the here and now. Therefore, many modern theologians have insisted that God must suffer with us, grounding God's being not in a transcendent or future reality but in God's presence with a suffering world. If God had been always removed from what happened in his creation, always spared the pain that characterizes life for so many, then God would not be worthy of that name. The argument runs that, if we suffer then God must suffer with us. There are, of course, modern theologians, motivated not only by a certain philosophical position but also by compassion and a desire for faithfulness to the Biblical evidence as they perceive it, who uphold a traditional understanding of the impassibility of God. Yet, as a whole, as Paul Fiddes points out, 'the belief that God is a suffering God has become compelling for recent theology'.[10]

This more recent desire to stress God's presence with the world here and now does not exclude reflection on an eternal future of the world without suffering. It is entirely understandable that the early Christian theologians stressed the freedom of God from change and suffering so strongly, for it was the only way they were able to speak with certainty of a suffering-free heaven. There were no other thought forms available with which they were able to express this future hope. Recent theologians, however, have found ways of expressing both suffering and change in God. They have done this without rendering God simply a victim in the world process, and so forfeiting any real concept of eternal salvation – although we will see that this is a path that could be taken – and without downplaying the reality of God's own suffering, another danger we shall encounter. Instead, we shall discover that it is by suffering in God's self that God overcomes what is evil in the world, and opens the way for a radically different future. Although we can remain in a broad agreement with the early Church Fathers about Christian hope, nevertheless our understanding of heaven, if we follow this line of thinking, must be different from theirs, for we have travelled along a very different path. In the final chapter I begin to explore some aspects of this eternal future with a suffering God.

Although suffering in everyday life has contributed to this revolution in thinking – Dorothee Sölle asserts that a 'fifty-year-old woman piece worker hangs on the cross no less than Jesus, only longer'[11] – it is the Holocaust in particular which has had a decisive effect on western thinking. This is not to devalue the experiences either of those who lived and died in the Holocaust or those who have suffered in countless other places by comparing one with another, but simply to recognize the particular effect of the Holocaust on subsequent theology and the resonance of the name Auschwitz. 'Theology after Auschwitz', both in its very possibility and its content, has therefore become something of a watchword in modern theology.[12] Through the account of his life, Wiesel challenges us to consider our 'talking of God' in the light of this particular experience, and in so doing we must relate God to suffering in general.

It is interesting that it is German theologians who, for the most part, have struggled with these themes, and in this book we will use the work of four such theologians – Jürgen Moltmann, Dorothee Sölle, Eberhard Jüngel and Hans Urs von Balthasar – to help us explore the strange Godforsakenness at the heart of the cross. These four writers tackle the juxtapositioning of God and suffering in different ways and from different traditions and backgrounds, but all are German and all are from roughly the same generation. For them the Holocaust is not simply an event in recent history but also a powerful factor in their cultural life. As German theologians who lived through, and have written after, the Second World War, they have had to face the experience of collective guilt.[13]

Sölle, reflecting on her own personal theological journey, begins with the assertion that the Holocaust 'is perhaps even also the most central event to have played an essential part in my intrinsic development, this legacy of gas, violence, war and murder. I have never understood how a theology after Auschwitz can be precisely the same as before'.[14] More recently still Sölle looks back to the beginning of her theological work, remembering that 'I did not want to write one sentence in which the awareness of that great catastrophe of my people was not made explicit'.[15] Moltmann is also acutely aware of the impact of history and describes *The Crucified God* as 'my attempt to find an answer for life in Germany "after Auschwitz"'.[16] Moltmann had begun this ground-breaking book with an autobiographical note about his return to Germany's lecture rooms from a British prisoner-of-war camp, needing to hear a theology that spoke of God 'in the sight of one who was abandoned and crucified'.[17] His personal experience of suffering was clearly more influential than his liberal Protestant upbringing.

Jüngel and von Balthasar generally avoid such autobiographical detail and their writing also has less of a practical orientation. Jüngel actually refers to his experience as a student under the Socialist regime in East Germany as a fundamental motivating factor for engaging in theology,[18] but no theologian of that generation could fail to be affected by Germany's turbulent history, and the themes of forsakenness and divine suffering present in their writing testify to this fact. All four authors, though to different extent and each in their own way, portray what Moltmann describes as 'a revolution in the concept of God'.[19] At the centre of this revolution is the necessity of thinking about God together with human suffering.

Although the sociological factor of human experience is a strong impetus towards a theology of divine suffering, it does not stand alone. As we have seen, at the centre of the church's life and integral to all Christian theology is the cross of Jesus Christ, whom the church has always proclaimed as sharing in some way the very being of God. And it is by wrestling with this mystery at the heart of God's relationship with the world that we gain a better insight into the reality of the world we encounter in the ordinariness of our everyday lives and in the depths of Auschwitz. For it is in the strangeness of the cross that we see the truth of God.

### 3. The cry

Seeking to explore this mystery at the heart of God, I will attempt to do three things in the pages that follow. First I will offer a careful analysis of the text of one biblical account of the cross, that of Mark's Gospel, with a particular focus on the cry of 'why?' with which Jesus died. Secondly I will consider the impact that Jesus' cry has had on the four theologians I have mentioned, leading them to explore the whole concept of Godforsakenness. It is this wider concept of Jesus' forsakenness by God which all these theologians have found to be of the utmost significance, but it is one which has been drawn from and is related to the Gospel text about the cry of Jesus in the darkness. Other themes, such as the question of God's passibility and the nature of God as Trinity, will necessarily be considered, but always through the particular lens of Godforsakenness.

Yet neither Biblical interpretation nor systematic theology can be seen as ends in themselves, and so, thirdly, I will conclude with some reflections on the Church's mission to engage with the world. These pastoral implications are not conceived as merely secondary, but as the very goal of this study. If any conclusions can be reached as to the meaning of Jesus' cry both in its Gospel setting and in its theological significance, then they must stand the test of the world as it is experienced by those who feel that they too have cried in dereliction.

### Notes to Chapter 1

[1] Karl Barth, *Church Dogmatics*, trans. G. W. Bromiley and T. F. Torrance (eds.), (Edinburgh: T. & T. Clark, 1936-75), II/2, p. 162.

[2] Eli Wiesel, *Night*, trans. Stella Rodway (Harmondsworth: Penguin, 1981), pp. 76-7.

[3] See Johann-Baptist Metz, 'Facing the Jews: Christian Theology after Auschwitz', in E. Schüssler Fiorenza and David Tracy (eds.), *The Holocaust as*

*Interruption* (Edinburgh: T. & T. Clark, 1984), p. 29: 'There is no other identification of God — neither as sublime as for instance in J. Moltmann nor as reserved and modest as in the case of D. Sölle – here as far as I am concerned, no Christian theological identification of God is possible'.

[4] Eli Wiesel, *All Rivers Run to the Sea* (London: Harper Collins, 1997), p. 84.

[5] Jürgen Moltmann, *The Crucified God. The Cross of Christ as the Foundation and Criticism of Christian Theology*, trans. R. A. Wilson and J. Bowden (London: SCM, 1974), pp. 273-4.

[6] The idea of divine mutability was not entirely lacking in the Patristic era, although comparatively rare; see Joseph R. Hallman, 'The Mutability of God: Tertullian to Lactantius', *Theological Studies* 42 (1981), pp. 75-88.

[7] The particular evaluation of patristic dependence on Greek philosophy influences the resulting doctrine of God. The majority of modern theologians read the Church Fathers with some kind of critical eye, aware of the influence of Greek philosophy, although some do embrace patristic thought whole-heartedly. Thomas Weinandy, for example, *Does God Suffer?* (Edinburgh: T. & T. Clark, 2000), offers a very positive evaluation of patristic theology and argues for the positive role of philosophy in the development of Christian doctrine. He seeks to show, p. 114, that the God of philosophy and of Christian revelation are the same.

[8] Irenaeus, *Against Heresies,* Book V, Preface, in *Ante-Nicene Christian Library*, Vol. IX (Edinburgh: T. & T. Clark, 1869), p. 55.

[9] Athanasius, *Against the Arians*, III, xxvi. 34, in *The Library of the Fathers*, Vol. XIX (Oxford: John Henry Parker, 1844), p. 449.

[10] Paul S. Fiddes, *The Creative Suffering of God* (Oxford: Clarendon, 1988), p. 16. In contrast, Thomas Weinandy in *Does God Suffer?* offers the most recent extended defence of the traditional belief in the impassibility of God, although Weinandy concurs with Fiddes' summary; indeed, he presents this as the reason for the book; see pp. 1-26.

[11] Dorothee Sölle, *Suffering*, trans. E. R. Kalin (London: Darton, Longman and Todd, 1975), p. 146.

[12] It was perhaps Johann-Baptist Metz who first coined this phrase in his article 'Facing the Jews: Theology after Auschwitz'.

[13] An important recent English contribution to the debate, and one to which extensive reference will be made in this study, is Fiddes, *The Creative Suffering of God*.

[14] This comes from an account of a fascinating symposium to mark Moltmann's 70th birthday, in which various leading German theologians talked

together about their theological journeys: see Jürgen Moltmann (ed.), *How I Have Changed* (London: SCM, 1997), p. 22. Sölle herself is actually one-eighth Jewish; cf. Dorothee Sölle, *Against the Wind*, trans. B. and R. Rumscheidt (Minneapolis: Augsburg Fortress, 1999), pp. 9-10.

[15] Sölle, *Against the Wind*, p. 16.

[16] Ibid. p. 19.

[17] Moltmann, *The Crucified God*, p. 1. See Moltmann (ed.), *How I Have Changed*, p. 13, for Moltmann's own experience of bereavement and survival during the Hamburg bombing of 1943.

[18] Moltmann, *How I Have Changed*, pp. 4-5.

[19] Moltmann, *The Crucified God*, p. 4.

# Part I
# The Scriptural Basis

# 2
# A Test Case?

We have seen that theologians of recent times have begun to reconsider the relationship between God and the world. In fact there is a real sense that this has been demanded of them, not simply by the devastating events of the twentieth century but also by the wider reaction to these events and the questions they have raised for many people. In our new 'post-modern' world such questioning can only increase, whether expressed in popular or academic terms.

The dilemma of theodicy ('How can we believe in a good and loving God when there is so much suffering in the world?') may have been sharpened by human experience and by our technological ability today to observe events on a world-wide scale, but theologically it has its epicentre at the cross of Jesus of Nazareth. It is the cross which functions both as initiator and critic of what theologians can and must say about suffering and God. And at the heart of the cross, at least in its earliest account, is a cry of Jesus expressing his abandonment by God. The cry of Mark 15:34 continues to inspire, provoke and haunt its readers, offering both spiritual comfort and theological challenge. A renewed interest in Mark's Gospel, combined with a searching reflection on the suffering in our lives and world, singles out this verse as a significant text for modern times. It is, perhaps, Jürgen Moltmann who has done most to bring Jesus' cry of dereliction and the wider theological issues it evokes to our attention, although he is not the only, or even the earliest, modern theologian to be fascinated by this biblical context. Mark 15:34 therefore becomes a test case for our theological discussion and the lens through which we will explore this particular area.

In line with much recent discussion of the literary nature of Mark's Gospel, we shall suggest, in the following chapters, that in this one verse three crucial themes unite for the Christian theologian. First, Jesus cries out using the words of Psalm 22:1. He takes a historical human expression of suffering and makes it his own, although in a whole new way.

Similarly, many people since have echoed these words both in prayer and in protest and in this cry is distilled the whole nexus of human suffering. Secondly, Jesus' cry is inextricably linked to the centurion's confession that Jesus is God's Son, 15:39. If we follow Mark's lead and find the cross to be a supreme occasion of revelation, then we must also take seriously the possibility that whilst being a cry of human pain, Jesus' words also point us to the deeper level of divine suffering. Finally, at the end of a life in which Jesus lived in close relationship to God, whom he addressed as Father, this verse plumbs the depth of the relationship between Father and Son, and so Jesus' cry opens up something of the nature of God's own Trinitarian relationships.

Although there has been a renaissance of interest in Jesus' cry in the latter half of the twentieth century, as theologians have found it to be a word for today, it was also the focus of much theological discussion through the preceding nineteen centuries, not least for the difficulties and challenges it presented.[1] An early widespread patristic explanation, which received its defining form from Augustine, was that since Christ is the head of his body, the church, it is *humanity* as a whole crying out in Jesus' words. In many ways Augustine was guided towards this interpretation by a mistranslation of the Hebrew into the Latin Vulgate. Whereas the Hebrew of Psalm 22:2 reads 'Why are you so far from my salvation, from the words that I cry?', Augustine read: 'Why are you so far from my salvation, from the words of my sins?'. On the assumption, which we shall question a little later, that Jesus must have had the whole of the psalm in mind, and so must have been thinking of this verse as following on from 22:1, the only sins that could be attributed to Jesus were the sins of humankind. Thus his cry of forsakenness must be the cry of humankind.[2] This was not the only interpretation, however, and alongside it Origen and others did attempt to explain this verse, with the aid of Philippians 2, as a real 'abandonment' for Jesus in as much as he had taken the form of a servant.[3] Gérard Rossé claims that the normative patristic interpretation of the word 'abandoned' centred on the Father's non-intervention and quotes Theodoretus' explanation, that it was a 'granting permission' for the passion to take place.[4] In other words, the Church Fathers shied away from any direct activity by God the Father at the cross; the most they would say is that God did nothing.

The debates over Christological heresies which followed resulted in the classic definition of the two natures of Christ in the Chalcedonian formula. This provided a theological means for holding together the apparent opposites of divinity and humanity, and this in turn opened the way for the classic interpretation of Mark 15:34, that it was the *human nature* of Jesus that cried out on the cross and not his divinity.[5] This view prevailed, even though the Platonic background, with all its stress on the soul and a higher world, gave way in the Scholastic theologians to an Aristotelian emphasis on the experience of the human senses. With this interpretation of the cry of forsakenness, God became further removed from the world and the impassibility of God was more firmly cemented as orthodox belief.[6] Although Aquinas, for example, does portray a more subtle distinction between the lower and higher parts of Jesus' soul, Chalcedonian orthodoxy and the impassibility of God remain firm.

After the Middle Ages the interpretation of Jesus' cry developed in various directions. Mystical writers, for example, used their own experiences as a hermeneutical key, and so explained the events of the cross in the light of their own experiences of 'the dark night of the soul'. This led to their emphasis on Jesus' *feeling* of abandonment according to his humanity, which was real and like their own, but within a constant unity between Jesus and his God. The mystics also took the passive concept of abandonment which the Fathers had adopted much further and explained the abandonment as a deliberate act of the Father in withdrawing from his Son, once more corresponding to their own experience of the dark night as the path to the fullest relationship with God. John of the Cross writes:

> He was likewise annihilated in his soul and was deprived of any relief and consolation, since His Father left Him in the most intense aridity, according to the lower part of his nature. Wherefore He had perforce to cry out, saying, 'My God! My God! Why hast thou forsaken me?' This was the greatest desolation, with respect to sense, that he suffered in his life.[7]

In a different direction, but continuing with the theme of the Father's active involvement, Luther and Calvin interpret the cry in the context of a strong penal understanding of the atonement. Jesus' abandonment is thus the result of God's anger and wrath – not that God was angry with Jesus himself, but in so far as Jesus bore our sins he endures God's wrath and judgement. [8] So Calvin writes:

> It was expedient at the same time for him to undergo the severity of God's vengeance, to appease his wrath and satisfy his just judgement. For this reason, he must also grapple hand to hand with the armies of hell and the dread of everlasting death.[9]

However, just a few pages later, as Calvin's exposition of this grappling with everlasting death leads him to Jesus' forsaken cry, he insists that 'feeling himself, as it were forsaken by God, he did not waver in the least from trust in his goodness. This is proved by that remarkable prayer to God in which he cried out in acute agony'.[10]

Whilst working within the traditional two-nature formula, Luther differs from the reformed tradition by actually introducing language that suggests that God himself suffered on the cross.[11] By stressing that the 'exchange of properties' (*communicatio idiomatum*) between divinity and humanity in the God-man was not just a matter of words, but of reality, Luther is able to speak of the man who created the world and the God who suffered, died and was buried.[12] Although the language sounds very similar, Luther's theology, still working within the traditional two-nature formula, is different from some understandings of the cross that have been expounded more recently. But he has certainly prepared the way, and Jürgen Moltmann, for instance, writes out of this Lutheran tradition and is highly influenced by it.[13]

From here thinking moved in various directions. In the eighteenth century, for example, Reimarus began the process of attempting to write something like a historical life of Jesus. Rejecting the concept of universal revelation, and limiting himself to what he thought were the 'facts', he concluded that Jesus' cry was a very human expression of disillusionment, for Jesus was a political revolutionary who had failed. Writing of the cry of forsakenness, he says:

> This avowal cannot, without violence, be interpreted otherwise than as meaning that God had not aided him in his aim and purpose as he had

hoped. That shows that it has not been his purpose to suffer and die, but to establish an earthly kingdom and deliver the Jews from political oppression – and in that God's help failed him.[14]

Then, in vivid contrast, in the early nineteenth century Friedrich Schleiermacher championed the belief that the relationship between Jesus and his Father remained unaltered and unaffected even by the events of the passion. Despite some sense of sympathy with us, and a greater experience of human suffering on the cross, Jesus' own God-consciousness is unruffled even as he cries out before his death:

> The more so that this suffering arose out of the opposition of sin, and that therefore the Redeemer's sympathy with misery, ever present, though without disturbing his blessedness, from the time of his entrance into the corporate life of sin, had here to enter in its greatest phase.[15]

During these developments in interpretation and theology, Christology and soteriology were the central concerns. How can we explain Christ's *nature* in such a way that takes seriously the event of the cross? And furthermore, what is the significance of his abandonment for our *atonement*? These are indeed important issues, but we will find that it is a further question that actually preoccupies our thinking. In addition to Christology and soteriology, a characteristic of a number of modern writers is the insistence that Jesus' cry is the proper foundation for *the*ology in the strictest sense of the word, which means 'talking about *God*'. We must consider the significance of Jesus' cry for our understanding of the very nature of God. As Jürgen Moltmann puts it:

> To take up the theology of the cross today is to go beyond the limits of salvation and enquire into the revolution needed in the concept of God. Who is God in the cross of the Christ who is abandoned by God? . . . . All Christian theology and Christian life is basically an answer to the question which Jesus asked as he died . . . . Either Jesus who was abandoned by God is the end of all theology or he is the beginning of a specifically Christian theology and life.[16]

## Notes to Chapter 2

[1] See Gérard Rossé, *The Cry of Jesus from the Cross* (New York: Paulist Press, 1987), for a fuller treatment of the historical interpretations of Jesus' cry.

[2] Augustine's *Exposition of the Psalms*, PL 36, 882; cit. Rossé, *The Cry of Jesus*, p. 74.

[3] Origen, *Series in Mattheum*, 135 (PG 13, 1785-87); cit. Rossé, *The Cry of Jesus*, p. 75.

[4] Theodoretus, PG 80, 1010; cit. Rossé, *The Cry of Jesus*, p. 77.

[5] For a survey of the patristic view of impassibility in the face of Jesus' sufferings, see J. K. Mozley's classic, *The Impassibility of God* (Cambridge: Cambridge University Press, 1926). T. E. Pollard, 'The Impassibility of God', *Scottish Journal of Theology* 8 (1955), p. 358, suggests that Origen offers the only hint of divine suffering with his reference to the 'passion of love'.

[6] Pollard, 'The Impassibility of God', p. 359.

[7] John of the Cross, *The Ascent of Mount Carmel*, Bk 2, chap. 7, par. 11, in *The Complete Works of Saint John of the Cross*, trans. E Allison Peers, (London: Burns & Oates, 1953), p. 87.

[8] See Rossé, *The Cry of Jesus*, pp. 83-5.

[9] Calvin, *Institutes of the Christian Religion*, in Library of Christian Classics, volume XX, John T McNeil (ed.), (London: SCM, 1961), II. xvi. 10, p. 515.

[10] Ibid., II.xvi.12, pp. 519-20.

[11] Warren McWilliams, for example, *The Passion of God* (Macon: Mercer University Press, 1985), p. 14, asserts that Luther was 'the only major reformer who seemed receptive at all of divine passibility'.

[12] Quoted by Moltmann, *The Crucified God: The Cross of Christ as the Foundation and Criticism of Christian Theology*, trans. R. A. Wilson and John Bowden, (London: SCM, 1974), p. 233 and taken from the *Weimarer Ausgabe* of Luther's work, 39, II, 93ff.

[13] See Moltmann, *The Crucified God*, pp. 232-5, for Moltmann's critical but appreciative appraisal of Luther's thought. Like Moltmann, the Japanese theologian Kazoh Kitamori, in his book *Theology of the Pain of God* (London: SCM, 1966), writes in the Lutheran tradition.

[14] Reimarus, from the fragment *Von dem Zwecke Jesu und seiner Jünger* published by Gotthold Lessing, Brunswick, 1778, and quoted in Albert Schweitzer, *The Quest for the Historical Jesus: A Critical Study of its Progress*

*from Reimarus to Wrede*, (London: Adam and Charles Black, 1954, 3rd edition), pp. 19-20.

[15] F. Schleiermacher, *The Christian Faith*, trans. H. R. Mackintosh and J. S. Stewart (Edinburgh: T. & T. Clark, 1928), p. 436. Schleiermacher describes the argument that Jesus gave up his 'blessedness' for the purpose of atonement as 'a magical caricature'.

[16] Moltmann, *The Crucified God*, p. 4.

# 3
# A Climactic Point?

**Mark 15:34 in the Context of the Whole Gospel**

Whatever else we might say about Jesus' cry in Mark 15:34, it does not come to us without a context. We read it towards the end of an account that has stressed the closeness of Jesus to God, but which also has, for us, a disputed final ending. We know it to be a quotation from an Old Testament psalm written within a different time and so with a distinctly different perspective. How then can we make sense of Jesus' cry to God within the whole wider context that we have received it? It is true of course that we have received it in two places and so in two distinct contexts. As we shall see, there is much that is similar in Matthew and Mark, although within the similarity important differences are highlighted. Working on the generally accepted assumption that Mark is the most primitive of the four Gospels our thinking will concentrate on that account and then consider how Mark's portrayal of the cross stands alongside the other three Gospels. In addition I suggest that Jesus' cry has a more critical place in the structure and thought of Mark's Gospel than in subsequent accounts, which therefore weaken some Marcan aspects.

## 1. Approaching the Gospel as a whole

Now, the approach we adopt to read and study the Gospels will greatly influence our final conclusions. For example, in the early part of the twentieth century the rise of form criticism opened up a whole new way of understanding the Bible. Although this led to some new insights into the text, ultimately these methods have proved disappointing, particularly in relation to the earliest Gospel. The myriad of conflicting suggestions produced by this method of criticism make clear that its attempt to separate tradition from Marcan redaction can never be successfully achieved, and that its concept of the evangelists as merely compilers or editors has led to a distorted view of Mark's Gospel. Rudolph Bultmann famously described the passage in Mark's Gospel centring on Jesus' cry as 'badly

disfigured'.[1] More recently, Étienne Trocmé concluded, 'the point is settled: the author of Mark was a clumsy writer and unworthy of mention in
any history of literature'.[2]

A new way forward came with the rise of redaction criticism which,
while still working on small sections of the Gospel text, stressed that the
Gospel writers were intelligent authors who had thoughtfully put together
their material. More recently still and building on these insights, literary
or narrative criticism has further stressed that the meaning of the Gospels
is to be found in approaching them as whole works.[3] The development of
a narrative approach to Gospel criticism in general, and the renewed interest in Mark's Gospel in particular, are clearly connected, for it is in its
totality, rather than in its dissection into small pericopes, that the richness
of this Gospel is to be discovered.

The recent flurry of theological research into the earliest Gospel leads
to two initial conclusions. First, despite using Greek which is simple and
popular, and which even on occasions may technically be wrong, the
Gospel of Mark is a good story! It is carefully constructed and there are
important connections throughout the Gospel on dramatic, literary and
theological levels. Second, the entire Gospel is to be considered Marcan,
that is all the various inherited traditions have been carefully revised and
included in the final work. This is not to prejudge any discussion on
authorship, but simply recognizes that whatever sources the author used,
he (presumably) would take responsibility for the entire finished work.

Our study will not attempt to be exhaustive: there will be no consideration of Mark's authorship, provenance, date or development of
tradition. Neither will we consider some very specific approaches within
literary criticism, such as structuralism or deconstruction. But, believing
that the Gospel of Mark was written to be read as a whole, we will exam-
ine Jesus' cry in the context of the whole Gospel.

Turning to Mark 15:33-9, the pericope at the centre of our discussion,
we find a number of exegetical problems, pointed out by many different
scholars:

• the strict three hour schema is quite different from the timings in John;
• the meaning of the darkness is uncertain;
• there is confusion over the original language of Jesus' cry;

• the misunderstanding with the name Elijah is difficult to explain;
• the reason for offering the wine vinegar is unclear;
• Jesus' inarticulate cry could be understood as a doublet with the cry of forsakenness;
• it is unclear which of the temple curtains is torn in two;
• the centurion's geographical position in relation to the cross is unclear;
• exactly what prompted the centurion's response is debated;
• it has been suggested that some verses are intrusions into the text.

My conviction is that in approaching the text as a whole from a narrative viewpoint we can set some clear boundaries within which any interpretation of Jesus' cry must sit,[4] gain new insights into some of these problematical aspects by focusing on their literary function within the passion narrative and Gospel as a whole, and also develop a greater appreciation for Mark's literary abilities.

## 2. The climax of three themes

The general consensus among those who adopt a variety of approaches to the text is that no one theme dominates the Gospel and no definite, accepted structure has been found; rather there is a complex of themes.[5] In this pericope three themes stand out and a careful reading finds them intertwined through the Gospel and brought to a climax together here.

### a. Abandonment

Jesus' cry of abandonment by God is the final experience of a forsakenness which begins at the outset of the Gospel. Jesus is rejected by his family (3:31-35), and then by the people of his hometown (6:1-6). He is betrayed by a follower (14:10-11), left alone while his disciples slept (14:32-42), and denied by one of his closest friends (14:66-72), after which the disciples desert him and flee at his arrest (14:15). Jesus' warning of future family conflicts in 13:12 picks up his rejection by his natural family and points forward to the betrayal and denial by his new family.[6] He was handed over to the Gentiles by the Jews (15:1), forsaken by the Roman judicial system and deprived of justice (15:1-15), beaten and mocked by the soldiers (15:16-20), stripped naked[7] (15:24), and mocked by the Jewish leaders (15:31-2). Forsaken by his family and friends, handed over by the leaders of his own people, Jesus dies exclaiming his abandonment by God.

Jesus' cry is thus clearly the climax of his forsakenness which has been a dominant theme in the passion narrative.[8] R. H. Lightfoot was one of the earliest to recognize several of the important themes in Mark's Gospel and he highlights the increasing forsakenness in the passion, but then compares it with the achievements of Jesus in the first half of the Gospel.[9] Although intensified in the narrative of the passion, abandonment continues and develops a theme introduced at the beginning of the Gospel, rather than contrasts with the earlier section of the Gospel. Jesus' abandonment on the cross is the climax of the whole work.

The dramatic structure through which Mark portrays Christ's increasing isolation points to the centrality of this theme of forsakenness as a deliberate and intentional aspect of the Gospel, leading to this important climactic passage. Robert Gundry, however, presents an opposite view, suggesting instead that a 'theology of glory pervades Mark'[10] and that the pre-Marcan tradition is edited with material such as Simon carrying the cross in place of Christ,[11] and formal language such as *exepneusen* ('he breathed out/ he died')[12], which add dignity to Jesus in order to make the cross an object of faith rather than an obstacle to faith.[13] Yet such an argument is based on too many presuppositions. Gundry's central thesis is that Mark inherited a tradition that stressed Jesus' suffering, including the cry of forsakenness, which he felt obliged to include in his Gospel as accepted tradition, but which he redacted in order to lay the emphasis on Jesus' glory. Yet there is no certainty or even scholarly consensus about the content of Mark's sources which were the object of his redaction. This uncertainty is increased in the light of Luke and John's handling of the tradition, in whose accounts the cry of forsakenness is freely omitted, whereas we have actually suggested Mark highlights this very point. From the perspective of the whole Gospel, Jesus' forsakenness is an important theme that is deliberately brought to our attention.

*b. Identity*

The centurion's response to the death of Jesus is the climax of the revelation of Jesus' identity. The appellation of Jesus as the 'Christ' and the 'Son of God' begins the Gospel of Mark, and although there are textual variants, there is strong manuscript support for the inclusion of *huios theou* (Son of God), and the dominant view favours inclusion.[14] The title 'Son of God' is then used in a programmatic way through the Gospel reaching its conclusion with the centurion's declaration.[15] From a dramatic perspective, the first verse sets the scene for the readers by disclosing the most important fact. We read the Gospel knowing something that is so far hidden from the various characters involved and is revealed to them only gradually. The same technique is used in many media. The film *Titanic*, for example, to which I have already referred, begins with the current search for the wreck and introduces us to Rose, a survivor from the crash. The flashbacks are her story. Whatever else may happen in the film we know one thing – the heroine survives!

So in Mark's Gospel Jesus is called 'Son' at his baptism (1:11), but only he hears the heavenly voice. Demons address Jesus as 'Son of God' (3:11, 5:7), showing the spiritual realm's grasp of Jesus' identity, but again no one else responds or even seems to hear the cries. At Jesus' transfiguration (9:7), God speaks directly to the inner three disciples, although they do not grasp the significance of what they hear. The title 'Son of the Blessed One' is at the heart of the High Priest's question in 14:61, put in order to elicit a blasphemous response. Finally, it is in a most unexpected situation, Jesus' Godforsaken death on the cross, through a most unexpected medium, the Gentile centurion, that the conclusion of this question of identity is reached. For the first time a human being confesses that 'this man was the Son of God'[16].

The exact meaning of this declaration has been disputed. The Greek *huios theou* is what grammarians call 'anarthous', that is, having neither a definite article ('the') nor an indefinite article ('a'); this is grammatically quite acceptable in Greek, and so the phrase can be translated either as '*the* Son of God' or '*a* son of God'. It has been argued by Earl Johnson Jr. on both linguistic and sociological grounds that the centurion could only have meant '*a* son of God'.[17] He considers here the often-quoted

'Colwell's rule' in grammar, which has been an accepted guide to translating Greek. This states that a predicate nominative, that is a noun used
in connection with the verb 'to be', when used without an article is taken
to be definite when it precedes the verb. The text of Mark 15:39 has the
word order 'this man Son of God was', and so if the rule is followed it
would mean, 'this man was *the* Son of God'. Johnson demonstrates quite
clearly, however, that the rule does not in fact hold for New Testament
writers at significant points. He also considers the often-made suggestion
that the tense of the verb 'to be' in the centurion's confession can be
treated as a historic present ('this man *is* Son of God'), which would
imply a state of continuing divinity and so lend weight to the translation
'*the* Son of God'. In reply, Johnson argues that the imperfect tense here is
normally used to imply that something is past and gone, so whatever the
centurion meant it was something that finished with Jesus' death; this
would support the translation 'this man was a Son of God'.

Moving away from purely grammatical arguments, Johnson insists
that these words on the lips of a worldly-wise professional soldier could
not mean 'the Son of God' and would not have been read that way by
Mark's readers. Therefore Johnson concludes, 'there is a lack of sufficient
evidence both inside and outside the Gospel to compel the contention that
such a confession is a necessary or probable conclusion to the Gospel'.[18]
I suggest that Johnson is right to reject the language that speaks of the
centurion's 'conversion',[19] but that he has failed to consider the climactic
nature of this passage.

Philip Harner had earlier also recognized the inadequacies of
Colwell's rule, and therefore the ambiguity of 15:39.[20] Having studied the
sentence structure throughout Mark's Gospel, he concludes that usually
the word order clearly indicates a definite or indefinite noun. Yet at this
crucial point Mark chooses to be ambiguous. Harner suggests that the
structure of this sentence in Mark 15:39 deliberately places the words
'man' and 'Son of God' as close together as possible ('this man Son of
God was').[21] If we combine this with the significant Marcan emphasis,
writing *houtos anthrōpos'* ('this man') as compared to the simple
Matthean *houtos* ('this one'), then we can see Mark's stress on the divine
sonship of this suffering man. In a Gospel which consistently contrasts
the divine and the human, Jesus' identity is established as the unique

human who is also divine.[22] Tae Hin Kim, in a fascinating historical article, also dismisses Johnson's concern with the absence of an article and argues that this anarthous phrase has a significant history as one of the principle titles, or even names, for Augustus.[23] Not only does *huios theou* have a very definite meaning, it would also have been a known phrase. Our linguistic conclusions must be that both translations – 'a son' or 'the son' – are grammatically possible and could be considered Marcan in style. The decision must be based on the context of the verse within the whole narrative.

The confession of the centurion contrasts sharply with those who either have rejected or failed to recognize Jesus' sonship, and this is further emphasized by the use of the word *idōn* ('seeing') at the beginning of 15:39. In Mark 'to see' often has a spiritual connotation, involving understanding as well as literally observing events. In the more immediate context, Jesus replies to the High Priest's question that he, the High Priest, will *see* the Son of Man come in glory, for only then will he understand. The mockers at the cross taunt Jesus to come down so that they might *see* and believe, the clear implication being that they have not understood or believed. The crowd at the cross want to *see* if Elijah will come, for they too have not understood. Elijah has come in John but they did not recognize him, and Jesus' appropriation of Isaiah's prophecy (Mark 4:12, cf. Isaiah 6:9-10) that they would look and not *see*, is proved to be true. Earlier in the Gospel (10:51), at the end of the journey to Jerusalem which is the significant narrative form of the middle section of the Gospel, and as the climax approaches, Jesus heals Bartimaeus whose request is that he might *see*.

True sight forms part of the messianic secret, in which what is already known by the reader is gradually revealed to the characters, and this provides the literary framework for the presentation of Jesus' identity. The authority of Jesus seen in healings, exorcisms, the offering of forgiveness and the stilling of the storm leads the disciples to ask, 'Who is this?' (4:41). The ironic question, 'Isn't this the son of Mary?', at the synagogue in Nazareth brings the themes of identity and rejection together and this is closely followed by the first presentation of popular ideas concerning Jesus in 6:14-16. This in turn anticipates Peter's watershed confession of Jesus as the Christ (8:29), in which 'seeing' is again important.

Immediately after Jesus chastises his disciples for having eyes but not seeing (8:18), and immediately before Peter's declaration and subsequent rebuke, Mark recounts the other healing of a blind man (8:22-26). In the same way that the blind man's sense of vision was at first very vague and only later could he see clearly, so Peter's grasp of Jesus' identity is a step beyond the perception of the crowd, but still only partial.

The title 'Christ' is also used carefully through the Gospel, appearing in 8:29 for the first time since 1:1 where it equated with *huios theou* ('Son of God'). In 14:61 it is linked to 'Son of the Blessed One', a reverent form of 'Son of God', so that there is a clear development of Jesus' identity throughout the Gospel, in which *huios theou* ('Son of God') plays an important, although not isolated, part. The facts that Mark uses this title so precisely, that on other occasions in the Gospel it clearly means 'the Son of God', and that the centurion's confession is the climactic ending so carefully prepared for, lead to the conclusion that this confession, despite being on the lips of a Gentile before the resurrection, is meant to carry full Christological weight. There is certainly the sense in which the acclamation is pregnant with meaning beyond the centurion's own comprehension.[24] Mark's readers, then, are clearly intended to hear the centurion speak of *the* Son of God.[25]

*c. Temple*

The third theme to find its climax in these verses, caught up between Jesus' cry and the centurion's response, is that of the temple. Although references to the temple only begin in Chapter 11,[26] Jesus' first visit to Jerusalem in the Marcan narrative, this later emphasis picks up and develops the wider motif of opposition against him. Conflict is first hinted at in 1:22 where Jesus is described as teaching with authority, unlike the teachers of the Law and this leads to the first explicit threat in 3:6, importantly on account of Jesus' supposed blasphemy. As the Gospel proceeds this opposition is aimed more directly at Jesus,[27] and the changing of the scene of conflict from Galilee to the temple, God's House, serves to heighten the tension.[28]

Throughout the passion narrative judgement on the temple is inextricably linked with the identity of Jesus, in such a way that Jesus' words and actions in relation to the temple ask fundamental questions about the one who can speak and act in this way.[29] Thus, in driving out the merchants from the temple (11:15-19), Jesus is clearly enacting God's judgement and it is this action which leads to his subsequent dispute with the Jewish leaders (11:27). The dispute was about the authority Jesus had to do such things, that is about his identity, which is further raised as Jesus taught in the temple about the Son of David (12:35). The contrast between Jesus and the teachers of the law, first noted in 1:22, comes to the fore again in the juxtaposition of Jesus' warning against those teachers who devour widows' houses (12:40) with the account of the widow putting all she had into the temple treasury (12:41-4). It is particularly striking how this one short scene both looks forward, exemplifying Jesus' complete giving of himself, and also looks backwards, exemplifying the abuse of the poor by the temple leadership. This pericope then leads in to the important discussion between Jesus and the three disciples about the future destruction of the temple (13:1-3) in the 'apocalyptic' section of the Gospel, which includes a warning against messianic impostors (vv. 21-3). We return to Jesus' own identity as the crowd come to arrest him as if a bandit, even though he 'taught in the temple each day' (14:49), which then acts as a foil to the High Priest's questioning and the subsequent mockery on the cross ('You who would destroy the temple and build it in three days' 15:29), before the climactic tearing of the temple curtain in 15:38.

Donald Juel has written extensively on the Christological significance of the temple motif. Although for the main part he offers some excellent Biblical exegesis, the one weak point in his thesis is the contention that a fundamental part of Mark's messianic Christology is the image of Jesus as the destroyer and rebuilder of the temple. Such a picture emerges if the false allegations in the trial and at the foot of the cross are really seen as true at a deeper level.[30] The problem is that Juel has failed to see that the two key references, 14:58 and 15:29, are deeply ironic. The allegations against Jesus are indeed false because Jesus only predicts that the temple will be destroyed and never mentions its rebuilding. The charges are not true at a deeper level in the sense that Jesus did actually threaten to destroy the temple, but are ironic, for we are to understand the temple as Jesus himself, whom others will destroy but God will rebuild! The reference in both these verses to 'three days' clearly shows that the resurrection is in view.[31] Jesus' human body will be destroyed, but in three days one not made by human hands will be built. Juel's suggestion that this new temple symbolizes the Christian community introduces a new element not otherwise present in the narrative, whereas the interpretation of the new temple as Jesus' resurrected body keeps the focus on Jesus' identity, which is in keeping with Mark's literary motifs[32]. In the trial and the mockery scenes, temple and Christology are thus held firmly together to point us clearly towards Jesus' identity. It would therefore be no surprise if this linking had the same effect at the point when Jesus dies.[33]

### 3. The relation of the three themes in 15:37-39

We have already noted important connections between the themes of abandonment, identity and temple as the narrative has gathered pace. If Mark has deliberately brought them to a climax in the same passage then we can expect a relationship, both dramatic and theological, between Jesus' Godforsaken death, the tearing of the temple curtain and the centurion's confession.[34] At this point two exegetical issues present themselves: (a) what is the focus of the centurion's attention? (b) what is the cause of his proclamation?

(a) The phrase *ex enantias autou* (in 15:39) could be translated 'in front of *him*' or 'in front of *it*'. Most scholars prefer the former translation, so locating the centurion in front of Jesus, although *autou* could be neuter and refer to the temple as Robert Gundry, for example, suggests.[35] The focus on Jesus seems the more likely, since theologically the dominant theme at this point is Christological: Jesus' abandonment by God, Jesus as the new temple and Jesus the Son of God. Moreover, my following discussions will show that this pericope is constructed so that both verses 38 and 39 depend on verse 37.

(b) The cause of the confession is indicated by *houtōs (thus or 'in this way')*: 'When the centurion, who stood in front of him, saw that he *thus* breathed his last, he said . . . '. This small word has always been problematic, as is seen from both the textual variants and the varying interpretations. The textual problem is the most straightforward: those manuscripts which insert some form of the word *kraxas* ('cried out') following 'thus' seem clearly to be secondary readings, since they make explicit that *houtōs* refers back to the manner of Jesus' death, whereas there is no good reason why *kraxas*, if original, should have been omitted.[36] But to what does this simple word 'thus' refer?

Howard Jackson seeks to develop a dramatic connection between these events[37] by suggesting that the phrase 'he breathed out' (*exepneusen*) refers to a release of the Spirit on Jesus' death, that this caused the rending of the temple curtain, and that this in turn was the miraculous sign which prompted the centurion's confession.[38] This, he feels, fulfills his own criteria that the centurion must be a real character in the drama and not just a puppet, and that the death of another accused man on a cross would not be enough to prompt such a confession.[39] Jesus' death is still indirectly the cause of the centurion's response, but it is the miracle which directly prompts this confession. On such a view it is necessary for the centurion to be able to see the curtain. Jackson therefore must suppose that it was the outer curtain which was torn and Jesus must have been crucified on the Mount of Olives, the only place from where the east side of the temple would be visible. Hence the word 'thus' (*houtōs*) refers back to all that has happened, but especially the tearing of the curtain in verse 38. Gundry adds to this interpretation by suggesting that the centurion responds to what he *saw* (*idōn*), that is the temple veil, in contrast to those in verse 35 who responded to what they *heard*, the cry.[40] Contrary to this view, we have already outlined the spiritual meaning of 'seeing' in the Gospel which adequately explains the presence of *idōn* in the text, without the need for the distinction which Gundry proposes.

Jackson is certainly right to expect the centurion to be more than a puppet, but Jackson's unproved view that the Gospel was written in the Jewish martyrological genre, in which the protagonist is acquitted through a miraculous sign, has strongly influenced his interpretation here and overall Jackson's whole interpretation of this pericope is not convincing. He does, however, make some helpful specific suggestions, particularly a comparison between Jesus' baptism, his first appearance in the Gospel (1:9-11), and the crucifixion, his last appearance. Although not the first scholar to notice this important link, Jackson usefully compares the 'rending' of the heavens with the 'rending' of the curtain (the only two occasions the verb is used in the Gospel), and the giving of the Spirit in baptism with the giving up of the Spirit in death. He thus draws attention to the significance of the double use of the unusual *exepneusen* ('breathed out' or 'died') in 15: 37 and 39, and the declaration on both occasions that Jesus is the 'Son of God'.[41] These two scenes bracket the whole Gospel and Mark uses the connection to explain the significance of both events.[42] Both contain a sense of scandal: Jesus is declared to be the Son of God at his baptism for *repentance*, a scandal which Mark, unlike Matthew and Luke, does nothing to blunt[43], and the Son of God dies on the cross, considered a curse. Yet both scenes also picture an opening of a new way to God, through the heavens and the temple curtain, and the present tense of the verb 'rend' in 1:10 becomes an aorist in 15:38, suggesting that what was begun in Jesus' baptism is completed on his cross. For Mark the powerful nature of these two events is emphasized by the strength, even violence, of the verb *schizō* (to rend or tear) which is weakened in the baptism scenes in Matthew and Luke. A number of translations also miss the strength of the verb in Mark's portrayal of the baptism, and so the intended parallel with the crucifixion.[44]

The obvious conclusion is that there is more involved in the account of Jesus' crucifixion than a simple narrative of events, and Mark is clearly working here at two levels, that of the story itself and that of the deeper significance.[45] Johnson's mistake is to confuse these two levels and make Mark's theological message necessary for the dramatic flow. Mark clearly suggests a theological link between the expelling of Jesus' Spirit and the tearing of the curtain, but this does not mean that those at the cross had to observe the curtain being torn.

One of Jackson's reasons for wanting to connect verse 38 (the tearing of the curtain) to verse 39 (the confession) on the dramatic and literary level is to avoid the situation in which the motive clause of verse 39 ('thus . . '.) is related directly to verse 37 (the death), so leaving verse 38 high and dry and thus considered to be an intrusion.[46] However, our survey of these three major themes has shown that even if 'thus' (*houtōs*) does linguistically refer back to Jesus' death, the tearing of the curtain is neither an intrusion dramatically, nor out of place theologically. In the passion narrative the motifs of the temple and Jesus' identity are woven together, but not narratively dependent on one another. In the questioning before the high priest, which is then repeated in the mockery on the cross, Jesus is asked first about the temple and then about his identity. The second question does not depend on the first, nor is it a logical consequence, but the two themes are deliberately intertwined. Thus we see, later on, a two–fold response to the death of Jesus in the tearing of the curtain (verse 38) and the confession of the centurion (verse 39). *Both* verse 38 and verse 39 relate back to verse 37; there is a direct causal relationship between Jesus' death and the tearing of the curtain and between Jesus' death and the centurion's confession; these two themes of temple and Christology are thus intertwined. Which of the two curtains Mark has in mind no longer matters, and neither does the geographical site of the crucifixion.[47] The centurion does not need to see the curtain because the two events are not connected in this way. If the Gospel were changed into the medium of film, the camera would show three snapshots, Jesus death, the tearing of the curtain and the response of the centurion. They are evocative images that appeal to our imagination and, juxtaposed, they create their own unity.[48]

Similarly, Mark's own intention that his readers should understand the centurion's confession with full Christological content does not require this meaning to have been necessarily the original intention of the centurion. The frequent use of irony explains the one phrase working on two distinct levels. Even so, the fact that Mark's description of Jesus' death is typically brief and offers no reason for the centurion's confession is problematic. Whereas Matthew and Luke clearly link the response to the wonders observed, Mark deliberately connects it only to Jesus' death. The only credible defence that Mark does not make the centurion a puppet is that he is relating what he believed to be the facts.[49]

Our theological interpretation must accordingly reflect the two-fold reaction to Jesus' Godforsaken death. Whereas at first sight they seem to be quite distinct responses, a negative judgement on the temple and a positive confession of Jesus, on further reflection they can be seen to be linked more closely together. Here Harry Chronis makes an intriguing proposal. He notes that the passive verb *eschisthē* ('was torn') and the somewhat redundant *ap anōthen heōs katō* ('from top to bottom') point to the tearing of the temple curtain as God's action and that *ex anantias autou* ('in front of him') is an idiomatic expression for entering the temple, standing in the presence of God.[50] Remembering again the intentional connection with the baptismal scene, there is the strong sense that not only is the tearing of the curtain, negatively, a sign of judgement on the temple cult it is also, positively, an act of divine revelation. The curtain is torn, and face to face with Jesus, the centurion stands in the presence of God. This also strengthens our claim that the tearing of the curtain and the centurion's declaration are parallel responses to Jesus' death. The tearing of the curtain becomes a dramatic presentation of the Christological confession. The temple has been surpassed and it is now to those who stand in front of Jesus that God 'shows his face'. Mark's careful narrative construction links forsakenness and revelation together.

### 4. The three themes in the wider context of 15:33-39

Our clearer understanding of the three themes – abandonment, temple, identity – and their mutual climax can now shed light on some of the problems in the rest of the crucifixion scene. Kent Brower, for example, has pointed out that the introduction of the name of Elijah through the misunderstanding of the bystanders is unnecessary on a dramatic level.[51] According to Mark's account, the opening words of Jesus' cry of forsakenness, *Eloi, Eloi* ('My God, my God'), are taken to be an appeal to the prophet Elijah (verses 35-6). But redaction critics have long argued that the story flows well without verses 35-6, which have a number of exegetical difficulties, and they have tended to find a number of different traditions in these verses which have been brought together, comparatively unsuccessfully, by Mark.[52]

By contrast, I have consistently argued that Mark is a careful and thoughtful author, which suggests that the inclusion of apparently unnecessary detail serves a purpose at the theological level. Since there is no clear evidence for the tradition of calling on Elijah for help,[53] it is difficult to argue that these words would have been added by the early Church. There is no compelling reason why the earliest tradition would have been expanded with these details and there seems no other explanation for the inclusion of the Elijah incident other than it being an integral part of the remembered account. Equally it is impossible to conceive of this incident without a cry of some kind to provoke it. It is simply implausible that verses 35-6 have an independent tradition from the cry of verse 34. On the other hand, Brower offers a convincing analysis of this pericope as carefully constructed using chiastic brackets, in which each incident has its proper place.[54] From a literary critical viewpoint, having noted the climactic importance of this passage, such literary precision seems much more likely.

Exactly how the misunderstanding arose can never be fully answered,[55] but in the finished Gospel the *theological* significance of the event has two clear elements. First, the incident reinforces the sense of Jesus' forsakenness, for Elijah is one more person who does not come to help. The offer of vinegar in this context is best seen as mockery rather than a genuine attempt to help, which in this instance is also the sense conveyed by Psalm 69:21. Secondly, the Elijah incident is also part of Mark's widespread use of irony in the Gospel. All through his ministry Jesus' whole mission and his talk of God has been misunderstood; even his final words, which point again to God, are misunderstood.[56]

The pericope begins (verse 33) with the mention of three hours of darkness, linked closely to Jesus' death, although in the dramatic sequence the darkness actually occurs while Jesus is still alive and ends at the point of death. The darkness is not therefore strictly speaking representative of death, but may better be seen as symbolic of Jesus' forsakenness. Jesus cries out in the dark, looking for God, and in the same way that there is no divine answer so the darkness obscures any heavenly light. Gundry's alternative explanation that with the darkness God hides his son from the mockers fits well his own interpretation of glory, but not the understanding of forsakenness which has emerged from our literary considerations.[57] As the Gospel proceeds, the timing of the action becomes more specific, moving firstly to days at the beginning of the Passion and then to hours as the Passion reaches its culmination.[58] The three-hour schema in which the crucifixion is set, especially with the repetition of the ninth hour, is part of this building crescendo and points to this climax of Jesus' forsaken death.[59]

The status of verse 34 (the cry of forsakenness) on a literary level is also bound up with the question of the ending of the whole Gospel. If

Mark really intended to end his Gospel at 16:8 with the stark phrase *ephobounto gar* – 'for they were afraid' – then this places more importance on 15:34-9, since there is no other climax and the Gospel has an 'open' ending. Brower describes the remainder of the Gospel after 15:39 as having the character of dénouement.[60] However, the weakness of the manuscript support for any longer ending must be placed against the fact that 16:8 is a unique example of the ending of a sentence, let alone a whole book, with the particle *gar* ('for'). This must mean that the proper ending of the Gospel remains an open question and certain conclusions are impossible to reach. What we can say is that Jesus' forsaken death, with the theological significance this entails, is the great climax of the Gospel as we have it.[61]

## 5. Conclusion

Undoubtedly, questions still remain. How could there have been such a misunderstanding between the names for God and Elijah? Exactly what in Jesus' death prompted the centurion's confession? Recognizing we will never be able to answer such questions in complete confidence, I have focused on that which Mark has evidently set out to communicate, and I have shown how, at a literary level, the different elements both of this scene and earlier sections of the Gospel have been carefully formed into a unified narrative. The preparation has been laid through Mark's previous chapters, so that this moment prompts the two-fold response of the tearing of the curtain and the confession of the centurion, which both declare the Christological importance of Jesus' death. It will be important for our later doctrinal considerations that these two responses are so intimately linked to Jesus' Godforsaken death. It is not in spite of this forsakenness that God reveals God's Self, but precisely because of it. The scandal of the cross is tackled head-on, for it is only in suffering and death that divinity is fully revealed.

## Notes to Chapter 3

[1] Bultmann judges that it is 'stark entstellt'; Rudolph Bultmann, *Die Geschichte der synoptischen Tradition*, (Göttingen: Vandenhoeck and Ruprecht, 1957), p. 295.

[2] Étienne Trocmé, *The Formation of the Gospel of Mark* (London: SPCK, 1975), p. 72.

[3] Howard Kee's claim, in his *Community of the New Age: Studies in Mark's Gospel* (London: SCM, 1977), p. 64, that 'the attempt to deal with Mark exclusively or even largely on literary terms is doomed to failure' has been refuted on many fronts. For an interpretation of Mark's Gospel which sees it as a literary whole see Norman Perrin, 'Interpretation of the Gospel of Mark', *Interpretation* 30 (1976), pp. 115-24; Donald Juel, *Master of Surprise – Mark Interpreted* (Minneapolis: Fortress Press, 1994); Kent Brower, 'Elijah in the Passion Narrative', *Journal for the Study of the New Testament* 18 (1983), p. 86; Howard M. Jackson, 'The Death of Jesus in Mark and the Miracle from the Cross', *New Testament Studies* 33 (1987), p. 16; Harry L. Chronis, 'The Torn Veil: Cultus and Christology in Mark 15:37-9', *Journal of Biblical Literature* 101 (1982), pp. 97-8. For a very recent interpretation of the whole of the Gospel from a narrative perspective, see Donald Juel, *The Gospel of Mark* (Nashville: Abingdon, 1999).

[4] For example, the ingenious but clearly mistaken interpretation offered by Rabbi Dan Cohn-Sherbok, 'Jesus' Cry from the Cross – An Alternative View', *Expository Times* 93 (1981/2), pp. 215-6, would be ruled out by the wider context of Jesus' cry. He suggests that Jesus spoke in Aramaic, the last word being 'sabbahtani' rather than 'sebaqtani', so his cry would mean 'My God, why have you praised me?' This, he argues, was then misunderstood as Psalm 22:1 because, when transliterated into Greek, they are identical.

[5] See Howard Kee, *Community of the New Age*, pp. 56ff.

[6] Juel, *Master of Surprise*, p. 83.

[7] Rossé, *The Cry of Jesus*, p. 71, n. 5, states that 'according to Jewish symbolism, nudity also expresses the loss of relationship with God'.

[8] Rossé, *the Cry of Jesus*, p. 64: 'for the evangelist, as well as for his source, the cry of abandonment is found at the narrative and theological climax of the account of the passion of Jesus'.

[9] R. H. Lightfoot, *The Gospel Message of Mark* (Oxford: Clarendon Press, 1950), p. 55.

[10] Robert Gundry, *Mark, A Commentary on his Apology for the Cross* (Grand Rapids: Eerdmans, 1983), p. 1024.

11 Ibid., p. 944.

12 Ibid., p. 949.

13 Ibid., p. 966.

14 See Donald Juel, *Messiah and Temple* (Missoula: Scholars Press), p. 80; C. S. Mann, *Mark* (Garden City, New York: Doubleday, 1986) p. 194; Robert Guelich, *Mark* (Waco: Word, 1989), p. 6, where he suggests that the very similar abbreviations for 'Jesus Christ the Son of God' may have led to the omission of the final two words.

15 Jackson, 'The Death of Jesus in Mark', p. 21.

16 See Jack D. Kingsbury, *The Christology of Mark's Gospel* (Philadelphia: Fortress, 1983), p. 132.

17 Earl S. Johnson Jr., 'Is Mark 15:39 the Key to Mark's Christology?', *Journal for the Study of the New Testament* 31 (1987), pp. 3-22.

18 Ibid., p. 15.

19 Ibid. Similarly, Kingsbury's conclusion, *The Christology of Mark*, p. 131, that Mark characterizes the centurion as a 'convert' is unhelpful and misleading.

20 Philip B Harner, 'Qualitative Anarthous Predicate Nouns: Mark 15:39 and John 1:1', *Journal of Biblical Literature* 92 (1973), pp. 75-88.

21 The disputed 1:1, which begins this question of identity, also has this anarthous formula, although on that occasion with no verb present.

22 See Philip Davis, 'Mark's Christological Paradox', *Journal for the Study of the New Testament* 35 (1989), pp. 11-14. He rejects both Johnson's and Harner's arguments and argues that the reader will interpret the title based on its previous use in the Gospel and not on grammatical niceties. But then Davis continues to offer intricate grammatical arguments against Johnson in respect of Mark's use of the imperfect here!

23 Tae Hin Kim, 'The Anarthous υἱὸς θεοῦ in Mark 15:39 and the Roman Imperial Cult', Biblica 79 (1998), pp. 221-241.

24 Kingsbury, *The Christology of Mark*, p.131.

25 Chronis, 'The Torn Veil', pp. 101-2, is surely right in seeing *huios theou* as having more than just royal and messianic implications and as including the concept of divinity. He is specifically critical of Juel at this point who claims that it is synonymous with 'Christ'. For Juel's argument see *Messiah and Temple*, pp. 80-4 and 108-14.

26 There is mention of the 'House of God' in 2:26, but only in the context of an Old Testament reference to David entering the temple. Set within a series of controversies, which end with the plot to kill Jesus, it is possible that this temple reference is important and intentional, but this is by no means certain.

27 Jack D. Kingsbury, *Conflict in Mark* (Minneapolis: Fortress, 1989), p. 68.

28 Juel, *Messiah and Temple*, p. 102.

29 Theodore J. Weeden suggests, in 'The Cross as Power in Weakness', in Werner Kelber (ed.) *The Passion in Mark: Studies in Mark 14-16*, that Christology eclipses the temple motif, in such a way that the temple leads us to Christology; this is preferable to George Nicklesburg's view, in 'The Genre and Function of the Marcan Passion Narrative', Harvard *Theological Review* 73 (1980), p. 180, that Christology diffuses the temple theme, in which he finds contradictions rather than any unity.

30 Juel, *Messiah and Temple*, *passim* but especially pp. 169ff. Nicklesburg, 'Genre and Function', and Chronis, 'The Torn Veil', both rightly criticize Juel in this respect. Nicklesburg's own thesis ties everything to Mark's Gospel being written in a specific persecution/ vindication genre. Not only is this unproved and unlikely, he also ignores some of the key literary aspects of the passion narrative.

31 This is paralleled in John 2:19-22 where the destruction of the temple is clearly a reference to Jesus' death and resurrection.

32 'In one of Mark's profoundest ironies 'temple destruction and rebuilding' finally applies to the career of Jesus', Chronis, 'The Torn Veil', p. 112.

33 For Chronis, 'The Torn Veil', p. 113, the torn curtain has primarily a positive Christological significance and only functions as a secondary metaphor for the destruction of the Temple.

34 Nicklesburg, 'Genre and Function', p. 179, again misses the clear literary connections by insisting that the temple and Christology are explicitly dissociated by linking the confession to the death, not the curtain.

35 Gundry, *Mark*, p. 973, argues that if the *autou* referred to Jesus then the centurion would be described as both *by* Jesus (*parastēkōs*) and *opposite* him, which would be a contradiction.

36 See Jackson, 'The Death of Jesus in Mark', p. 33, n. 3 and 4, for a discussion of the support for *houtōs* with *kraxas*.

37 Ibid., *passim*.

38 Jackson, 'The Death of Jesus in Mark', pp. 16, 19, is specifically critical of Chronis, 'The Torn Veil', who 'with a vagueness matching that of Luke commentators too numerous to mention refers the Marcan centurion's confession to the whole manner of Jesus' death'.

39 See Jackson, 'The Death of Jesus', p. 18, who is critical of Chronis here: 'But to ground the centurion's confession in a sudden recognition of the apocalyptic and christological significance of what to a Roman soldier can have been little else than a death rattle makes of him a simple puppet of the Christian

kerygma and does violence to his independence as a character . . . Mark is not so inept a storyteller as to allow the urgency of inculcating his particular christology to blind him to the literary necessity of rooting its confession firmly and plausibly in the various contexts of the story'.

[40] Gundry, *Mark*, p. 950. Gundry follows Jackson's basic interpretation here.

[41] Jackson, 'The Death of Jesus in Mark', pp. 21-3; see Juel, *The Gospel of Mark*, p. 59.

[42] Juel, *Messiah and Temple*, pp. 44-6.

[43] See Juel, *Master of Surprise*, pp. 39-41.

[44] The New English Bible and New International Version do use 'torn' in both places. The Authorised Version, the Revised Standard Version and the Good News Bible all simply have 'opened' in 1:10. The Revised English Bible improves this slightly with 'break open', and a number of 'paraphrase' translations, such as JB Phillips, the Message and the New Living Translation all use 'split open'.

[45] Brower, 'Elijah in the Marcan Passion Narrative', pp. 86-93, also notices what he describes as the 'dramatic level' and the 'reader level' at work throughout the Gospel.

[46] Jackson, 'The Death of Jesus in Mark', p. 23. For example, Kee, *Community of the New Age*, p. 32, still considers that Bultmann is right to point to the disorder in this pericope and that this results from Mark's imperfect combination of complex traditions.

[47] Lightfoot, *The Gospel Message of St Mark*, pp. 55-6, exemplifies those who do not treat Mark on its own terms and argues for the inner curtain based on the reference in Hebrews 9:3.

[48] Juel, *Master of Surprise*, p. 32, suggests that the author trusts the imagination of his readers!

[49] Tae Hin Kim's suggestion that *huios theou* referred to Augustus makes it a well-known phrase, but even more radically significant when applied to Jesus. He is probably right that Mark is challenging the Roman cult, but this entails that the centurion had a greater understanding of the significance of what he was saying. His conviction, in 'The Anarthous υἱὸς θεου in Mark 15:39', p. 240, that Mark would not credit such a saying to so unlikely a person also overlooks that this is precisely the point. It is a Gentile who 'sees'.

[50] Chronis, 'The Torn Veil', pp. 109-10.

[51] Brower, 'Elijah in the Marcan Passion Narrative', pp. 85-6.

[52] For example, Frank Matera, *The Kingship of Jesus* (Chico: Scholars Press, 1982), p. 31, suggests that the quote from Psalm 22 and the Elijah incident came together from originally different traditions.

[53] Rossé, *The Cry of Jesus*, p. 17, thinks that this was a popular Jewish belief, but Jeremias shows that this is the earliest example of Elijah understood as a helper, a concept that had no place in the early church. See the article ʹΗλ(ε)ιας in G. Kittel (ed.), *The Theological Dictionary of the New Testament* (Grand Rapids: Eerdmans, 1964), p. 930.

[54] Brower, 'Elijah in the Marcan Passion Narrative', pp. 88f.

[55] See below, pp. 57-60, for further discussion of the language of the cry and its historical basis.

[56] Brower, 'Elijah in the Marcan Passion Narrative', p. 94.

[57] Gundry, *Mark*, p. 947.

[58] Kingsbury, *Conflict in Mark*, p. 49.

[59] See Rossé, *The Cry of Jesus*, p. 34. Although the hours mentioned do conform to the Jewish hours of prayer, to introduce some new liturgical theme, at a time when Mark is focusing our attention on Jesus' forsakenness seems unlikely. More possible may be some intended link between the three hours of darkness and the three days from crucifixion to resurrection. If there is this intended meaning, and the possibility cannot be pushed too far, it must be in addition to the three-hour schema pointing to a climax.

[60] Brower, 'Elijah in the Marcan Passion Narrative', pp. 92-3.

[61] See Juel, *The Gospel of Mark*, pp. 167-76, for a discussion of the ending of the Gospel from a literary perspective.

# 4
# A Happy Ending?

## Mark 15:34 in Relation to Psalm 22

### 1. The themes of the psalm

Although we have thus far been careful to interpret the cry of forsakenness in Mark 15:34 within the context of the Gospel itself, it is
immediately obvious that these words are in fact taken from the first verse
of Psalm 22. In addition to this one direct quotation there are numerous
Old Testament references and allusions in the final scenes of Jesus' passion, particularly to other parts of Psalm 22 as well as to other psalms of
lament. The casting of lots for Jesus' clothing in 15:24 picks up words
from Psalm 22:18, and the reference to the mocking of Jesus in 15:29
echoes Psalm 22:7, with even the same Greek phrase, *kinountes tas
kephalas* ('shaking their heads'), being used.[1] Psalm 69:21 is alluded to in
the offer of wine in 15:23 and 15:36, and also Psalm 69:9 in the insults
Jesus endures in Mark 15:32.[2]

Given the climactic nature of this passage and the significant usage of
Old Testament quotations and allusions throughout the Gospel,[3] the reference to Psalm 22:1 in Mark 15:34 raises two central and important issues.
First, did Jesus actually say these words, or was an Old Testament phrase
put on his lips by Mark or the earlier tradition? This will be the subject of
the next chapter. Secondly, should these words simply be taken at face
value or does the significance of Jesus' cry depend in some way on the
original context of Psalm 22? Do these words stand alone, or is more of
Psalm 22 implied by this short cry?

The question is of some significance because Psalm 22 includes contrasting ideas, weaving together lament, prayer and thanksgiving. The
psalmist begins with the starkest declaration of his situation: God has
abandoned him. He has cried out, but heard only silence. The following
verses then spell out some of the reasons for feeling this way. The
psalmist is like a worm, despised and mocked by others who shake their
heads at him (verses 6-7); it is as if he is surrounded by bulls (verse 12)

and lions (verse 13) and a pack of dogs (verse. 16); he feels weak and ill and close to death (verses 14-15). And in this state of forsakenness the psalmist cries out to God again, that even now God might come close and save him (verses 11, 19-21). But then in verse 22, the tone of the psalm changes completely. It is as if there is a time delay between verses 21 and 22, and in between something has happened; God has answered the prayer, God has come close and acted to save. So the psalmist announces his intention to declare God's goodness before all the people, and give testimony to what God has done. For God does not neglect those who suffer, but answers their call for help (verse 24). Peter Craigie suggests that the psalm ends with the gathered congregation joining in this litany of thanksgiving,[4] and the psalm concludes with an offering of praise to the God who saves his people (verse 31).

Such diverse material has suggested to some exegetes that two distinct psalms have been joined together at a later date.[5] Leaving aside such questions, for it has been handed down and was read as a unified work, we must ask again about the meaning of Mark 15:34 in the light of Psalm 22 as a whole. Whereas the cry 'my God, why have you forsaken me?' is the pivotal thought of the first half of the psalm, the second half counteracts this blunt assertion by rejoicing in the experience of salvation, and ends not with despair but a deep trust in God. So did Jesus and/or Mark – and we must be open to the possibility that they meant different things – intend the words of the cry of dereliction to be understood simply as they are, or was the whole of the psalm in view with its concluding prayer of trust? Does the cry of dereliction, in spite of all its bleakness, really contain within itself a happy ending?

## 2. The influence of the psalm on Mark's account

In spite of the various allusions to Psalm 22 in the crucifixion of Jesus, I propose that there is overwhelming evidence that Mark intends the words of the cry to be understood on their own merit in the context of the Gospel story, without introducing the theme of trust or thanksgiving from the *end* of the psalm. Jesus cries out expressing his abandonment from God.

It is often suggested that we should not be surprised that Jesus quoted words from the Old Testament at his death, for as a Jew he would have been able to quote many of its verses. No doubt others called on God at times of trouble using these or other scriptural words. Thus Joachim Jeremias is content to conclude that 'the Psalter . . . was evidently Jesus' prayer book'.[6] Such a view, at least in respect of Psalm 22, may receive some support from Craigie's interpretation of the original Psalm, which he conceives of as liturgy.[7] Although no doubt originating in the experiences of one person, he suggests that it appears in the Psalms as a liturgy for individuals to use within a corporate setting. People who themselves felt that God was distant would use this psalm to express such grief to God and pause after verse 21 and wait for an oracle from the priest or prophet. On hearing good news from God they would continue with the latter verses as an expression of thanksgiving and trust.[8]

Although this may be the case in Old Testament liturgy, John Reuman has shown that Jeremias' opinion of personal prayer in the first century is an unjustified assumption, since examples of any sections of the Old Testament used in such piety are lacking, let alone specifically the first verse of Psalm 22. There is one often quoted occasion when Psalm 22:1 is used in this kind of way, in the Midrash on the Psalms. This retells the story of Esther who calls out with the words of Psalm 22:1. But this, as Reuman points out, offers no comparison to Mark 15:34.[9] The Midrash is a purely literary work in which the words are placed by an author on the lips of someone in the past and so actually offers no evidence of what a Jew might have spontaneously cried. In addition the problem of dating means that this particular piece of midrash may actually be later than Mark's Gospel itself. No doubt Jesus would have been familiar with the psalms and there is no evidence that Jews did not use such quotations in their own prayers, but we can draw no conclusions about the meaning of Mark 15:34 on such a tendentious basis.[10]

Lorren Fisher attempts to make a case that the first line of psalms or other biblical songs were used as a title and stood for the whole of the psalm or song.[11] He cites as evidence the more certain example of Exodus 15:21, in which Miriam sings the song of Moses contained in Exodus 15:1-18, with only the first line reappearing in the text, and then the less certain example of Psalm 68, claiming this to be a collection of first lines of ancient psalms. Fisher also produces an example from the Mishnah in which whole psalms are referred to by their first line, but the context is more akin to the index of a hymn-book than a narrative. Further, he cites a psalm from Qumran in which the theme of forsakenness is taken up in a new psalm of thanksgiving that God has not in fact forsaken the worshipper. Despite the fact that the Mishnah and Qumran passages are so different in style and context to Mark and that he can offer no evidence of such a practice in the New Testament,[12] Fisher concludes that 'it is impossible to speak of God forsaking Jesus'[13]. The central purpose of Fisher's article is to argue that Jesus was not forsaken by God but abandoned by his friends. He puts forward these two themes as opposites without realising that they are actually connected together in Mark's Gospel. The article as a whole betrays the fact that theologically Fisher cannot accept the forsakenness of Christ,[14] and so resorts to the most tenuous arguments against it.[15]

Despite the various references in Mark 15 it seems most unlikely that the evangelist has used Psalm 22 as a whole to provide the structure or framework for this section of the Passion narrative, since the experience of Jesus does not in fact mirror the remaining details of Psalm 22. In the psalm the sufferer begins by proclaiming his abandonment by God and this then leads to his mocking, trouble and sickness. But in Mark's Gospel the progression is reversed. Beginning with the desertion of his family and friends, followed by the mocking of his enemies, Jesus' forsakenness by God is the culmination of his experience. Even ignoring the second half of the psalm, which announces the sufferer's thanksgiving, verses 1-21 do not correspond to the Marcan portrayal of Jesus' life and especially his passion. Mark, in common with other New Testament writers draws on Psalm 22 in his presentation of Jesus, but not for a framework for the Gospel.

### 3. Mark's use of scripture

Light may be thrown on the meaning of Mark 15:34 by considering the way in which the evangelist uses Scriptural quotations throughout the Gospel. It is clear that Mark exercises a comparatively free hand in this respect, for example blending and merging texts, such as the conflated quotation from the prophets Isaiah and Malachi in 1:2-3,[16] or relying on specific details of the (Greek) Septuagint translation of the Hebrew

Bible.[17] Robert Gundry asserts that all New Testament writers draw on verses from the start, middle or end of Old Testament passages with only those verses in mind.[18] Yet some interpretations of Gospel passages depend to a large degree on their original context. Donald Juel, while recognising an 'atomistic exegesis' in many cases, argues that we can only understand Jesus' strange description of the Temple as a 'den of robbers', especially compared to John's much milder 'market' (2:16), in the light of its context in Jeremiah 7:11. The original passage speaks of the forthcoming destruction of the temple, explaining why the reference to robbers is chosen here.[19]

Mark 15:34 is unique, in that the rest of the quotations on Jesus' lips are in the context of his teaching, either to the disciples or crowds, or disputing with the Jewish leaders. Here alone does Jesus speak Old Testament words to express his own inner life and relationship with God. Yet despite this uniqueness we can expect the Old Testament to be handled in the same way throughout the Gospel. The only conclusion we can thus draw is that although, on some occasions, Mark may have drawn on a particular verse because its original context suggested its suitability that is certainly not always the case. In addition, in Juel's example above, although the charge of banditry itself may not be a justified response to the fleecing of tourists, but owes more to the original Old Testament context, the general thrust of Jesus' charge is clear without reference to or knowledge of Jeremiah. It is the *strength* of Jesus' denouncement that is clarified by the Old Testament background, not the very denouncement itself. If Jesus' cry of Psalm 22:1 is meant to convey the meaning of the whole of the psalm, and thus an attitude of trust and thanksgiving, then it can only do so both with detailed knowledge of Psalm 22, and on the assumption, not at all proved, that the first line would be understood to imply the whole psalm. If either aspect is absent the opposite meaning is implied by the actual words used. Although the original context may sometimes be important in the choice of an Old Testament quotation, there is no suggestion that any such quotation in Mark *only* makes sense if the original context is known. The original context may add depth to the reader's appreciation of the significance of the words employed, but in no case does it change the meaning entirely. If Mark was attempting to convey the theme of trust, then using Psalm 22:1 is a most inept way to proceed![20]

## 4. The context of the cry

Whatever the original background and subsequent use of words from Psalm 22:1, the cry must be understood in its context, and this is the most important clue to its correct interpretation. As we have already seen this clearly points to the theme of abandonment, especially as the cry, the tearing of the curtain and the response of the centurion form the climax of the whole Gospel through which Mark stresses that it is precisely in his Godforsaken death that Jesus' divinity is seen. Jesus' death is of course not the end and is turned around in the resurrection, but that is still to come and not at all in view in this passage. To interpret the cry in such a way that the first line stands for the whole psalm is to take the verse completely out of the context of the passion narrative and the whole Gospel. Moltmann is surely right when he insists that Jesus' cry is not to be read in the light of Psalm 22 but 'it is more correct to interpret the words of the psalm in the sense of the situation of Jesus'.[21]

The exact nature of the relationship between Psalm 22 and Mark's Gospel is impossible to prove. The two primary possibilities are either that Mark, or the earlier tradition, inherited a very simple account of Jesus' death and used Psalm 22:1 and other material to create a fuller version,[22] or that Jesus actually died with the words of Psalm 22:1 on his lips and Mark found in the psalm other material that fitted the traditions surrounding Jesus' crucifixion.[23] We will turn to the historical question in the next chapter, but – whatever might be the case historically – there is no evidence to support a 'happy' interpretation of the words as given; a precise reading of the Gospel clearly implies that when we hear Jesus' cry we are to understand it as indicating Jesus' forsakenness by God.

A subsequent question would then be whether Jesus *was* abandoned or only *felt* abandoned by God. This demands an answer at two levels, of history and theology. Historically, we shall be considering in the next chapter whether Jesus himself actually said these words. If we were to conclude that Jesus did say these words, biblical exegesis can only understand this as an accurate expression of Jesus' experience; that is, we can legitimately state that Jesus *felt* abandoned. Whether Jesus' experience on the cross indicates a real breaking in the relationship between Jesus and God is a theological question, which includes our understanding of Jesus' divinity and the whole nature of God. Through the climactic nature of this passage and the ever-deepening theme of forsakenness Mark himself seems to present this as more than just a felt experience, and so as a reality. This debate between feeling and reality will be considered further in subsequent chapters and will be central to our interpretation of the cross.

### 5. The sense of abandonment

For those theologians who have sought to play down the theme of forsakenness the emphasis on trust and thanksgiving at the end of Psalm 22 has naturally been welcomed as wider Biblical evidence for their interpretation. However, those who have sought to resolve the harsh climax in 15:34 into a happier ending have also sought exegetical support in other ways. We have already noted Gundry's contention that the whole purpose of the Gospel is to redact the tradition of the cross into a motif of Jesus' glory and power. So the time of darkness during the crucifixion is God hiding his Son from mockery, and the loudness of Jesus' subsequent cry – for Gundry believes there was only one – testifies to his superhuman strength, which is enough to tear the curtain of the Temple.[24] An alternative view, which accepts two distinct cries (verses 34, 37), imagines that this portentous event was caused by the second cry, a cry of victory, which thus balances the earlier cry of abandonment.[25] Kingsbury, on the other hand, stressing the suffix 'my' in the appeal *Elo-i* ('My God') concludes that Jesus is pictured as going to his death as one who places his total trust in God.[26] Although this cry is certainly a cry for God and Jesus is certainly looking for God in the midst of abandonment, to describe this as 'total trust' risks a docetic interpretation which seems to play down the reality of Jesus' forsakenness.

A further popular misreading of the earliest Gospel is to harmonize Mark with the later accounts of Luke and John, with the result that the dramatic climax of Mark's Gospel is always lost, softened by its juxtaposition to the more positive words from the cross in these Gospels.[27] Such interpretations may reveal more about the preconceptions of the various commentators than about the meaning of the biblical text. In the next chapter we will consider in greater detail the different Gospel accounts together with these difficult historical questions, but it is vital that we first treat each of the Gospels as a separate and unified account.

## 6. Conclusion

Our discussion of Mark's use of the Old Testament in general, some consideration of the meaning of Psalm 22 and our focus on the context of Jesus' cry, combine to offer the strongest evidence that, in the context of the Gospel of Mark, Jesus' cry must be taken at face value and understood to express the depth of abandonment Jesus experienced at the cross. There is no secondary meaning implied or hidden behind the text, so that what appears to be a cry of abandonment can be turned into a cry of trust or thanksgiving. Clearly the cry must be understood in the light of the subsequent resurrection – Moltmann is right to insist repeatedly that we must always speak of the death of the risen Christ[28] – but balancing the forsakenness of the cross with the joy of the resurrection is very different from reinterpreting the cry itself.

## Notes to Chapter 4

[1] Mark's Bible was the Septuagint (the Greek translation of the Hebrew Bible) and the verbal comparisons in 15:34 are with that version. Similarly *ōneidizon* ('insulted') in 15:32 is also an echo of the language of Psalm 22:7. It is interesting that there is no allusion in Mark to Psalm 22:16, 'they have pierced my hands and my feet', although similar details are mentioned in John 20:25.

[2] For a comprehensive survey of both the Old Testament influences in the crucifixion scene in Mark and the use made of Psalm 22 through the whole of the New Testament see John Reuman, 'Psalm 22 at the Cross: Lament and Thanksgiving for Jesus Christ', *Interpretation* 24 (1974), pp. 39-58.

[3] It is clear that Mark himself had a good grasp of the Old Testament, and expected a similar understanding from his readers. See Juel, *The Gospel of Mark*, pp. 35-9.

[4] Peter C. Craigie, *Psalms 1-50*, (Waco: Word, 1983), pp. 201-2.

[5] See A. A. Anderson, *The Psalms vol. 1* (New Century Bible, London: Marshall, Morgan, & Scott, 1972), p. 184.

[6] Joachim Jeremias, *New Testament Theology: Vol 1* (London: SCM, 1971), p. 205. Previously, p. 189, Jeremias also writes: 'Jesus was fond of praying in the words of the Psalter: that is particularly true if the quotation of the beginning of Psalm 22 is meant to indicate that Jesus prayed the whole psalm'.

[7] Craigie, *Psalms 1-50*, pp. 197-202.

[8] Artur Weiser, *The Psalms* (The Old Testament Library, London: SCM, 1962), p. 219, and A. A. Anderson, *The Psalms vol. 1*, pp. 184-5, had expressed similar ideas. Anderson also suggests that the purpose of the psalm may be thanksgiving, with the initial lament looking back to the past.

[9] Reuman, 'Psalm 22 at the Cross', pp. 55-7. The passage of note from the Midrash on the Psalms is in Midr. Teh. xxii. 2. Tr. in *The Midrash on the Psalms*, Vol. I (New Haven: Yale Judaica Studies, 13, 1959), pp. 297ff. Reuman himself is indebted to the quotation of this passage in Gustav Dalman, *Jesus-Jeshua: Studies in the Gospels* (London: SPCK, 1929) p. 206. Rossé, *The Cry of Jesus*, p. 40, refers to Th. Boman's claim, in 'Das letzte Wort Jesu', *Studia Theologica* 17 (1963) p. 111, that Jesus was not in the habit of expressing himself with Old Testament quotations, from which Boman concludes that the cry is not historical.

[10] Reuman's last paragraph is an unexpected and quite unjustified conclusion, in which, despite all he has said previously, he pictures the cross as offering a lament in suffering, and thanksgiving for what God did in response, implying that the whole of the psalm is in view.

[11] Lorren R. Fisher, 'Betrayed by Friends – An Exposition of Psalm 22', *Interpretation* 18 (1964), pp. 20-38. Rossé, *The Cry of Jesus*, p. 103, refers to S. Del Paramos' suggestion, in *Vangelo secundo Matteo*, Nuovo Testamento (Rome: Città Nuova, 1970) p. 413, that it is probable that Jesus spoke the first verse in a loud voice and then the rest of the psalm quietly to himself. Rossé quite rightly gives this little consideration.

[12] Fisher, 'Betrayed by Friends', p. 24, admits 'examples are not easy to find'. The only New Testament reference is to Matthew 12:18-21, where Fisher concedes Matthew quotes the whole of that servant song.

[13] Ibid., p. 37.

[14] See, for example his judgement: 'It may be that some theologians have a need of a forsaken Christ in their theological systems . . . but when these passages are put in their context, it becomes important to put the blame for betrayal on man rather than God'. Ibid., p. 37.

[15] Rossé, *The Cry of Jesus*, p. 104, quotes E. Fromm's general claim, in *Voi sarete come dei* (Rome, 1970), pp. 155f, that it is probable Jesus and his contemporaries referred to psalms by their first line because that has been more recent

practice. Rossé does not accept this point, but is surely being too generous in considering this to be a serious argument.

16 Malachi 3:1, Isaiah 40:3

17 Kee, *Community of the New Age*, p. 46, has a list of eighteen examples of this in Mark 11-16.

18 Gundry, *Mark*, p. 966.

19 Juel, *Messiah and Temple*, p. 133.

20 Gundry, *Mark*, p. 966.

21 Moltmann, *The Crucified God*, p.150.

22 Martin Dibelius, *From Tradition to Gospel* (London: Ivor Nicholson and Watson, 1934), pp. 193ff, argues that the early Christians used Old Testament passages to explain the passion, which they found offensive, as the will of God. Yet words from Jesus at this climactic point seem to accentuate the offensive aspect of the cross rather than diminish it.

23 Reuman, 'Psalm 22 at the Cross', p. 54, also notes these two possibilities.

24 Gundry, *Mark*, pp. 947-8; also see his discussion of *phōnē* on p. 950.

25Reuman, 'Psalm 22 at the Cross', p. 51, notes this suggestion but offers no references.

26 Kingsbury, *The Christology of Mark*, p. 130.

27 For example, David Atkinson, 'A Cry of Faith', *Expository Times* 96 (1985), pp. 146-7.

28 This is a formulation, together with 'the resurrection of the Crucified Christ', which appears throughout Moltmann's work.

# 5

# A True Account?

## Mark 15:34 in the Wider Gospel Traditions

Mark's message to his readers seems evident – in the Godforsakenness of the cross the divinity of Jesus is revealed – but what judgement can be made as to the authenticity of Mark's interpretation? There are obvious differences with the other three Gospels, behind which lies the more vexed question of historical accuracy.

### 1. Jesus' cry in relationship to the other Gospels

Matthew, like Mark, contains the cry of dereliction as the only words of Jesus on the cross. It is well attested how Matthew has used Mark as a major source, using all but fifty verses of his Gospel,[1] and so, as might be expected, the vast majority of the Marcan themes are also found in Matthew. In general terms, however, Matthew has different concerns. Although the cry of Jesus is retained its theological import is changed by the wider context of the passion and the whole life of Jesus. The progressive motif of abandonment, for example, while still present in Matthew, has neither the coherence nor importance that it has in Mark.

Whereas a deliberately arranged cycle of conflict-narratives begins in Mark as early as chapter two, the parallel passages in Matthew lack the same tight structure and emphasis; they do not occur until chapter nine, with the first direct opposition of the Jewish authorities to Jesus.[2] Furthermore, the comment in Mark 3:21 that Jesus' family came to find him because he was 'out of his mind' is completely omitted from the beginning of the Beelzebub controversy in Matthew 12:22. Similarly, Matthew retains the declaration that Jesus is the 'Son of God' at his baptism, transfiguration, trial and crucifixion, but it is no longer used in a programmatic way. Instead of introducing the Gospel with this title, Matthew begins with the alternative appellation of Jesus as the 'son of David' and 'son of Abraham'. Again, the messianic secret, which produces such an emphatic climax in Mark 15:39, is not part of the dramatic

style of Matthew's Gospel, for Jesus speaks to the disciples about his
Father (see 11:27), and they confess him as the Son of God both collec-
tively (14:33) and through Peter (16:16).

The condensed and nuanced interrelation of themes in the Marcan climax is dissipated in Matthew's longer account. The connections between
cry, curtain and confession are disrupted by additional material, such as
the earthquake and the raising of the dead (27:52-53), and weakened by
the added motif of the fear of the centurion in response to such portentous
events. Matthew makes other additional changes in the parallel pericope
to Mark 15:33-39, beyond the merely stylistic. Inserting *peri* ('about') in
the clause referring to the ninth hour (27:46), having also earlier omitted
the reference to the third hour in Mark 15:25, makes Mark's precise
chronology into an approximation, thus reducing the climactic emphasis
of Jesus' cry. Matthew further removes the ambiguities from Mark's
account; with regard to the two cries, his insertion of 'again' (*palin*) in
27:50 clarifies that the inarticulate cry was distinct and later, and with
regard to the centurion's position he omits *ex anantias autou* ('in front of
him/it'), which is redundant in the light of the earthquake's impact. One
change, however, actually emphasizes a strong Marcan theme, for the
phrase 'he gave up his spirit' (*aphēken to pneuma*) connects the baptism
and crucifixion even more strongly.[3] Although Matthew is clearly dependent on Mark and the two accounts are similar on the dramatic level,
small redactions lead to significant theological differences.

Luke and John both offer accounts of Jesus' life and death which are
theologically complete within themselves but contain striking differences
from each of the other Gospels.[4] 'Father, into your hands I commit my
spirit'[5], is a fitting end to Luke's portrayal of Jesus in the whole Gospel in
which the theme of obedience dominates. In the same way that Jesus resolutely sets out for Jerusalem knowing what would befall him (9:51), so
he offers his life in the same spirit of obedience. The quotation from
Psalm 22 would not fit theologically in this context whereas the prayer
from Psalm 31 acts, for Luke, as a fitting climax.[6] Jesus' final cry in John,
'it is finished' (*tetelestai*), brings to a climax both the theme of fulfilment
and the great Johannine motif of Jesus' enthronement and glorification on
the cross. Again, forsakenness is ill at ease in a narrative in which giving

freely of his life and demonstrating control over events are important features in the portrayal of Jesus.

Although there are dominant themes in each Gospel, this is not to say that a theme highlighted by one evangelist is absent completely from all the others. The references in Mark to the atoning purpose of the cross (10:45), and the repeated promises of his resurrection mean that Jesus' cross is not portrayed as a failure, in spite of the stress on abandonment. Jesus' forsakenness is neither meaningless nor final, but rather necessary for salvation. Neither does Jesus walk that way unwillingly, but *gives* his life as a ransom for many. Matthew, who retains the motif of forsakenness, also reminds us of Jesus' authority (28:19) and adds to Mark the repeated address of Jesus as 'Lord'. Luke, alongside his stress on the obedience of Jesus, retains the Marcan material of betrayal, denial and mockery, and there is the clear sense that Jesus, at least humanly speaking, is alone. Even in John's portrayal of the passion there is a glimpse of the Jesus who suffers and is in need, to the point that he cries 'I am thirsty'.[7] Finally there is the cross itself, for however much the themes of obedience, salvation and victory are drawn out, at least in a Jewish setting, to be crucified was to be under God's curse.

Any comparative study of the four Gospels must conclude that a proper understanding of each 'word from the cross' can only be achieved in the light of the Gospel in which it appears.[8] Each of the seven statements of Jesus makes perfect sense within its own setting and in some way brings to a climax important themes for each evangelist. Jesus' conflict with the Jewish authorities, his betrayal, denial, arrest, appearance before the High Priest and Pilate and his subsequent crucifixion form the plot in all four Gospels and in this context the identity of Jesus is developed. Within this central framework the significance of the story is brought out by the evangelists in different ways. Theologically, the differing emphases, abandonment in Mark and, though to a lesser degree, Matthew, obedience in Luke and victory in John, can be successfully combined in an overall understanding of Jesus' death. It is much harder, however, to unite the seven words of the cross as historical sayings, because the differences are so sharply highlighted. For those interested in the historical Jesus, one crucial question will be which word Jesus said last. In other words, how did Jesus die? Such a consideration is beyond the scope of this study, which focuses more exclusively on Mark's Gospel. I have suggested that because the sense of abandonment is present in the very fact of the cross it is included in some way in all of the Gospels. But in Mark's Gospel more than any other this is made a focal point. Is, then, Mark's particular interpretation valid?[9]

## 2. The historicity of Jesus' cry

If Mark had omitted verse 34 and portrayed Jesus dying only with a loud inarticulate cry, the underlying meaning of the crucifixion scene would not be significantly changed. There is still the progressive abandonment of Jesus by all those around him culminating in his death on the cross, considered from a Jewish perspective to be under God's curse. There is obvious dramatic and theological weight in the fact that Jesus himself speaks these words, but Mark's theology does not rest exclusively on this cry, and in this sense the historicity of the cry could be considered a secondary consideration. Paul, for example, makes no mention of such a cry but can argue for a similar theology in which Jesus is considered both 'sin' and 'a curse' based on the incontestable historical evidence of Jesus' death on the cross.[10] But the cry is the dramatic climax of the Gospel, and brings this underlying meaning of the cross to centre stage. Does this result from artistic licence, or is the cry part of the historical framework on which the Gospel is built?

### a. External evidence

Textual study highlights the weakening of Jesus' cry in later biblical manuscripts, particularly the change from 'why have you forsaken me' to 'why have you reproached me?' (*ōneidisas*) in Codex Bezae and related manuscripts.[11] There is a similar weakening in other, non-canonical sources, such as the change to 'my power, why have you left me?' (*hē dunamis mou kateleipsas me*) in the Gospel of Peter. Although we have seen that Luke and John both offer theologically coherent Gospels in which a cry of dereliction would be inappropriate, it is also true that the alternatives they offer seem theologically easier and less dramatic. There is a general trend to move away from the more difficult theme of abandonment. Therefore, not only does *egkatelipes* (*abandoned/forsaken*) stand out as the earliest reading, but we may judge that the clear move away from abandonment in later material suggests that it is unlikely that such a cry would have been added by the Church to the earlier tradition.

Gérard Rossé, however, considers this argument to be weak for three reasons. (i) Adding this cry in a Palestinian Church would not be misunderstood because it would have been recognized as Psalm 22 and so – Rossé argues – a prayer of trust. (ii) The cry corresponds well to the earlier parable of the tenants in which they killed the son and 'threw him out the vineyard'. (iii) The cross itself is a symbol of abandonment. Therefore 'the community not only did not have any difficulty in placing, if necessary, such a cry on the mouth of Jesus, but also had to do so because it had to look the cross in the face; it could not avoid it with the entire burden of its curse'.[12] In response, we may judge that individually Rossé's arguments have little merit and when combined contradict each other. First, we have already shown that there is no good reason to interpret Jesus' cry as one of trust and equally no sure evidence to suggest that Mark was written in a Palestinian milieu.[13] Second, connecting Jesus' cry with the parable of the tenants, especially given the Old Testament's symbolic presentation of Israel as the 'vineyard', seems to contradict Rossé's own argument that the main point of the prayer is one of trust, since the parable evokes a sense of real forsakenness; further, to argue that Jesus' cry simply arose from a parable fails to express the significance of Jesus himself speaking these words at his death. Third, Luke and John both face the horror of the cross without using this cry, while its addition clearly adds dramatic and theological weight.[14]

A related external argument for historical authenticity is that of double dissimilarity: neither the cry nor the misunderstanding about Elijah are found either in contemporary Jewish spirituality or in the life of the early church. We have already highlighted the fact that there is very little evidence to suggest that Psalm 22:1 was routinely spoken by pious Jews in trouble and that this is also the earliest evidence for Jews calling on Elijah for help. Certainly there would have been no tradition in the early church either of Jesus or Christians calling on Elijah for help, so the passage gives no insight into contemporary experience within the Marcan community. Thus, while external factors offer no certainty, they present evidence that quite strongly points towards the historicity of the cry.[15]

## b. Internal evidence

The internal evidence of the narrative at this point also suggests that the cry is at least part of the early tradition. Bultmann considered that the cry of Jesus was probably a secondary interpretation of Mark 15:37, where a simple fact of a loud cry is narrated,[16] and was added by the Christian community to help explain this inarticulate cry. A number of exegetes since have followed Bultmann in seeing the two cries as a doublet, two references to one event. But the distinctiveness and authenticity of Jesus' articulate cry makes much better sense of the composition of the narrative. Although Matthew's addition of *palin* ('again') clarifies the point, verses 34 and 37 function in Mark's Gospel as presenting two separate cries within a consecutive series of events. Rossé's suggestion that the inarticulate cry is a repetition of the first cry, that Jesus died with the first cry and that this is the reason he did not drink the offered vinegar, highlights the forsakenness of Jesus at his death but at the expense of twisting the narrative sequence.

The confusion between the names of God and Elijah is clearly dependent on Jesus saying something that could be misunderstood. The suggestion that Mark has badly joined together two separate sources, the cry from one and the Elijah incident from the other, both fails to see the careful way that Mark has crafted his Gospel and struggles to provide an adequate reason why there should be any mention at all of Elijah in any tradition. It is possible that 15:36, with its reference to waiting to see whether Elijah would come to rescue Jesus, stood independently in the tradition and that the confusion of names in 15:35 is a narrative connection to explain the introduction of Elijah. But given the lack of evidence for Elijah as a helper and the great difficulty involved in the confusion of names, there seems no literary or theological reason to have included an independent tradition of an Elijah motif and then engineered so tenuous a link. Whatever the place of these motifs in the tradition, Mark puts the whole incident to significant theological use. Although no definite conclusions can be reached, it seems most likely that Jesus' cry and the waiting for Elijah were always linked in the tradition and have the same origin. Given the external evidence for both the uniqueness of the cry and the role of Elijah, the historicity of this event appears the most satisfactory conclusion.[17]

Whether Jesus' cry is a historical fact or a later expansion of the narrative, there remains the difficulty of how these words from Psalm 22:1 – written by Mark as *elōi elōi* ('My God, my God . . '.) – could be misunderstood as *Elijah*. Mark gives us few clues as to the make-up of the crowd at the foot of the cross, apart from indicating that there were both Jews and Gentiles. Jewish hearers, who alone might have been aware of an Elijah tradition, would be likely to understand both the Aramaic itself and the origin of the quotation. Gentiles, on the other hand, may have had an inadequate grasp of Aramaic, with resulting confusion, but then would not be expected to think of Elijah as a helper. There are also a number of differences in the actual events portrayed by Matthew and Mark. In Matthew 27:47-9 some of the bystanders misunderstand Jesus' cry, one of whom offers Jesus the wine and then the group of bystanders caution they should wait for Elijah. In Mark 15:35-6 the wine is offered by an individual, quite possibly distinct from the first group and perhaps a soldier, who alone cautions to wait for Elijah. Yet in both Gospels it is the crowd of bystanders who misunderstand Jesus, a crowd that it seems most natural to suppose from the preceding events is made up of Jews.

A. Guillaume offers the intriguing suggestion that Jesus cried out '*Eliya*', the normal word for 'God' with a Semitic first person suffix, thus making the misunderstanding more feasible. Subsequently such a word form became redundant, the suffix was dropped and a shortened form, in line with an established Old Testament text, appears in the Gospel.[18] Guillaume's assumption is that the Hebrew of Matthew's account (*ēli ēli*) is actually the more original, despite being the later Gospel, and that Mark contains a translation into Aramaic.[19] Such a hypothesis can, of course, never be proved. Any discussion of the exact words of the cry is hampered by the immensely complex textual traditions and the confusion created by the scribal use of uncial abbreviations and the copying of unfamiliar and foreign words. *ēli ēli lema sabachthani*' in Matthew 27:46 and *elōi elōi lama sabachthani* in Mark 15:34, the texts printed most frequently in Greek editions of the New Testament, are not actually found complete in any major manuscript, and both versions have slight differences from the Septuagint text of the psalm. There is clear agreement as to the root words used, but the preferred text draws the exact spelling of each word from different manuscripts.[20] In addition, the traditional distinction that Matthew records the cry in Hebrew and Mark in Aramaic may itself be too simplistic.[21] Although in some manuscripts the spelling in one Gospel has influenced the text of the other, we cannot be certain exactly what Matthew and Mark wrote, and so are unable to deduce the nature of any Matthean redaction.

### c. Other historical factors

Two further aspects of Jesus' cry have raised historical problems in some theologians' minds. In the first place, the loudness of Jesus' cry is highlighted, twice, by Mark. We have seen that Gundry finds a theological significance in this loudness,[22] but from a historical perspective it is generally thought that those who were crucified would have struggled to speak at all. After presenting the arguments against Jesus' ability to cry out in a loud voice, Rossé simply concludes, 'In spite of these data, the otherwise surprising report that Jesus dies uttering 'a loud cry' undoubtedly has historical value'.[23] The second problem, again raised by Rossé, is Bowman's contention that Jesus was not in the habit of exposing his inner life to public view and so certainly would not have done so at this point.[24] Both features are certainly exceptional and cannot simply be dismissed. Although evidence suggests it would be difficult for a crucified man to cry out, it does not follow that such a cry was impossible and that Jesus must have died silently. All four Gospels testify that Jesus spoke and even the suggestion that only the inarticulate cry in Mark 15:37 is original implies that Jesus cried out. Similarly, while Jesus' cry of forsakenness may be different from all his other words in Mark's Gospel, it is impossible for any commentator to know enough of the experience of crucifixion to dismiss any exclamations as *prima facie* impossible. Furthermore, the particular crucifixion of Jesus itself was an exceptional event and this may be the reason for its unique characteristics.

Secondly, the centurion is reported as responding with the declaration that Jesus was the Son of God. We have already noted that this confession is important in its Marcan context, that Matthew retains the same response, although attributes it to the centurion's observation of the miraculous portents, and that Luke replaces *huios theou* ('Son of God') with *dikaios* ('righteous', so reading: 'Truly this man was *innocent*'). Although it seems quite different, the Lucan redaction can actually be read with a very similar meaning to the other synoptics. Not only does *dikaios* mean 'innocent', thus fitting Luke's portrayal of Jesus as a religious teacher who bore no threat to the Roman state despite being tried and crucified, but Frank Matera points out that the word can also mean 'righteous' with reference to a relationship with God,[25] and perhaps is intended to convey messianic imagery.[26] The motif of Jesus' identity is thus central to the Lucan confession, for one word portrays Jesus as in a right relationship with both God and the Roman state.

Recognizing that all three synoptics draw on this one response to the cross, can any conclusions be drawn about its historicity? It seems certain that this confession in all three Gospels acts on two levels. In Mark it is certainly meant to be understood by the reader with full Christological significance, but that does not imply that Mark considered this to be exactly what the centurion himself meant. Similarly, the double meaning of *dikaios* adds a greater depth to the meaning the centurion may have intended. The particular apologetic concerns of Luke suggests that *huios theou* ('Son of God') is the more original, which has been carefully redacted so that while the original meaning is not lost, the two layers of meaning are sharpened more clearly. But would a centurion have made any such declaration, or is he a puppet of the evangelists? Ultimately there can be no certain answer. There are enough positive appearances of centurions in the Gospels and Acts to rule out generalized arguments based on how all centurions would have reacted, and the use of irony obviates the need for the centurion to have intended a full Christian confession. In this instance any decision on historicity can only be made on the basis of wider judgements on Mark's intertwining of story and significance. Faced with a most unusual execution and witnessing both the death of Jesus and the reaction of the crowd, that a centurion made some such response is certainly not impossible.

### 3. Conclusion

We have seen that Jesus' cry of dereliction is not out of place in Mark's passion narrative, but is the dramatic climax to which the Gospel moves. Neither is the cry out of place theologically, for it articulates the very meaning of the cross. In this respect, the historicity of the cry is of secondary significance. But Jesus' cry and the centurion's response are at the very heart of the drama of Mark's Gospel. While it is never possible to verify completely the authenticity of any direct speech in the Gospels and John Reuman correctly concludes that arguments for the genuineness of Mark 15:34 fall short of definite proof,[27] the varying evidence we have considered points firmly in the direction of the historicity of Jesus' cry. If this is the case then it is reasonable to assume that the account of Jesus' Godforsaken death has been formative in the development of the themes and structures of the whole Gospel.

In these last four chapters I have suggested that the Gospel of Mark has been carefully written, drawing on the historical tradition to present both the story of Jesus and its theological significance. I have also attempted to argue that a correct understanding of the Gospel centres on Jesus' cry of forsakenness. Mark deliberately highlights this aspect of Jesus' death and has prepared us, in the rest of the Gospel up to this point, to understand its significance. But what is most striking is that it is not in response to the miracles Jesus performs or the sermons that he preaches that those around him glimpse his identity. Jesus is seen for who he is only in the cross. In Jesus, the experience of Godforsakenness and the revelation of divinity are inextricably linked, for it is at the cross that we stand in the presence of God. This insight comes from the very beginning of Christian reflection on the life and death of Jesus, but it is an insight that has been rediscovered and reinterpreted most profoundly in recent years.

## Notes to Chapter 5

[1] Graham Stanton, *The Gospels and Jesus* (Oxford: Oxford University Press, 1989), p. 63.

[2] The theme of opposition has been introduced only indirectly, through Herod's slaughter in chapter 2 and John's denouncement of Jewish leaders in chapter 3.

[3] See above, p. 32.

[4] Rossé, *The Cry of Jesus*, pp. 28-33, delineates the main points in Luke and John's portrayal of the crucifixion and considers all the 'words from the cross'.

[5] Luke 23:46.

[6] For a detailed study of the crucifixion scenes in Mark and Luke see Frank Matera, 'The Death of Jesus according to Luke: A Question of Sources', *Catholic Biblical Quarterly* 47 (1985), pp. 469-85.

[7] See below, pp. 179-80, for Hans Urs von Balthasar's interpretation of this cry, which connects it with a theme of forsakenness.

[8] Rossé, *The Cry of Jesus*, p. 32, makes this point well.

[9] To conclude that Mark's interpretation is 'right' may imply that the other evangelists are 'wrong'. To conclude it is valid admits a spectrum of justified interpretation within which boundaries Mark's Gospel sits.

[10] See Galatians 3:13; 2 Corinthians 5:21.

[11] While 'reproach' is still a negative word, in the context of the cross it is weaker than 'abandon'. Other Latin manuscripts offer different translations of *ōneidisas*, such as 'exprobasti me', 'me in opprobium dedisti' and 'maledixisti me'. See Mann, *Mark*, p. 651.

[12] Rossé, *The Cry of Jesus*, p. 37.

[13] Rossé seems confused about Mark's provenance, writing in *The Cry of Jesus*, p. 48, n.17, 'It is necessary, in fact, to situate oneself better in the context of a Jewish community of Palestine', although stating on p. 37, 'but was Mark not also written to a Hellenistic community?' Later, pp. 103-7, Rossé argues that Jesus' words here should not be interpreted as a cry of trust. The whole of this argument is quite unclear.

[14] Rossé concludes that there is no certain proof either for or against the historicity of the cry, but he does argue that there are strong indications that the cry dates back to the origin of the tradition of the passion.

[15] Gundry, pp. 964-5, argues for the historicity of the cry on the grounds that it would not have been added by the Church, but this is more the consequence of his central thesis, that references to suffering form the inherited tradition and the

references to power and glory are the Marcan apology for the cross, than a clear consideration of the cry itself.

[16] Bultmann, *Geschichte der synoptischen Tradition*, p. 342.

[17] So Brower, 'Elijah in the Marcan Passion Narrative', p. 86.

[18] A. Guillaume, 'Matthew 27:46 in the Light of the Dead Sea Scrolls of Isaiah', *Palestine Exploration Quarterly* (1951), pp. 78-80.

[19] See Rossé, *The Cry of Jesus*, pp. 42-4, for a variety of other approaches to this problem.

[20] In Mark's Gospel, *elōi* is read by χ A B C et al., *lama* by B D θ et al., and *sabachthani* by θ et al.

[21] Joseph Fitzmeyer, 'Qumran Aramaic and the New Testament', *New Testament Studies* 20 (1974), p. 394, proposes that Matthew 27:46 may be in Aramaic on the basis of a Qumran fragment. Jeremias, *New Testament Theology Vol I*, p. 5, suggests that Matthew seems to be composite, *ēli* being Hebrew and *lema sabachthani* being Aramaic, but on the basis of the Targum of Psalm 22:1 concludes that Matthew gives a totally Aramaic rendering. G. D. Kilpatrick, *Origins according to the Gospel of St Matthew* (Oxford: Clarendon Press, 1946), pp. 104-5, considers the manuscript support in each Gospel and surmises that the cry could have originally been written in either language in both Gospels, but from other factors considers it more likely that Mark is Aramaic and Matthew is Hebrew.

[22] Others also find a theological significance in the loudness of the cry, such as Werner Kelber, *Mark's Story of Jesus,* p. 81 and Frederick Danker, 'The Demonic Secret: A Re-examination of the Cry of Dereliction', *Zeitschrift fur die neutestamentliche Wissenschaft* 61 (1970), pp. 48-69, but these suggestions are obscure speculations.

[23] Rossé, *The Cry of Jesus*, p. 41.

[24] Ibid., p. 40. See above, p. 51 n. 9.

[25] Matera, *The Kingship of Jesus*, p. 47.

[26] Luke uses *dikaios* as a title for Jesus in Acts 3:14 and 7:52. Mann, *Mark*, p. 654, describes 'Righteous one' as 'an elusive messianic title, certainly as old as Isaiah 53:11 and maybe much older'.

[27] Reuman, 'Psalm 22 at the Cross', p. 57.

# Part II
# The Theological
# Implications

# 6
# Jürgen Moltmann:
# Exploring the Opposites

We have seen in Mark's account a kind of hellish irony that Jesus' identity as God's Son is revealed in the very moment he becomes forsaken. His cry of abandonment proclaims the same God with whom he has lived in such intimacy, while the centurion's confession asserts the true identity of the Godforsaken Jesus. His reaction prompts the conclusion that divine revelation occurs in the very midst of forsakenness. This is central to the whole theology of Jürgen Moltmann, according to which Jesus' cry from the cross is the key to our understanding of both Jesus and God:[1]

> Jesus' death cry on the cross is 'the open wound' of every Christian theology, for consciously or unconsciously every Christian theology is a reply to the question 'Why?' with which Jesus died.[2]

With the horizon firmly set on the theodicy question, deeply moved by world events such as the Holocaust and the ecological crisis, Moltmann seeks a renewed understanding of God, theologically defensible, practically orientated and demanded by Jesus' dying words.

Moltmann has not been the first in recent years to place such emphasis on Jesus' cry of dereliction, but is certainly the most widely read, in English at least. Of our four theologians, Hans Urs von Balthasar's book *Mysterium Paschale* (1962) led the way, followed by Jüngel, who shows himself acquainted with *Mysterium Paschale* at least, in his essay 'Of the Death of the Living God' (1968).[3] Moltmann only picks up the theme after this, culminating in *The Crucified God* (1972), having read both von Balthasar and Jüngel. From then onwards Moltmann is involved in an ongoing dialogue – all four authors were writing at the same time – as well as drawing significantly on the resources of the theological tradition which formed some important presuppositions.

Moltmann, revealing here his heritage from the older theologian Karl Barth,[4] insists that theology cannot start with some universal or prior understanding of God and into this framework then fit the life and death

of Jesus. This was done, he claims, both by those who held to the philo-
sophical concept of God's *apatheia* (non-suffering nature) and also by
those enlightenment theologians who advocated subjective Christologies.
For both ways of thinking, Jesus' cry represented a fundamental problem.[5] By contrast, Moltmann affirms that it is the very particularity of
Jesus' life and death which opens for us a window through which we see
God's true nature; we can *only* understand God in the light of the cross.[6]
The same sentiment expressed by the centurion, that in the death of Jesus
is the revelation of God, is taken up by Moltmann as a founding principle
for his work. Moltmann is right to lay such stress on the particularity of
the cross and consequently on the historical becoming of God, that the
cross is more than just a revelation of God's eternal nature, but introduces
something new both for us and for God. However, we shall see that
Moltmann encounters a persistent difficulty in describing the exact nature
of the relationship between the particularity of Jesus' cry from the cross
and two realities: on the one hand, God's eternal life and, on the other,
universal human suffering.

Mark's theological climax, that the revelation of Jesus' identity
occurred in the midst of forsakenness, is adopted by Moltmann into a
kind of 'eschatological dialectic', thus also showing a significant influence from the nineteenth century philosopher, G. H. F. Hegel. Hegel had
proposed that the meaning and goal of existence was to be found in the
continual resolution of opposites (a 'dialectic'), and that this was also true
for the life of 'Absolute Spirit', or God. Moltmann stresses that the cross
and resurrection represent opposites: death and life, God's absence and
God's presence, this present sinful world and God's transforming future.
The identity of Jesus is found precisely in this contradiction as the one
who was wholly dead and wholly raised,[7] and because of the revelatory
nature of the event of cross and resurrection, this dialectic has implications for the way that we know God. God is revealed in God's opposite,
so life is revealed in death and God in Godforsakenness. Through all his
theological life Moltmann has struggled both with his appreciation of
Hegel's new approach and his awareness of its inherent problems, and
despite, recently, offering his clearest critique yet of Hegel, he has never
finally shaken off his influence.[8] This will have continual, and essentially
negative, implications for Moltmann's interpretation of Jesus' cry.

## 1. The biblical perspective: the meaning of the text

*a. The historicity of Jesus' cry*

Of our four theologians Moltmann makes the most specific comments about Mark 15:34, and does so in a number of his books. These various passages all share a basic similarity and on some occasions Moltmann has simply repeated a section from an earlier work with only minor amendments. Overall, Moltmann seems uncertain about the historicity of Jesus' cry. In *The Crucified God* he clearly distinguishes between the inarticulate cry of 15:37 and the earlier cry of forsakenness (15:34) in very much the same way as Rudolph Bultmann.[9] It is 15:37 which 'we can probably rely upon as the kernel of historical truth',[10] whereas the cry of dereliction is 'certainly an interpretation of the Church after Easter'[11] but 'as near as possible to the historical reality of the death of Jesus',[12] and Moltmann 'regards this interpretation as the most accurate'.[13] Jesus' inarticulate cry in 15:37 was interpreted by the Church with the words of Psalm 22, showing that Jesus died 'with every expression of the most profound horror',[14] and it was gradually weakened in later passion narratives.[15]

At this point Moltmann's exegesis of the Gospel text lacks the necessary precision. It was surely not the loud inarticulate cry that expressed horror and was later weakened, for such a cry alone would convey an uncertain meaning, but the words of forsakenness themselves. On Moltmann's rendering of the text, the Church first interprets Jesus' loud cry with words that convey profound abandonment by God, only gradually to weaken them later. Moltmann attempts to accept a traditional view that only the wordless cry was historical but fills it with the meaning supplied by the cry of forsakenness.

Yet later, in *The Trinity and the Kingdom of God*, Moltmann now concludes that the cry of forsakenness itself 'must surely be the very kernel of the Golgotha story, historically speaking', because the Church would not have added such a statement. But Moltmann immediately qualifies this, for such a notion, he insists, would never have taken root if Jesus had not uttered these words, 'or if the despair had not been at least perceptible in Christ's death cry'.[16] How such despair would have been evident without at least similar words to the cry of forsakenness being spoken is never answered. In his book *The Way of Jesus Christ* Moltmann offers an even more ambiguous alternative, for these terrible words must have been uttered or 'at least been heard in Jesus' death cry'.[17] Most recently, in *Jesus Christ for Today's World*, in a section which owes its structure and the majority of language to the passage in *The Trinity and Kingdom of God*, Jesus' cry is again described as 'historically, the very kernel of what happened on Golgotha',[18] for these words must either have been uttered or at least been 'evident in Jesus' death cry'.[19] There is clearly a definite shift after writing *The Crucified God*, in which the 'historical kernel' is increasingly applied to the words of forsakenness themselves rather than the inarticulate cry.[20] Yet, although Moltmann seems to want to accept the historicity of the cry, he never feels able to do so without a variety of vague and unclear qualifications. Moltmann also fails to distinguish properly between Jesus' *feeling* of abandonment, which is open to historical verification, and the *actuality* of abandonment which is the provenance of faith, both easily slipping from one to another and also assuming the reality of Jesus' abandonment to be historical fact,[21] doubly difficult given the absence of any definitive statement by him on the historicity of Jesus' cry.

*b. The relationship with Psalm 22*

Moltmann is much more consistent in his interpretation of the relationship between Psalm 22 and Mark 15:34, which features in all his discussions of Jesus' cry. That Jesus prayed or meant the whole psalm is regarded as simply far-fetched – Jesus' cry is followed by his own death, not salvation as in the psalm,[22] and the crucified Jesus would not have been capable of speech[23] – although Moltmann does refer to the unlikely notion that in Jewish tradition the first line stood for the whole.[24] The one occasion that Psalm 22 takes precedence is the interpretation of Jesus' cry as a 'legal plea'. Like the psalmist, Jesus 'is not calling for the compassion of God upon his own person, but for the revelation of the righteousness of God',[25] he calls upon God 'for God's sake'. Jesus here is not lamenting his own fate or indulging in self pity, but has put his whole theological proclamation at stake for God's righteousness.[26] Jesus' cry is a cry of protest and a search for theodicy. While Moltmann is essentially right in this interpretation of the cry, Jesus' words must be interpreted from the context of the cross and not simply from Psalm 22. It would be legitimate to argue that the Gospel writers used this understanding of Psalm 22 to shape their own presentations, but we must be cautious about introducing an interpretation of Psalm 22 into the words of Jesus' cry. Jesus' cry as a cry to God must stand on its own merits alone.

### c. Possible answers to Jesus' question

Moltmann's primary concern is the overall significance of the cry for God, but he does offer, even if in passing, a number of different 'answers' to Jesus' dying question. Critical of those who move immediately to a specific theory of the atonement, Moltmann takes seriously the reality of Jesus' Godforsakenness as a particular experience. The only response must be another experience, for as Moltmann explains it in a sermon 'there is only *one* satisfying and liberating answer to the question "My God, my God, why have you forsaken me?" It is the answer of the resurrection'.[27] Every other answer would fall short, either giving death eternal significance or failing to take it seriously. Elsewhere Moltmann describes this as an eschatological response, which is in effect a postponing of the answer until the final event of history (the 'eschaton'), when 'God will wipe every tear from their eyes'.[28] Moltmann is aware that any attempt to give an answer will at best be provisional and must await both God's final revelation and resolution of suffering and evil. Moltmann imagines the Father answering the Son, 'For a brief moment I forsook you, but with great compassion I will gather you'.[29]

Yet despite his own warning, Moltmann does, in a later book, offer a mystical answer, drawn from Catherine of Sienna, who, when crying out to God with her own 'why?', heard God reply, 'I was in your heart'. Thus Moltmann's 'answer to the God-cry of the God-forsaken Christ', in language which echoes his earlier thought, is:

> For a brief moment I forsook you, so that you might become the brother
> of the forsaken human being, and so that in fellowship with you nothing
> can separate anyone at all from our love. I did not forsake you eternally,
> but was beside you in your heart.[30]

Although this passage contains some important themes in Moltmann's thought, especially the solidarity of Christ with us in our suffering as the basis for our fellowship with God and salvation, its relation to the rest of his theology is unclear. Moltmann's intention in offering this 'answer' is practically orientated, that we might discover God's pain in our pain and see our suffering as a participation in 'the sufferings of Christ'. But his language is clearly mystical rather than theological. Although the unity of Father and Son at the very point of disruption in the divine life is a familiar theme in Moltmann's writing, the notions of God being 'beside [Christ] in his heart' and forsakenness for 'a brief moment' are not explored, nor is any explicit connection made to his earlier sermon.

However, Moltmann's most consistent and also controversial 'answer' to the question 'why?' is his 'theology of surrender', in which the Father gives up the Son and the Son gives himself 'for us'.[31] Here Moltmann begins to explore the relationship between the Father and the Son in the context of Christ's passion. Gethsemane is 'the first time that he [Jesus] does not want to be alone with God' and Moltmann concludes, 'he [Jesus] is evidently afraid of him [God]. That is why he seeks the protection of his friends'.[32] In *Jesus Christ for Today's World*, in a passage of great similarity, one notable change is the omission of the phrase, 'he is evidently afraid of him', replaced by the more subtle rhetorical question, 'protection from whom?'[33] Central to Moltmann's theology of surrender is the conviction that Jesus experiences 'suffering from God' which is 'the real torment in Christ's passion. This godforsakenness is the cup he is not spared'.[34]

Without doubt Moltmann grapples with the historical-critical issues of Mark 15:34, particularly the historicity of Jesus' cry and its relationship to Psalm 22. Despite such work, however, problems still remain, particularly the continuing imprecision of Moltmann's assessment of Jesus' cry and the failure to distinguish between feeling and reality. Yet it is through grappling with this text that Moltmann arrives at his well known, though problematic, theology of surrender, at the heart of which is the concept of Godforsakenness. It is this we will explore in some detail.

## 2. The divine perspective: the meaning of the cry for God

Traditionally, discussion of the cross, and within this the cry of dereliction, has focused on its implications for salvation. All four of our theologians, and Moltmann in particular, wish to give priority to a more radical question: what does the cross mean for God?[35] Any doctrine of God must be developed within earshot of the dying cry of Jesus.[36] Jesus' cry of forsakenness is at the heart of the cross and so we can expect this to be at the heart of his *theo*-logy.

Moltmann describes his first encounter with Jesus' cry in a prisoner-of-war camp as the key to grasping God's presence with him in his own sense of Godforsakenness. From this existential experience Moltmann develops the theological conviction that the cross is the basis for our understanding of God's ability to suffer.[37] He is aware and accepts that the depth of human suffering is a further compelling reason, most famously demonstrated by his interpretation of Wiesel's story of the boy on the gallows at Auschwitz,[38] but it is from the conviction that God is in Christ that the cross becomes the theological foundation for divine passibility.[39] If God were incapable of suffering then the cross would just be a human tragedy.[40] Moltmann therefore explicitly rejects the impassible God of metaphysical theism, together with its image in atheism,[41] in his search for a new divine understanding. The cry of abandonment indicates that Jesus did not die serenely and at peace, but disturbed and forsaken. The centurion's confession goes further than revealing the identity of Jesus and firmly links God and suffering together. The passion of Jesus is the passion of God.[42] Within the context of divine passibility Jesus' cry of forsakenness is significant because it adds to our understanding of the *kind* of suffering that God experienced on the cross.[43]

### a. Godforsaken suffering

Moltmann consistently refers to the Godforsaken death of Jesus in order to stress the universality of God's suffering. The phrase 'godless and godforsaken' resonates throughout Moltmann's work and it indicates both the very extremities of life and the very essence of suffering,

Godforsakenness. This does not suggest that Jesus somehow suffered to a greater extent than any other, in an exclusive way, but indicates that in the death of Jesus God experienced the 'breadth and depth'[44] of our history, a phrase which has a rather generalized, indeed vague, meaning, but which is intended to signify the inclusive nature of God's suffering. Because Jesus became one with all the Godless and Godforsaken, in solidarity with them, no one stands outside the suffering love of God.[45] At this point the confession of the centurion gives added significance to the forsaken cry of Jesus: a Gentile confirms that the cross was a divine event that happened on 'the boundary of human society' and so 'for all'.[46] Here Moltmann's dialectic contains significance for salvation. God identifies with what is opposite in order to overcome it; because the conflict of history is in God, 'all feuds have an end'.[47] In the light of the human situation it was important that in the incarnation God stands along side all, and, therefore, God endured Godforsaken suffering.

Although Moltmann's stress has always been on the particularity of Jesus' cross, he also refers to God's universal suffering. 'God suffers, where love suffers',[48] which seems to imply that all that is wrong somehow impinges upon God. Moltmann does join this universal suffering with Jesus' Godforsaken death, although only by juxtaposing the two ideas, which results in a merely grammatical link. How Moltmann connects theologically the particular Godforsaken death of Jesus and God's universal suffering remains unclear. The cross is more than just the death of one man, but includes a universal dimension within itself, for in some way the cross 'contains' all human suffering. 'There is no death which has not been God's death in the history of Golgotha';[49] 'forsaken men are already taken up by Christ's forsakenness into the divine history'.[50] Moltmann's aim in understanding salvation like this is clear, and thus the desire to use such inclusive language: Jesus' Godforsaken death opens the way for *all* to know God's embrace, so all suffering is taken up into God. But one critic, Paul Fiddes, concludes that the description of the cross as 'containing' all suffering cannot be taken literally.[51] Although such language does provide a link between the cross and all other suffering, this kind of link must be entirely subjective and emotive; the significance of the cross seems to be dependent on our noticing God in our suffering. Such a connection is only of limited value. Fiddes' criticisms are confirmed in Moltmann's more recent book, *Jesus Christ for Today's World*. In considering how God helps us, Moltmann writes that we discover, perceive and recognize God in our suffering and find strength to love.[52] Even when he speaks of atonement through Christ's vicarious suffering, it is the 'knowledge of Christ' which liberates.[53]

At the same time, Moltmann drops the language of the cross as 'containing' all suffering and speaks instead of the 'sufferings of Christ' which 'are not exclusive; they are inclusive – our sufferings too'.[54] Moltmann illustrates this with the history of the Jews – Jesus experienced the same fate as many of his own people – with the experiences of the Christian apostles and martyrs who suffered with Christ at the hands of their persecutors, with Auschwitz, and even with the sufferings of the whole groaning creation.[55] Christ who in his Godforsakenness 'has suffered everything which has happened to us, and more even than that'[56] is *present* in our sufferings so that they become his sufferings. The universalizing element is God's presence with Christ on the cross through the Spirit and then with us in our sufferings, through this same Spirit.[57] Jesus dies a Godforsaken death in which he experiences the Godforsakenness of hell. Because God was in Christ on the cross, hell is thereby transformed and that which was Godforsaken is a place of hope. God is then present with us in our hells.[58]

Acknowledging that not all those who suffer will subjectively feel anything of God, Moltmann insists Christ is still 'objectively' present, and 'hell has been objectively transformed', although he fails to elaborate on these broad outlines. But an unfortunate consequence of such a system is that specific experiences of suffering are denied their very concrete harshness, even to the point that they are almost justified.[59] Particularly critical are post-Holocaust theologians who fear that Moltmann, among others, reduces the significance and impact of historical events like Auschwitz.[60] Moltmann repudiates such a claim and insists that his focus on Jesus' Godforsakenness does not rob other suffering of its dignity,[61] but because Moltmann's system seems to place greater importance on the generic nature of suffering rather than its individuality his protest is unconvincing.

Yet Moltmann's greater problem is due to the Hegelian dialectic lurking in the wings. Drawing on the pivotal event of the centurion's response to Jesus' Godforsaken death, Moltmann speaks in various ways of God's revelation in the opposite, a dialectical principle of knowledge that undergirds and makes possible analogical knowledge. First, God is revealed in what is opposite to natural theology's understanding of God, 'not through power and glory, but in suffering and the cross'.[62] The self-humiliation and suffering of the cross is contrary to the expected glory of God, but not opposite to God's own self. The cross shows such self-humiliation to be the revelation of God's eternal nature and by no means strange for God.[63] Second, God is revealed in the context of what is opposite; hate does not reveal love, but love can be seen for what it is in the context of hate.[64] Third, God reveals himself in God's opposite, which Moltmann defines as 'godlessness and godforsakenness'[65] and refers to 'the despisers of men and those who have been forsaken by men, the oppressed and those who have become guilty of their oppression'.[66]

Moltmann's essential problem is that he has taken what is portrayed in Mark's Gospel as a particular event and recast it as a fixed theological axiom,[67] and it is this concept of a dialectical *principle* which conveys undertones of necessity. To say, as Moltmann does, that God's profoundest revelations have always been in suffering[68] can be taken as an historical assessment, but to invoke a principle is to put constraints on God. There is the suggestion that God *must* be revealed in suffering. While his more appreciative critics see the dialectics of Luther and Barth at play, Moltmann has constantly been dogged by the suggestion that he has drawn too heavily on Hegel's necessary descent of Absolute Spirit into nothingness in a 'speculative Good Friday', in order for Spirit to return to itself in fuller life.[69] Moltmann is clearly appreciative of Hegel's emphasis both on trinitarian theology and on dialectic. In considering the empowering aspect of God's suffering in the death of Jesus, which Hegel sees as characterizing the life of the mind, Moltmann quotes:

> mind is this power *only* by looking the negative in the face and dwelling with it.[70]

> 'God himself is dead', as it is said in a Lutheran hymn; the consciousness of this fact expresses the truth that the human, the finite, frailty, weakness, the negative, is itself a divine moment, is in God himself.[71]

Moltmann has responded to criticism by explicitly defending himself against the charge of eternalizing suffering,[72] but his insistence on dialectic as a principle still lays him open to the charge that his theology perpetuates this approach despite his stated intention. Bauckham, who is one of Moltmann's most appreciative critics, suggests that it was 'probably a mistake' for Moltmann to include the cross under some general dialectical principle;[73] better would be to stress God's free revelation springing from his love. Moltmann himself does move in this direction. In *The Future of Creation*, he suggests that Schelling's notion that 'every nature *can be* revealed *only* in its opposite', is better changed to read 'is in actual fact' revealed only in its opposite.[74] However, Moltmann still describes it as a dialectical *principle*.[75] While from the human perspective, revelation in opposite is necessary for any understanding of God, from the divine perspective, the dialectic of cross and resurrection is only the consequence of love. Those other profound occasions of revelation in suffering – Moltmann refers to the cry of the slaves in Egypt and the sighing of the whole enslaved creation – are not so much examples of a principle but revelations of love.

The whole issue of God's freedom and necessity, encapsulated by the Hegelian dialectic, remains unclear throughout Moltmann's work. Moltmann is right to stress that the kind of suffering that God experiences must be 'Godforsaken', but we must look for a clearer account of what this might mean.

### b. God's new suffering

Jesus' cry of dereliction points to God's suffering the depths of human Godforsakenness, as the result of divine freedom, but how does this relate to God's own eternal life? Is such suffering in any sense new for God? In this regard Moltmann consistently upholds his belief in the historical becoming of God. 'The nature of God does not stand behind the appearance of history as eternal, ideal being; it is that history'.[76] God is not an eternal present who appears at all points in history timelessly, nor a closed system who reveals his own self to the world in a one-way relationship. Instead Moltmann develops an eschatologically orientated notion of God, constantly open to creation,[77] and with a future ahead so that God will be as Trinity-in-goal different from being Trinity-in-origin. Within this history of God the cross has a unique place. It is not just one of many encounters with creation or a supreme example of God's love. Jesus' Godforsaken death on the cross is unique in revelation, and certainly corresponds to God's inner life, but more importantly it has significance for God and changes God.[78] The cross then is certainly something new for God.

> In the night of his death on the cross, in the abandonment of the Son by the Father and of the Father by the Son, God himself experiences surrender in the form of death and rejection. We might add that here God has a new experience . . .[79]

However, the same lack of clarity in Moltmann's connection between particular and universal, which we noted earlier, persists in his discussion of the particularity of the cross and God's eternal nature. In *The Crucified God*, Moltmann uses language that suggests that the event of the cross itself *is* the history of God, that 'the trinitarian God-event on the cross becomes the history of God which is open to the future'.[80] The cross has priority not only for our *understanding* of God, but also for the very *being* of God, and thus the cross has retroactive force, 'acting from below upwards, from without inwards, out of time back into the divine eternity'.[81] Fiddes continues his criticism here, suggesting that the language of 'beginning' and 'constituting' the divine history of suffering gives the perplexing impression of 'instituting' it, as if God was not the suffering Trinity before the cross.[82] Yet this is clearly not what Moltmann believes. In *The Crucified God* he draws eagerly on Abraham Heschel's work on the pathos of God revealed in the Old Testament prophets,[83] in which God suffered with his people, and speaks of a number of stages of God's self-humiliation starting with creation.[84]

Bauckham also recognizes this problem with Moltmann's language, but claims that Moltmann quickly retreated from this position.[85] Yet, while it is true that in his later books Moltmann does place a greater emphasis on the function of the cross in God's *eternal* trinitarian history, the idea of God 'constituting' himself on the cross still reappears. In an essay in *The Future of Creation*, Moltmann links the historical sending of the Son to the eternal procession of the Son from the Father. Thus 'as God appears in history, as the sending Father and the sent Son, so he must have previously been in himself'.[86] A little later, Moltmann suggests that the cross offers God a new experience, that of pain,[87] despite God being 'from eternity to eternity the crucified God'[88] who has always been involved in suffering.[89] In a later book Moltmann still writes that God, whose being and existence is love, 'in Christ constitutes himself as love. This happens on the cross'.[90]

Moltmann's language of novelty fluctuates and is simply inconsistent. The fundamental question as to what is new in the cross is never satisfactorily answered. It is significant that once again thinking of God together with negativity has proved difficult for Moltmann as Hegelian undertones emerge. God is unconditional love, and this love can be contradicted and crucified, 'but in crucifixion it finds fulfilment and becomes love of the enemy'.[91] For Hegel the negative provides that which is new for God in the fulfilment of divine self-realization. Without the 'Good Friday' moment God's own being is not fully realized. As a whole system, Moltmann does reject Hegel's synthesis but in stressing the cross as the central feature in God's historical becoming Moltmann has not escaped Hegelian associations. Once again in outline I believe Moltmann to be right in seeking in the cross a new experience for God, but its exact nature must be more carefully explored.

We may say that God had always been sharing in the suffering of his dying people, but only in the cross did Godforsakenness and death enter the divine life to the point of disruption. In the cross God went further and deeper into human life and death and hell, to the point that it was a unique experience. We can thus say, with Moltmann, that 'in Christ's cross, history is found concentrated in God'[92] and that 'God's self-humiliation is completed and perfected in the passion and death of Jesus'.[93] Fiddes categorizes God's experience on the cross as being both different in degree and different in kind, recognizing the fluidity of the boundary between the two. There is an important connection here with God's experience of suffering in other places, but God encounters death to such a unique degree on the cross that it is also a unique kind of experience.[94] Bauckham also helpfully distinguishes between incarnate and non-incarnate suffering, but then unfortunately classifies the former as God experiencing suffering as human, and the latter as God experiencing suffering as God. God must experience *both* as God, although differently in each.

This again raises the issue of degree and kind. If one takes a more 'functional' Christological approach, based on the continuity between God's involvement in human lives and the life of Jesus, the difference in degree will be stressed. If one adopts a more 'ontological' Christology, based on a unity of being between Jesus and God (as Moltmann with his Lutheran heritage seems to do), then the difference in kind will be stressed. But in *both* approaches the incarnation can be described as 'unique' and so a new experience for God. Jesus' Godforsaken death is a unique revelation of God, for here divine humility and vulnerability is shown most clearly. This Godforsakenness is also a unique experience for God, in harmony with the whole of God's history, yet also new. Finally this Godforsakenness is unique in its effect, as the basis for soteriology.

### c. God's active suffering

Moltmann characterizes God's involvement in the cross as 'active suffering', that is as the result of God's freedom.[95] This is thus a third way, a middle path, between the two alternatives that God was either impassible or the unwilling recipient of suffering from another. Moltmann begins with Jesus' resolve to set out for Jerusalem and his decision to 'actively take the expected suffering upon himself'.[96] This experience of forsakenness is not blind fate nor imposed against his will, but the result of his active love, which Moltmann frequently describes using the Pauline notion of Jesus' self-giving,[97] 'the suffering of love, in which one opens himself to the possibility of being affected by another'.[98] Although perhaps Moltmann's earliest statement of this idea it remains one of the profoundest, and is echoed and repeated in later books.[99]

Moltmann thus reinterprets the patristic doctrine of impassibility by stressing that legitimate divine suffering cannot be imposed unwillingly from outside but must be the result of God's eternal freedom.[100] Here Moltmann enters the debate between the source of God's action being his will or his nature,[101] but seeks to move beyond it by turning to the concept of 'desire'[102] and characterizing God's freedom not as mere free-choice, familiar from our consumerism, but being free to love, not out of a deficiency but from an overflowing of love.[103]

> God is not incapable of suffering, if this means that in the freedom of his love he would not be receptive to suffering over the contradiction of man and the self-destruction of his creation . . . . God is not invulnerable, if this means that he could not open himself to the experience of the cross.[104]

Vulnerability is the key concept,[105] for it allows for God's suffering to be the result of God's own freedom and not imposed by creation. Such a vulnerability embraces both an openness to suffering, without suffering being the logically necessary outcome, and an understanding of suffering as something that befalls us. Moltmann has clearly grasped something of the profundity of this idea. It appears as a light of hope on the horizon, but it does not illuminate the rest of his thinking and especially the shadow cast over God's freedom in creation.[106] Thus, the unresolved Hegelian dialectic remaining in Moltmann's thought suggests that this suffering is *necessary* for God rather than the result of God's openness to creation.[107] In addition, Moltmann's frequent description of God's suffering as the action of the Father on the Son, which we will explore more fully later, suggests that suffering does not befall God through the actions of the world. 'Vulnerability', for Moltmann, is little more than a synonym for suffering.

Building on Moltmann's hint of God's 'openness' to suffering, but moving on further, we might distinguish between 'metaphysical imposition' and 'contingent imposition' of suffering. In the first, God would be the author of God's own suffering; but in the second, God out of freely chosen vulnerability opens the divine life to creation, with the real possibility that what is created will inflict and impose suffering on God. Paul Fiddes argues passionately for this second kind of understanding, and the main thrust of his book *The Creative Suffering of God* is that suffering, if it is to be real, must be something which *happens* to God.[108] In my view, it will be important to hold onto this concept of vulnerability, since it will enable us to hold together the activity of both Father and Son in the Godforsakenness of the cross without dissolving the cross into conflict. It will also be the foundation stone on which the whole interpretation of Jesus' cry is built.

If we presume that Jesus' passion is God's passion, and that God experiences a suffering on the cross which is Godforsaken, new and active, the cross reveals God to be *essentially* vulnerable. Jesus resolutely sets out for Jerusalem knowing what may befall him there, but in doing so he puts his immediate future into the hands of others, so that his life is affected and changed by them. This is exactly what God does on the cross, opening the divine life to humanity. Moltmann draws on various Jewish writers, notably Abraham Heschel and Franz Rosenzweig to interpret the Old Testament as showing this same divine characteristic. God is open to the world, willingly affected by creation. If God's relationship to creation is open then this will lead to new experiences for God in sharing creation's life.

Something, nevertheless, of God is unchanging. God is faithful to God's own self and we can never speak of God's unfaithfulness. In this sense we might say that God's nature[109] is eternal and unchanging, and, in a clear echo of Barth, Moltmann asserts that we must learn from the cross that 'God is like this'.[110] As suffering love God undergoes new experiences of suffering due to choosing a covenant partner. God both suffers human sin and shares in human suffering. Moreover, God seeks a new experience of glorification, God does not want to be God without us and desires creation to be included in the trinitarian glorification.

> God does not want to come to his rest without the new creation of humanity and the world through the Holy Spirit. God does not want to become at one with himself without the unification of all things with him.[111]

The Trinity-in-goal is different to the Trinity-in-origin because in between is God's history with an elected covenant partner, and within God's history with us there are countless new experiences for God, of both joy and pain. John McDade criticizes Moltmann for turning a narrative account of God's history, which in itself he finds attractive, into a divine ontology, or an account of God's *being*. The basis of narrative, he points out, is a sequential order of past, present and future and such a sequence is inappropriate for God. In this way McDade, although he never makes this explicit, rules out any real experience of suffering for God.[112] He prefers Karl Barth's view that God's inner being only 'corresponds' to God's actions in the world, rather than the two being identical. But he only presents one aspect of Barth's whole approach here. Barth also asserts that if God elects humankind as a covenant partner and if this relationship is to have any significance, then God's free choice of humankind must include the choice to *be* God in time, with all its movement from past to future.[113]

Here we must be certain that we finally escape the Hegelian dialectic. God does not need creation in order to become fully God; rather God's divinity is such that God *chooses* to share that divinity with creation, which is a decision to be for us. If my life is to make any difference to God then it cannot leave God unchanged. A narrative description of God, far from being read to present one unified picture, is necessary to describe the God who lives in relationship with creation. Such a God is essentially vulnerable and is revealed as such in Jesus' Godforsakenness on the cross.

### d. Trinity and forsakenness

Moltmann deliberately begins his main argument in *The Trinity and the Kingdom of God*, a more systematic presentation of some themes first expounded in *The Crucified God*, with a discussion of God's passion and only on that basis argues for the necessity of understanding God as Trinity.[114] Starting with a phrase from B. Steffen, that 'the shortest expression of the Trinity is the divine act of the cross', Moltmann examines the specific significance of Jesus' Godforsakenness.[115] If Jesus was God and died expressing his abandonment by God then it means God cannot be *simplex esse* ('being in simplicity') but must be Trinity. The rejection of the classic distinction between two natures, human and divine, and the acceptance that the totality of Christ was involved in the abandonment on the cross, are the precursors for faith in a God who suffers.[116]

Jesus' death on the cross reveals a God who suffers. This suffering includes the forsakenness of God by God, thus requiring there to be real distinctions within God, and so the Trinity is no longer speculation but 'a shorter version of the passion narrative'.[117] In the light of God's suffering both theistic and atheistic concepts of God falter; the crucified God is the trinitarian God. This links the unique Godforsakenness of the cross and the Christian doctrine of the Trinity inextricably together in such a way that strengthens Moltmann's insistence that Godforsakenness only happens on the cross. If this is the case then the doctrine of the Trinity can be derived uniquely and directly from Jesus' Godforsaken cry.

### e. A social Trinity

Jesus' Godforsakenness at the heart of the cross also has important implications for Moltmann's doctrine of the social Trinity. Unhappy with trinitarian theology based on the concepts either of divine substance or absolute subject, Moltmann draws more heavily on Eastern Orthodox thinking to propose a doctrine of the Trinity based on relationships.[118] In the light of this he speaks of both the unity of will in surrender[119] and also the 'union' of God.[120] It is not possible to consider Moltmann's whole trinitarian doctrine in any detail, but simply to point out the significance of Moltmann's dual emphasis on Godforsakenness and social trinitarianism. By giving priority to God's trinitarian distinctions rather than to one divine nature, whether conceived in terms of substance or subject, Moltmann's notion of God allows for a greater degree of distinction or difference. A social doctrine of the Trinity allows Moltmann to speak more easily of a disruption in the very heart of God. It is interesting that Moltmann criticizes Barth for not being trinitarian enough,[121] by which he means that Barth's notion of the Trinity is too modalistic, that is, too close to the ancient error of thinking of the persons in God as simply three 'modes of action' of one divine subject (often popularly expressed as 'one God working in three different ways'). Whatever the merits of Moltmann's claim against Barth, a more modalistic approach to the Trinity will always necessitate a more limited interpretation of disruption in God at the cross. Moltmann's interpretation of Jesus' Godforsakenness and his doctrine of the social Trinity are important partners.

## *f. Trinitarian experiences of forsakenness*

One of Moltmann's particular contributions to recent trinitarian theology is the consistent distinction he draws between the experience of the forsaking Father and of the forsaken Son. The Son suffers *dying* in forsakenness but not *death*, because it is the living who experience death, in the sense of being bereaved through the deaths of others; so the Father experiences the death of his Son.[122] Although the experiences of Father and Son are distinguished, the grief of the Father is just as important as the death of the Son.[123] Although Moltmann's earliest explorations of these ideas are almost exclusively binitarian, he later develops a similar understanding of the Spirit who suffers but not in the same way, so suffering the death of the Son, but not dying.[124]

When Moltmann first introduces this idea in *The Crucified God*, he pointedly distances himself from a number of previous theologies. He rejects Luther's phrase, 'the death of God', preferring instead to speak of 'death *in* God'[125] and claims his own theology cannot be described as either 'patripassian', meaning that the Father suffered and died, or 'theopaschite', as is implied by speaking of the 'death of God'.[126] Instead he coins the phrase 'patricompassionism' to express his own trinitarian approach.[127] Although Moltmann retains and repeats this distinction in divine experiences frequently, it is possible to notice some gradual changes. After *The Crucified God*, the phrase 'death in God' no longer features, nor does the insistence that his theology is neither patripassian nor theopaschite.[128] In *Jesus Christ for Today's World*, Moltmann uses explicitly theopaschite language when he concludes, from his discussion of these different experiences, 'God too experiences death on the cross'.[129]

Paul Fiddes has rightly criticized a number of aspects of Moltmann's theology outlined above.[130] If Jesus is God, as Moltmann himself maintains, then the death of Jesus can and must be referred to as the 'death of God', especially in the light of Christianity's insistence on the perichoresis of the Trinity. Obviously, those like Luther and Jüngel, who use this phrase in a positive way, are using it equivocally. The 'death of God' does not mean God has died and is no more, but rather that God has experienced death. It may be that avoiding this ambiguous phrase is partly

behind Moltmann's preference for 'death in God'. Equally, Moltmann
may be anxious to avoid being branded as perpetuating an ancient heresy,
and his theology is indeed different to the original understanding of patripassian and theopaschite theologians, but Moltmann's final result seems
quite clearly to fit into these broad headings.[131]

Although Fiddes criticizes Moltmann for making too great a distinction between dying and death, which in turn produces too great a conflict
within God, he too speaks of the different experiences of Father and Son,
based on a different anthropological model.[132] The dying already experience their own death, at least in some sense, so Jesus experiences dying
and also, in anticipation, his death. The Father endures the death of the
Son and also dying, in as much as the Father is involved in the struggle
between life and death which Fiddes, drawing on Jüngel, describes as a
process of 'perishing'. The triune God suffers death and dying but is not
dead.

Both Moltmann and Fiddes are seeking to give full value to the historicity of Jesus' death. It is Jesus of Nazareth who is put to death on a
Roman cross, and although, in Christian reflection, Father, Son and Spirit
are all involved in that death, their experiences of this human death must
be different. In *The Crucified God*, Moltmann's language is almost exclusively centred upon the action of the Father, 'In the forsakenness of the
Son, the Father also forsakes himself. In the surrender of the Son the
Father also surrenders himself'.[133] In later books we see a much greater
balance of the suffering of the Father and Son, 'The Son endures being
forsaken by the Father . . . the Father endures being forsaken by the
Son',[134] and this mutuality of experiences is greatly needed, protecting
against too great a separation of Father from Son. This mutuality could be
deepened by adding that both Father and Son suffer some sense of loss
and bereavement and that by representing sinful humanity Jesus stands
with those who forsake the Father, and thus experiences forsakenness
himself. Moltmann's fundamental problem in expounding these trinitarian
distinctions is that they do not spring from God's relationship with creation but are wholly the result of God's action upon God.

## g. God against God?

Although Moltmann's social Trinity allows for a high degree of distinction within God, are these differences too great? Is it really possible to describe the cross as an event of 'God against God' without descending into meaninglessness and does it introduce conflict into the very being of God?[135] Although this is a phrase very much associated with Moltmann in recent years, it already had a comparatively long history. Luther had already affirmed not only that God was in Christ but also that Christ is God and on this basis Moltmann concludes, 'what happened on the cross was a happening between God and God; there God disputes with God; there God cries out to God; there God dies in God'.[136]

It is in Gethsemane when his prayer is rejected that Jesus' 'true passion begins: his suffering from God'.[137] It is this that is the 'real torment in Christ's passion'.[138] Moltmann explores two aspects of the New Testament presentation of the cross. First the assertion in Acts that the Jews killed Jesus, but God raised him from the dead,[139] and second, the Pauline theme of the handing over of Jesus by God, drawing here on Wiard Popkes' detailed discussion of *paradidōmi*.[140] This one verb is used in the Gospels with a variety of meanings, but in reference to Jesus only in the negative sense of either being handed over by those in authority or betrayed by Judas.[141] In Galatians 2:20 and Ephesians 5:2, 25 it is used positively of Christ's willing self-sacrifice and in Romans 8:32 we have the one clear occasion when God 'hands over' his Son.[142]

Moltmann discusses *paradidōmi* twice in *The Crucified God* and not entirely consistently. On the first occasion Moltmann specifically contrasts its meaning of 'deliver over, betray and abandon', used as passion terminology, with its use in Romans 8:32 where it is 'an expression of the love and election of God'.[143] In the later and fuller account Moltmann concludes, 'according to this, God gave up his own Son, abandoned him, cast him out and delivered him up to an accursed death'.[144] Both discussions are connected with the same quotation from Wiard Popkes' doctoral dissertation, *Christus Traditus*.

That God delivers up his Son is one of the most unheard-of statements in the New Testament. We must understand 'deliver up' in its full sense and not water it down to mean 'send' or 'give'. What happened here is what Abraham did not need to do to Isaac: the Father quite deliberately abandoned Christ to the fate of death: God subjected him to the power of corruption, whether this be called man or death. To express this idea in its most acute form, one might say in the words of the dogma of the early church: the first person of the Trinity casts out and annihilates the second... A theology of the cross cannot be expressed more radically than it is here.[145]

God was at work not only in the resurrection but also in the cross, the result of divine as well as human action. In one of his most startling comments Moltmann refers to 'the God who raised him as the God who crucified him'.[146]

Dorothee Sölle has led the way in criticizing Moltmann here for portraying a sadistic God. Despite all the expressions of God's own experience of suffering, it is still the Father who causes the suffering of the Son.[147] Although some of Sölle's criticisms are overstated,[148] Moltmann's language in *The Crucified God* clearly suggests that God is also the author of suffering as well as the one who endures it.[149] Not only does Moltmann approvingly use Popkes' phrase about the first person of the Trinity 'casting out' and 'annihilating' the second, he independently develops his own understanding of the cross based on Luther's description of 'God against God'. Moltmann seeks to answer Sölle's basic charge in *The Way of Jesus Christ*,[150] where he recognizes the difficulty of using such terminology. The phrase *nemo contra Deum nisi Deus ipse* ('no one is against God except God himself') is omitted, as is any quotation from Popkes, and Moltmann's main line of defence is to answer Sölle's criticisms by passing the blame onto Popkes, carefully ignoring the fact that by quoting Popkes approvingly he was agreeing with his thoughts.[151] It is also notable that before he tackles Sölle's criticism Moltmann offers a précis of his previous work in which there is a distinct and subtle change in tone, for without admitting as much, Moltmann has modified his language.[152] He wholeheartedly agrees that it would be wrong to talk of the cross in terms which put Father and Son on different sides, oppose them or divide them: the Father is always on the side of his Son. Moltmann then considers six possible answers to the question 'where is God?' as

Jesus cries in abandonment, three of which are rejected and three of which are endorsed.[153] Here at least Sölle's criticisms are successfully and eloquently refuted, and Moltmann's three positive answers will form the basis for chapter 12 in this study.

But Moltmann is not completely consistent in this respect, and his writing fluctuates and still leaves him open to Sölle's original criticisms. In *The Spirit of Life* Jesus experiences 'suffering from God' and 'the hidden, absent, even rejecting Father'.[154] In *Jesus Christ for Today's World* Moltmann specifically asks whether God gave up Christ to death while at the same time being present in him. The only answer he offers is the Jewish story of God's own exile and restoration with Israel.[155] At other times Moltmann could be accused of portraying a masochistic, rather than sadistic, God, who inflicted suffering upon himself. So on the cross, 'God is acting in his own Son and in so far in himself'[156] and 'here the Father acted on himself'.[157] There is simply a basic inconsistency in Moltmann's language, which continues right up to the present. Although he does specifically reject any notion of one person in the Trinity being the cause of suffering from another, he does not follow this conviction through in all that he writes.

Barth speaks of God experiencing God's own contradiction of sinful humanity, which happens in the Son's Godforsakenness on the cross, but also affirms that this means God does not contradict God's self.[158] Moltmann's consistent problem in taking Jesus' cry seriously[159] is not that God suffers, but that, in contrast to Barth, the Father is the cause of the divine suffering. What Moltmann's theology needs is a clear and consistent exposition of God's openness towards the world resulting in the suffering of Father, Son and Spirit. God does not choose to suffer – that would still be masochistic – but God chooses to love that which is other, Godless and Godforsaken humanity, although knowing that such love would involve the real possibility of suffering. From the very beginning of his thinking on Jesus' Godforsaken death Moltmann reaches for this very point. In *The Crucified God* he writes, in what seems to be an echo of Dietrich Bonhoeffer,

> God allows himself to be forced out. God suffers, God allows himself to
> be crucified and is crucified, and in this consummates his unconditional
> love that is so full of joy.[160]

In a later book he goes further in the place he gives to sin in affecting the
divine life:

> ultimately the crucified figure of the incarnate God is actually deter-
> mined by the evil of law, sin and death. God has taken this evil upon
> him in order to give man his own goodness.[161]

Unfortunately, such an insight appears all too infrequently in Moltmann's
work, thus the repeated and frustrating inconsistency. Behind this inconsistency seems to be a fundamental uncertainty about the nature of God's
vulnerability, causing Moltmann to fluctuate between a belief in the openness of God's trinitarian history to the world and a desire to keep God still
in control over events, as suggested by the phrase 'Master of pain'.[162]

On the cross the Father and Son are so deeply separated that their
relationship breaks off, but God does not cease to be God as Trinity.
Moltmann speaks of the unity of God in the midst of separation in two
ways, first as the conformity of will and purpose between the Father and
Son, profoundly united in their mission at the point of deepest separation,
and second as the bond between Father and Son through the work of the
Spirit.[163] What is missing from Moltmann's thinking is any account of the
temporality of Jesus' forsakenness. The silence and separation of the cross
becomes directly the joy and unity of the resurrection. Hegel's pervasive
influence seems to have reduced the significance of the historicity of the
cross and the whole of the created order.

Does God open up the divine life to the extent that creation can
change God, or does only God really change God? Based on Origen's
insistence that Jesus' sufferings could not be under his control, but were
'in the power of the men who were disposed to inflict the pains and griefs
upon him', Paul Fiddes suggests that the same principle can be applied to
the very nature of God.[164] This is not to say that God's future is now
entirely in human hands, for the coming victory over sin and evil is
clearly an act of God, but that God chooses a real element of mutuality in

engaging in a relationship with the world. Bauckham urges that Moltmann is indeed thinking of such a genuine two-way relationship, and that it is as Trinity that God affects and is affected by the world, that is, the Trinitarian Persons are open to the world 'in such a way that those relationships change and thereby change the world'.[165] There is, however, still the lingering doubt that it is in fact simply God who changes God in the context of entering world history.[166] It remains unclear whether God's interest in the world is really an expression of interest in God.

Moltmann certainly sets out the reciprocal nature of the relationship between God and the world as a basic assumption, so that the world is an object of God's passionate interest and also puts its impress upon God in its own way.[167] Yet Moltmann also concludes that 'creation is a work of divine humiliation' and that 'the suffering of love is God's supreme work *in himself*'.[168] For Hegel the world was not significant in itself, but only in as much as it provided the negative through which *God* achieved self-realization. It may still be the influence of Hegel that limits the significance that Moltmann ascribes to the actuality of the world, for Moltmann's treatment of the historical concreteness of the cross shows the same tentativeness. Without doubt God is passionately interested in his creation, but does Moltmann really present creation with a free and real part to play in the ongoing drama or is creation simply the stage on which and the audience to which God performs a 'one-man' play?

In linking Jesus' Godforsaken cry so closely to the nature of God, Moltmann has steered the whole of Christian theology in a new direction. His works contain important pointers towards key elements in this revolutionary understanding of God, God's love and self-humility, God's vulnerability, and God's mutuality with the world. Unfortunately, the system that transmits these ideas contains a number of residual tensions. Once free from Hegelian influence Moltmann's insights could have a greater effect on the whole of his thinking.

### 3. The human perspective: the meaning of the cry for us

As we call out to God in our suffering our cries echo Jesus' own cry of forsakenness and we find God's presence with us. Human cries for God are intertwined with Jesus' dying words in a reciprocal relationship. We experience the benefit of knowing God with us - our salvation – and we are caught up in Jesus' cry, leading to imitation and discipleship.[169] Orthopraxis ('right practice') is as important to Moltmann as orthodoxy and an integral part of his conviction that all Christian theology has to do with the Kingdom of God.[170]

> Christian theology finds its relevance . . . by suffering in 'the sufferings of this present time' and makes the groaning of the creation in travail its own cry for God and for freedom . . . and this is why brotherhood with the 'least of the brethren' is a necessary part of brotherhood with Christ.[171]

*a. Self-knowledge*

The first consequence of being drawn up in Jesus' dying cry is *self-knowledge*. We recognize who we really are and what the world is like, and any of the myths created by natural theology are broken. I am one of the 'godless and godforsaken'.[172] Such knowledge 'shatters everything to which a man can hold', namely pride and self-deification, recognizes God in the passion of Jesus and is open to the suffering of others. Moltmann links closely together knowledge of God and knowledge of self. Natural theology, which pictures God in terms of power and possession, leads to the human quest for these same qualities in life now and in future salvation. By contrast, the trinitarian theology of the cross finds God in suffering and self-humiliation and is reflected in a discipleship of the cross, which expresses the community and mutuality at the heart of God. When Christian trinitarianism has been reduced to a mere monotheism, it has produced a God conceived of in terms of power and control and subsequently absolute rulers in both Church and state, abusing the theology of the cross.[173] Christian theology must challenge all such abuse of power, including any remnant of patriarchy, and overcome hierarchical, and especially sexist, behaviour and language.[174]

## b. Solidarity

Jesus' cry shows that he stands with the Godforsaken, and so the consequence of such a discipleship of the cross is a profound *solidarity* with those who suffer. In one of his fundamental and recurring themes, Moltmann draws us back to his basic dialectical understanding of the cross and resurrection. Jesus identifies with the Godless and Godforsaken, those who are opposite to him, but contradicts this Godforsakenness in the resurrection. Jesus, therefore, destroys the pattern ingrained in human culture that 'like seeks after like' and calls those in fellowship with him to seek those who are other or different and to live in solidarity with them.[175] Freed from our narcissistic tendencies we can love that which is opposite to us. The insistence by classical theism on God's *apatheia* led to the human desire to be like this God, separating people from each other. The suffering God points us to a new way of living, to what Moltmann calls the *homo sympatheticus*.[176] The 'suffering in suffering' is forsakenness and this can be ended through solidarity in the depths.

## c. Protest

Jesus' cry was a cry to God and echoing this cry leads from solidarity to *protest*.[177] Luther had already seen that the cross itself was God's protest against the misuse of Christianity and the politicized medieval Church,[178] and appreciating this insight, Moltmann himself draws on and interprets Marx's famous dictum that 'the point is not to understand the world but to change it'.[179] Since Jesus was crucified as a political rebel, preaching the cross must involve this dimension,[180] although Moltmann insists that Christian protest must never be reduced to a political ideology; rather discipleship must be lived out in the political sphere[181] and the Church must not be afraid to take sides in concrete social and political situations.[182] To live in the light of Jesus' dying cry is to stand in solidarity with those who are Godforsaken and to protest to the powerful and Godless on their behalf. In *The Crucified God*, Moltmann highlights the vicious circles of poverty, exploitation, violence, racism, pollution of nature and Godforsakenness as specific areas where Christian protest and action is needed.[183] In later books he develops new interests in nature as a sphere of God's presence, leading to ecological concerns[184] and in human rights, which becomes the focus for many of his other concerns.[185]

## d. Concrete situations

There has never been any doubting Moltmann's commitment to 'ortho-praxis', but the detail of his theological presentations has sometimes been received critically. José Miguez Bonino, who praises Moltmann's 'coher-ent and brilliant argument', finds there is no concrete expression of identification with the oppressed. In order to avoid political ideology Moltmann describes God as on the side of the poor, but without country or class. Yet the poor *are* a class and *do* have a country, Bonino counters, and if God and Christians are on the side of the poor it means concrete political choices. In general terms Bonino finds Moltmann's description of alienation and oppression too general and impressionistic, lacking rig-orous social-political analysis and failing to grasp the basic challenge of Latin American theological thought.[186] Rebecca Chop and Richard Bauckham make the same general criticisms.[187] It may be said in Moltmann's defence that he attempts to integrate political theology into the whole theological task, integrating practical action with the nature of God, leaving it to others to work out the details in individual concrete sit-uations, which a number of liberation theologians have done. Yet it is certainly true that Moltmann does little of this himself.

However Moltmann approaches specific situations of suffering and injustice, a more serious problem is the fundamental flaw in his whole theological framework underpinning his orthopraxis. Moltmann's praxis is based so closely on his understanding of God, that the doubts which remain about the Hegelian dialectic and about the language of conflict in which the Father is the cause of the suffering of the Son will undermine his concern for protest and solidarity. As Randall Bush points out, how can a Father who forsakes the Son in order to be one with the Godforsaken, really be sympathetic with those who are truly forsaken?[188] There must be lingering doubts as to whether the Father is really on the side of the oppressed, and it is such practical considerations that fire Dorothee Sölle's stringent opposition to Moltmann's whole theology. Specific discipleship must be worked out in individual and separate situations, and however specific Moltmann had been this would still need to be the case. A vulnerable God, open to the world, suffering its pain and protesting against its sin is the only solid foundation for radical discipleship.

## Notes to Chapter 6

[1] Moltmann, *The Crucified God*, p. 193, firmly links the confession with the cry, hinting at the programmatic use of 'Son of God' outlined in Chapter 3 above, and pointing to Jesus' progressive forsakenness; see Moltmann, *The Way of Jesus Christ*, trans. M. Kohl (London: SCM, 1990), p. 138; Moltmann, *Jesus Christ for Today's World*, trans. M. Kohl (London: SCM, 1994), pp. 38-9, 65.

[2] Moltmann, *The Way of Jesus Christ*, p. 166; cf. Moltmann, *The Crucified God*, p. 153: 'In the face of Jesus' death-cry to God, theology either becomes impossible or it becomes possible only as specifically Christian theology'.

[3] The essay is not available in English. See Eberhard Jüngel, 'Vom Tod des lebendigen Gottes. Ein Plakat' (1968), repr. in Jüngel, *Unterwegs zur Sache* (München: Chr. Kaiser Verlag, 1972), pp. 105-25.

[4] For Barth see *Church Dogmatics*, trans. and ed. G. W. Bromiley and T. F. Torrance (Edinburgh: T. & T. Clark, 1936-75), IV/1, p. 59.

[5] Moltmann, *The Crucified God*, p. 96. See also Moltmann, *The Trinity and the Kingdom of God*, p. 22.

[6] Moltmann, *The Crucified God*, p. 190.

[7] See Richard Bauckham, *The Theology of Jürgen Moltmann* (Edinburgh: T. & T. Clark, 1995), p. 9.

[8] Moltmann, *The Coming of God*, trans. M. Kohl (London: SCM, 1996), pp. 326-330. The criticisms still seem to contain a hidden appreciation.

[9] See above, p. 58.

[10] Moltmann, *The Crucified God*, p. 146.

[11] Ibid.

[12] Ibid., p. 147.

[13] Ibid., p. 149.

[14] Ibid., p. 146.

[15] Moltmann contradicts his argument by reference to textual variants. He says, *The Crucified God*, p. 147, 'The Western group of texts of Mark 15:34 have watered down the words and read "My God, what hast thou to reproach me

for?"' This is the reading of D and it$^{c\cdot}$. Yet later, in *The Trinity and the Kingdom of God*, p. 78, he writes, 'Early manuscripts of Mark's Gospel express the cry of dereliction even more drastically: "why hast thou exposed me to shame?" and "why hast thou cursed me?"' These are the readings of it$^k$ and it$^i$. Yet all these manuscripts are related, are part of the Western text and essentially translate the same Greek variant reading. Cf. Moltmann, *The Power of the Powerless*, trans. M. Kohl (London: SCM, 1983), p. 118. Moltmann cannot have it both ways!

[16] Moltmann, *The Trinity and the Kingdom of God*, p. 78.

[17] Moltmann, *The Way of Jesus Christ*, p. 166.

[18] Moltmann, *Jesus Christ for Today's World*, p. 35.

[19] Ibid. Moltmann makes a similar assessment in a Good Friday sermon, in Moltmann, *The Power of the Powerless*, pp. 117-8.

[20] Bauckham has missed this subtle, but important, change in Moltmann's language. He simply takes the position in *The Crucified God* pages 146-7 as authoritative and claims Moltmann considers the cry not to be historical but an authentic interpretation. See Bauckham, *The Theology of Jürgen Moltmann*, p. 53 and Baukham, *Messianic Theology in the Making* (Basingstoke: Marshall Pickering, 1987), p. 97.

[21] Moltmann, *Jesus Christ for Today's World*, pp. 34-8.

[22] This is Moltmann's conclusion in his *Jesus Christ for Today's World*, p. 35. He makes similar statements in his *The Crucified God*, p. 150, *The Trinity and the Kingdom of God*, pp. 78-9 and *The Way of Jesus Christ*, pp. 166-7.

[23] Moltmann *The Power of the Powerless*, p. 118. Yet Moltmann had already said, p. 116, that after three hours of silence Jesus died with this cry. It is not clear whether Moltmann imagines that Jesus was capable of these few words but not the whole Psalm, or whether he still has in mind that Jesus himself only gave a wordless cry.

[24] Moltmann, *The Trinity and the Kingdom of God*, pp. 78-9. See above pp. 45-6.

[25] Moltmann, *The Crucified God*, p. 150.

[26] Ibid. Grace Jantzen, 'Christian Hope and Jesus' Despair', *King's Theological Review 5* (1982), p. 3, summarizes Moltmann's interpretation of Jesus' cry as being the result of disillusionment. But this is not Moltmann's position.

[27] Moltmann, *The Power of the Powerless*, p. 119.

[28] Moltmann, *The Way of Jesus Christ*, p. 172.

[29] Moltmann, *The Power of the Powerless*, p. 119.

[30] Moltmann, *The Way of Jesus of Christ*, p. 180; cf. Moltmann, *Jesus Christ for Today's World*, p. 46.

[31] Moltmann, *Jesus Christ for Today's World*, pp. 36-7.

[32] Moltmann, *The Trinity and the Kingdom of God*, p. 76; Moltmann, *The Way of Jesus Christ*, p. 166. Moltmann interprets the sleeping of the disciples as a response to this relationship, for he consistently describes their sleep as due to grief. Compare my earlier suggestion, p. 23, that the disciples forsake Jesus by sleeping and so *parallel* the relationship between Jesus and his Father. See Moltmann, *The Trinity and The Kingdom of God*, p. 76, *The Way of Jesus* Christ, p. 166, Jesus *Christ for Today's World*, p. 33.

[33] Moltmann, *Jesus Christ for Today's World*, p. 33. Moltmann had already written in this way in a sermon, *The Power of the Powerless*, p. 116.

[34] Moltmann, *The Power of the Powerless*, p. 117.

[35] Weinandy, *Does God Suffer?*, p. 173, criticizes this modern trend and seeks to reassert a strictly soteriological interpretation of Jesus' cry.

[36] Moltmann, *The Crucified God*, p. 201. Moltmann quotes Paul Althaus, 'Jesus died for God before he died for us'; cf. Moltmann, *The Freedom of Creation*, p. 62. Marc Steen, 'Moltmann's Critical reception of Barth's Theopaschitism', *Ephermerides Theologicae Lovaniensies* 67 (1991), p. 286, considers this to be a striking difference from Barth.

[37] Moltmann, *Jesus Christ for Today's World*, p. 2; cf. Moltmann, in Miroslav Wolf (ed.), *A Passion for God's Reign* (Grand Rapids: Eerdmans, 1998), p. 2, 'For me theology springs from a divine passion – it is the open wound in one's own life and in the tormented women and children of this world . . . from Christ's cry of forsakenness on the cross'.

[38] See Moltmann, *The Crucified God*, p. 274: 'To speak here of a God who cannot suffer would make God a demon'; cf. pp. 220-223.

[39] The background and horizon for Moltmann's discussion of God's suffering is the theodicy question, for this asks questions that only the cross can answer. See Chapter 12 below for a full discussion of this issue.

[40] Moltmann, *The Trinity and the Kingdom of God*, p. 22.

[41] See Moltmann, *The Crucified God*, pp. 214-216, 220ff., although this is at the heart of the book's central argument.

[42] Francis Fiorenza, 'Joy and Pain as Paradigmatic for Language about God', *Concilium 5* (1974), p. 74, suggests that New Testament authors would not have

linked Jesus' suffering to God's suffering, but it is Hellenistic metaphysics, which
Moltmann criticizes, which provide him with this identification. But Mark's narrative climax militates against this view.

[43] Our aim is to consider the specific treatment of Jesus' cry, which in all four
of our theologians will assume some measure of belief in the suffering of God; an
evaluation of the whole concept of divine passibility cannot be undertaken here.

[44] Moltmann, *The Future of Creation* (London: SCM, 1979), p. 93;
Moltmann, 'The Trinitarian History of God', *Theology 78* (1975), p. 643.

[45] Moltmann, *The Crucified God*, pp. 195, 276.

[46] Ibid., p. 194.

[47] Moltmann, *The Future of Creation*, p. 66.

[48] Moltmann, *The Crucified God*, p. 255.

[49] Ibid., p. 246.

[50] Ibid., p. 255.

[51] Fiddes, *The Creative Suffering of God*, pp. 11-12.

[52] Moltmann, *Jesus Christ for Today's World*, pp. 45-6.

[53] Ibid., pp. 55-6.

[54] Moltmann, *Jesus Christ for Today's World*, p. 39.

[55] Moltmann, *The Way of Jesus Christ*, pp. 155-6, 167-8.

[56] Moltmann, *Jesus Christ For Today's World*, p. 36.

[57] Randall Bush, *Recent Ideas of Divine Conflict*, (San Francisco: Mellin
Research University Press, 1991), pp. 247-8, suggests that Moltmann's stress on
the Spirit in later books eclipses his earlier concentration on the particularity of
the cross to the point that the necessity of the cross and resurrection are questioned.

[58] Moltmann, *Jesus Christ for Today's World*, p. 65-6. Moltmann intertwines
hell as both the experience of Godforsakenness and death and a descent into hell
between death and resurrection.

[59] Klaas Runia, *The Present Day Christological Debate* (Leicester: IVP,
1984), p. 44.

[60] Alice R. & A. Roy Eckardt, *Long Night's Journey into Day* (Detroit:
Wayne State University Press), p. 135, not only comment on this danger, they
even propose that the burning alive of Jewish children by the Nazis is a more significant event than the cross.

[61] Moltmann, *Jesus Christ For Today's World*, p. 65

[62] Jürgen Moltmann, *History and the Triune God*, trans. J. Bowden (London: SCM, 1991), p. 172.

[63] Moltmann, *The Crucified God*, p. 205; Moltmann, *The Trinity and the Kingdom of God*, p. 118-9.

[64] Bauckham, 'Moltmann's Eschatology of the Cross', p. 306, describes this as revelation in contradiction.

[65] Moltmann, *The Crucified God*, p. 27; cf. Moltmann, *The Future of Creation* p. 78.

[66] Moltmann, *The Future of Creation*, p. 60.

[67] Moltmann, *The Crucified God*, pp. 25-8.

[68] Moltmann, *The Trinity and the Kingdom of God*, p. 4.

[69] See Moltmann, *Theology of Hope* (London: SCM, 1967), pp. 168-9. For criticisms of Moltmann's Hegelianism see Klaas Runia, *The Present Day Christological Debate*, pp. 38-46; Brian Walsh, 'Theology of Hope and the Doctrine of Creation', *Evangelical Quarterly* 59 (1987); pp. 53-76, Alister McGrath, *The Making of Modern German Christology* (Oxford: Blackwell, 1986), Ch 8; Marc Steen, 'Jürgen Moltmann's Critical Reception of K Barth's Theopaschitism', esp. pp. 294-7, 309-11.

[70] Moltmann, *The Crucified God*, p. 254, quoting Hegel, *Phenomenology of Mind*, trans. J. Baillie (Allen and Unwin, 1931, revised ed.), p. 93 (italics mine).

[71] Moltmann, *The Crucified God*, p. 254, quoting Hegel, *Philosophy of Religion*, III (Routledge and Kegan Paul, 1968), p. 98.

[72] Moltmann, *The Future of Creation*, pp. 76-7. However, Moltmann does little more than simply state that he does not make suffering necessary. There is no careful argument or assessment of Hegel.

[73] Bauckham, *Messianic Theology in the Making*, p. 69.

[74] Moltmann, *The Future of Creation*, p. 78.

[75] Carl Braaten, 'A Trinitarian Theology of the Cross', *Journal of Religion* 56 (1976), p. 120, describes Moltmann as under the tyranny of the single category given the constant use of 'all', 'every', 'only' etc.

[76] Moltmann, *The Future of Creation*, p. 74.

[77] Moltmann, *The Crucified* God, p. 255; Moltmann, *The Church in the Power of the Spirit* (London: SCM, 1977), pp. 55-6.

[78] Moltmann, *The Future of Creation*, p. 60. See *The Trinity and the Kingdom of God*, p. 159 for Moltmann's commendation of Barth for breaking his theory of correspondence at this point.

[79] Moltmann, *The Future of Creation*, p. 93; cf. Moltmann, 'The Trinitarian History of God' p. 644.

[80] Moltmann, *The Crucified God*, p. 255.

[81] Ibid., p. 159. Moltmann also states that on the cross 'these persons constitute themselves in their relationship with each other', ibid. p. 245, that God is 'the event of Golgotha', ibid., p. 247, and that the cross is 'the beginning of the trinitarian history of God', ibid., p. 278.

[82] Fiddes, *The Creative Suffering of God*, p. 7. Also see Roland Zimmany, 'Moltmann's Crucified God', *Dialog* 16 (1977), p. 54.

[83] Moltmann, *The Crucified God*, pp. 270-2.

[84] Ibid., p. 272.

[85] Bauckham, *Messianic Theology in the Making*, p. 100; Bauckham, *The Theology of Jürgen Moltmann*, p. 155. In an earlier article, 'Moltmann's eschatology of the cross', *Scottish Journal of Theology* 30 (1977), p. 310, Bauckham summarizes Moltmann with 'the cross as an event of love initiates a trinitarian history of God', without comment or criticism.

[86] Moltmann, *The Future of Creation*, pp. 83-4.

[87] Ibid., p. 93; cf. Moltmann, *History and the Triune God*, p. 24, 'With the surrender of the Son to death on the cross the infinite pain of the Father begins'.

[88] Moltmann, *The Trinity and the Kingdom of God*, p. 159.

[89] See Fiddes, *The Creative Suffering of God*, pp. 4-12 for a discussion of this aspect of Moltmann's thought up to and including *God in Creation*.

[90] Moltmann, *The Way of Jesus Christ*, p. 175.

[91] Moltmann, *The Crucified God*, pp. 248-9.

[92] Moltmann, *The Future of Creation*, p. 66; cf. p. 75.

[93] Moltmann, *The Trinity and the Kingdom of God*, p. 119.

[94] See Fiddes *The Creative Suffering of God*, pp. 9-10, pp. 168-9. However, in my view Fiddes here is not entirely clear, for the impression is given in the earlier pages that Fiddes is seeking to contrast 'degree' and 'kind' rather than combine them. See also *Past Event and Present Salvation*, pp. 109-110.

[95] Fiddes, *The Creative Suffering of God*, pp. 61-2, traces back this notion to Kirkegaard.

[96] Moltmann, *The Crucified God*, p. 51.

[97] Ibid., pp. 243-4; Moltmann, *The Trinity and the Kingdom of God*, p. 81.

[98] Moltmann, *The Crucified God*, p. 230.

99 Moltmann, *The Church in the Power of the Spirit*, p. 62; *The Future of Creation*, p. 93; *The Trinity and the Kingdom of* God, p. 23; *The Way of Jesus Christ*, p. 178; *History and the Triune* God, p. 24; *Jesus Christ for Today's World*, p. 44.

100 Moltmann concludes that the *apatheia* axiom is not an axiom but a comparison. Thus God does not change or suffer as we do, but rather God is free to change himself. Don Schweitzer, 'The Consistency of Jürgen Moltmann's Theology', *Studies in Religion* 22 (1993), p. 204, perceives a dialectical approach to tradition which requires a 'yes' and a 'no'. Moltmann wants to be seen to be building on the basic perceptions of the early theologians in this area, but not in entire agreement with them. See Moltmann, *The Crucified God*, p. 229, *the Trinity and the Kingdom of God*, p. 23, *Jesus Christ for Today's World*, p. 44.

101 See Moltmann, *The Future of Creation*, p. 77 and Moltmann, *The Trinity and the Kingdom of God*, pp. 52-6, 105-8.

102 Moltmann, *The Trinity and the Kingdom of God*, pp. 99, 105-8.

103 Moltmann, *The Trinity and the Kingdom of God*, p. 23; *The Crucified God*, pp. 229-30. See Fiddes, *The Creative Suffering of God*, pp. 71-6 for a critical evaluation of Moltmann's thinking and a wider discussion of God's 'will' and 'desire'.

104 Moltmann, *The Future of Creation*, p. 93. The same phrase occurs in *The Church in the Power of the Spirit*, p. 62 and 'The Trinitarian History of God', p. 644. The section entitled 'The experience of God' in *The Church in the Power of the Spirit*, pp. 62-6, is repeated with a few changes in *The Future of Creation*, pp. 92-5.

105 'If we trace the thought of the sending of the Son consistently through to the end, we are bound to talk about God's vulnerability, the suffering and the pain'. Moltmann, *The Church in the Power of the Spirit*, p. 64; cf. Moltmann, *The Future of Creation*, p. 94.

106 Bauckham does not seem to explore this embryonic concept of vulnerability at all.

107 Steen, 'Moltmann's critical reception of Barth's Theopaschitism' p. 306.

108 Fiddes, *The Creative Suffering of God*, pp. 61-3, 108-9, 205-6, ch. 9 passim, pp. 261-3.

109 Nature here does not mean divine substance, but refers to what might be termed God's characteristics, such as love, faithfulness, justice etc.

110 Moltmann, *The Crucified God*, p. 205.

[111] Moltmann, 'The Trinitarian History of God', p. 644.

[112] John McDade, 'The Trinity and the Paschal Mystery', *Heythrop Journal* 29 (1988), pp. 175-91.

[113] e.g. Barth, *Church Dogmatics*, II/2, compare pp. 8-12, 52-60, 625-640.

[114] Moltmann, *The Trinity and the Kingdom of God*, pp. 4-5, 25.

[115] Moltmann, *The Crucified God*, pp. 241ff. Moltmann quotes B. Steffen, *Das Dogma vom Kreuz. Beitrag zu einer staurozentrische theologie* (1920), p. 152.

[116] Moltmann, *The Crucified God*, pp. 205-6

[117] Ibid., p. 246; Moltmann, *The Future of Creation*, p. 74.

[118] James Mackey, *The Christian Experience of God as Trinity* (London: SCM, 1983), pp. 202-8, criticizes Moltmann's broad brush and inaccurate presentation of Substance and Subject and his unspoken assumptions regarding relationships.

[119] Moltmann, *The Future of Creation*, p. 73.

[120] Ibid., p. 92; cf. Moltmann, *The Church in the Power of the Spirit*, p. 61.

[121] Moltmann, *The Future of Creation*, p. 64.

[122] Moltmann later develops an explicit anthropological model for this. See his *The Gospel of Liberation*, p. 134 and *The Coming of God*, p. 96.

[123] Moltmann, *The Crucified God*, p. 243; *Jesus Christ for Today's World*, p. 37; *The Church in the Power of the Spirit*, p. 95.

[124] Moltmann, *The Spirit of Life*, pp. 64-5.

[125] Moltmann, *The Crucified God*, p. 207.

[126] Bauckham, 'Moltmann's Eschatology of the Cross', p. 308, very early on characterizes Moltmann as 'boldly theopaschite'.

[127] Moltmann, *The Future of Creation*, p. 73.

[128] Moltmann's claim that his theology is not theopaschite appears for the last time in *The Future of Creation*, p. 73.

[129] Moltmann, *Jesus Christ for Today's World*, p. 37; cf. Moltmann, *History and the Triune God*, p. 23, 'This leads to the reacceptance of the statements of theopaschism and patripassianism which were rejected earlier'.

[130] For what follows see Fiddes, *The Creative Suffering of God*, pp. 195-198.

[131] Steen, 'Moltmann's Critical Reception of Barth's Theopaschitism', p. 297, describes this as 'trinipaschitism'.

[132] Fiddes, *The Creative Suffering of God*, pp. 195-200. Jantzen, 'Christian Hope and Despair', p. 5, is also concerned that two different experiences may lead to tritheism.

[133] Moltmann, *The Crucified God*, p. 243.

[134] Moltmann, *The Future of Creation*, p. 73.

[135] That Moltmann's conception of God includes conflict is a frequent criticism. Randall Bush, *Recent Ideas of Divine Conflict*, p. 148, for example, traces this back to the influence of Ernst Bloch, as well as noticing that the abandonment of the Son introduces a rift into God.

[136] Moltmann, *The Future of Creation*, p. 73. Moltmann quotes Goethe's 'nemo contra Deum nisi Deus ipse', and here refers to Carl Schmitt's suggestion that J. M. Lenz's poem *Catharina von Sienna* was the source. In *The Crucified God*, pp. 234-5, Moltmann draws on Luther, but also adds a criticism that this kind of phrase was misleading because it was not conceived in a trinitarian way and therefore leads to paradoxical statements.

[137] Moltmann, *Jesus Christ for Today's World*, p. 33.

[138] Ibid., p. 34. This sentiment echoes earlier works; cf. Moltmann, *The Crucified God*, p. 149, 'the torment in his torments was his abandonment by God'.

[139] Moltmann, *The Way of Jesus Christ*, p. 214.

[140] Wiard Popkes, *Christus Traditus* (Zurich: Zwingli Verlag, 1967)

[141] There is one intriguing exception in John 19:30. In the Synoptics the verb is sometimes used to mean 'give' or 'hand down' in a positive sense, but in the fourth Gospel the verb is always negative except this final occurrence when Jesus 'gave up' his spirit, suggesting both the negative connotation of dying and the positive one of purposefully giving the Spirit to the disciples.

[142] In Romans 4:25 the verb is used of Christ in the passive voice. Although the subject of the 'handing over' is not supplied, it is quite possible that God is also the implied subject here.

[143] Moltmann, *The Crucified God*, p. 191.

[144] Ibid., p. 242; cf. Moltmann, *The Church in the Power of the Spirit*, p. 94, 'In this respect what killed him was not only his people's interpretation of the law and Rome's power politics, but his God and Father'. This inconsistency continues as Moltmann develops both approaches in later books. Moltmann, *The Trinity and Kingdom of God*, p. 81, picks up the stress on abandonment; *The*

*Future of Creation*, p. 72 continues the theme of an expression of God's love in direct contrast to abandonment.

[145] Moltmann, *The Crucified God*, pp. 191 and 241, quoting *Christus Traditus*, p. 286. The second quote, p. 241, is longer and only this contains the most controversial statement, 'the first person of the Trinity casts out and annihilates the second'.

[146] Moltmann, *The Crucified God*, p. 190.

[147] Leonardo Boff, *Passion of Christ, Passion of the World* (Maryknoll: Orbis, 1987), p. 114, makes this same criticism for the sake of those who still suffer. Fiddes discusses Boff's critique of Moltmann in *Past Event and Present Salvation* (London: Darton, Longman and Todd), pp. 192-4.

[148] See below pp. 123-4 for more discussion of this point.

[149] Bush, *Recent Ideas of Divine Conflict*, pp. 217, 232, 242, agrees that although this is not Moltmann's intention, it is difficult to avoid drawing this conclusion.

[150] Moltmann, *The Way of Jesus Christ*, pp. 176-7.

[151] In private correspondence with me Popkes expressed the feeling of being misunderstood by Moltmann. His aim, for example, in discussing the Abraham/Isaac story was to pick up rabbinical criticism of Christianity – their God saved Isaac and substituted a ram, whereas the Christian God let his Son die – and to hold on to the difficult question as to what the New Testament meant by God handing over his Son.

[152] Moltmann, *The Way of Jesus Christ*, pp. 172-175 is a deliberate summary of the main points of *The Crucified God*, pp. 241-247. Much of the material is similar, with reference to the same biblical passages, such as Romans 1:18 and Galatians 2:20, although in *The Way of Jesus Christ* there is the addition of Philippians 2 and the self-giving of the Son.

[153] Moltmann, *The Way of Jesus Christ*, p. 177.

[154] Moltmann, *The Spirit of Life* (London: SCM, 1992), pp. 64-5.

[155] Moltmann, *Jesus Christ for Today's World*, pp. 37-8.

[156] Moltmann, *The Future of Creation*, p. 65

[157] Ibid., p. 67.

[158] Barth, *Church Dogmatics*, IV/1 pp. 186-7.

[159] Moltmann, *The Trinity and Kingdom of God*, p. 79, criticizes those theologians, ancient and modern, who water down its agony and profound theological implications.

160 Moltmann, *The Crucified God*, p. 248; cf. Dietrich Bonhoeffer, *Letters and Papers from Prison*, Eng. trans. (London: Collins/Fontana, 1953), p. 361.

161 Moltmann, *The Future of Creation*, p. 77.

162 Moltmann, *The Trinity and the Kingdom of God*, p. 23.

163 Ibid., p. 82; Moltmann, *The Way of Jesus Christ*, p. 174. In his earlier work Moltmann speaks of the Spirit as 'proceeding' from the event of the cross in similar fashion to the cross 'constituting' God – see *The Crucified God*, p. 244; cf. *The Future of Creation*, p. 73. In his article 'The Unity of the Triune God', *St Vladimir's Theological Quarterly* 28 (1984), p. 162, Moltmann speaks of a pneumatological Christology thereby stressing the work of the Spirit before the Incarnation, an emphasis that is worked out in *The Spirit of Life*.

164 Fiddes, *The Creative Suffering of God*, p. 61, quoting Origen, *Contra Celsum*, 2. 23.

165 Bauckham, *The Theology of Jürgen Moltmann*, p. 155.

166 Cf. Fiddes, *The Creative Suffering of God*, pp. 136-8.

167 Moltmann, *The Trinity and the Kingdom of God*, pp. 98-9.

168 Ibid., p. 99. My italics.

169 Moltmann, *The Way of Jesus Christ*, pp. 116-9. For further discussion see below, Chapter 11.

170 See Ellen Charry, in Wolf (ed.), *A Passion for God's Reign*, for Moltmann's defence of 'kingdom-of-God theology' and his *Jesus Christ for Today's World*, pp. 24-9 for this worked out practically in terms of relationships, democracy, economics and ecology.

171 Moltmann, *The Crucified God*, p. 24.

172 See Moltmann, *The Crucified God*, pp. 211-214.

173 Ibid., pp. 325-329, expanded in *The Trinity and the Kingdom of God*, pp. 131, 191-7.

174 Moltmann, *The Trinity and the Kingdom of God*, p. 165; *History and the Triune God*, pp. xv-xvi.

175 Moltmann, *The Crucified God*, p. 28.

176 Ibid., p. 272.

177 Moltmann, *Jesus Christ for Today's World*, pp. 69-70. Moltmann's earliest theology was written with a deep appreciation of much of the political concern expressed by Ernst Bloch, itself drawing on the thought of Karl Marx.

178 Moltmann, *The Crucified God*, p. 208.

179 Moltmann, *Theology of Hope*, p. 84.

[180] Ibid., pp. 144-5.

[181] Ibid., p. 318.

[182] Ibid., p. 53.

[183] Ibid., pp. 329-332.

[184] Ellen Charry in Wolf (ed.), *A Passion for God's Reign*, p. 90, notes Moltmann's move away from a purely historical understanding to stress God's presence in nature. See Moltmann, *God in Creation* (London: SCM, 1985) for a detailed exposition of Moltmann's ecological themes, and *Jesus Christ for Today's World*, chapters V & VI for a presentation of Christ in the paradigm of nature rather than history and for hope for creation after Chernobyl.

[185] See Moltmann, *On Human Dignity* (London: SCM, 1984), for the issue of human rights.

[186] José Míguez Bonino, *Revolutionary Theology Comes of Age* (London: SPCK, 1975), pp. 146-8.

[187] Rebecca Chop, *The Praxis of Suffering* (Maryknoll: Orbis, 1986), pp. 100-117; Bauckham, *The Theology of Jürgen Moltmann*, pp. 105, 117.

[188] Bush, *Recent Ideas of Divine Conflict*, pp. 236-7. Bush also points out here that Moltmann's distinction between the Son's experience of dying and the Father's experience of the death of the Son also reduces the sense in which the Father can sympathize with the oppressed.

# 7
# Dorothee Sölle:
# Interpreting the Story

God put himself at risk, made himself dependent on us, identified with the non-identical. From now on, it is high time for us to do something for him.[1]

With this evocative call Dorothee Sölle ends her first book: theology must be done within the matrix of social and political action. Questions about the identity of God, the importance of Jesus and the significance of the cross cannot be answered in some detached academic sphere; meaningful discussion needs the context of relationships and commitment. For Jesus was not the only person to cry out in agony and uncertainty to God. His cry has been echoed countless times since, and it is only with, and for, and through the suffering world that Jesus' Godforsakenness reveals its meaning and offers us hope.

Sölle, therefore, offers a consistently praxis-orientated interpretation of Jesus' cry of forsakenness. Of our four theologians Sölle offers the least explicit treatment of Jesus' cry – this occurs predominantly in her book *Suffering*, although particular aspects are picked up in later books – but the overall theme of Jesus' abandonment has implicit influence on much of what Sölle writes, reflecting her whole perception of contemporary human existence marked by this same sense of forsakenness. We will attempt to explore both this explicit and implicit significance of the cry of dereliction.

## 1. The 'myth' of the cross: the interpretation of Jesus' cry

The central category with which Sölle begins to understand the cross is that of 'myth'. What happened in those three days in Jerusalem is 'the mythical story of the death and resurrection of Jesus'.[2] By using the word 'myth' Sölle is not suggesting that the story is 'untrue', and neither is she denying any historicity to it at all; rather, she is intending to lay stress on

the fact that it has been told from the viewpoint of faith by the early
church, so that it now offers us the deepest insights into the human condition. The contentious issue of whether Jesus' experience was only a
feeling or a reality of his being is thereby neatly side-stepped and, in contrast to Moltmann, Jesus' cry does not enable us to explore inner
trinitarian relationships,[3] it is a symbol of reality as a whole.[4] The language of the cross which others have traditionally applied to God's being
is rethought and used instead to speak of the contemporary situation.
What is crucial is how Jesus' cry illumines our own experiences of forsakenness.

*a. Interpreting the cry positively*

We have repeatedly drawn attention to the paradox at the heart of Jesus'
cry of forsakenness, bracketed as it is by his experience of God's closeness and the declaration of Jesus' divinity. Whereas Moltmann holds on to
the paradox and introduces it into the inner life of God, Sölle's interpretation of the cry as myth resolves the paradox by recasting Jesus'
forsakenness itself in a positive light. Jesus cries out in pain, but it is not
the pain of despair, but a pain which entails a sense of victory; it is 'a
scream of growing up, the pain of this cry is a birth pang'.[5] The story of
Jesus is thus the story of coming of age in which the certainty of a benign
omnipotent God is replaced by learning to live, in Bonhoeffer's phrase,
*etsi deus non daretur* ('as if there were no God').[6] The negative experience of the loss of God entails within it a positive new freedom. To
describe Jesus' sufferings as 'birth-pangs' is to recognize the negative, the
'pangs', but to accentuate the positive, the 'birth'.

Jesus' cry is still treated as the real climax of the Gospel story, but
instead of being the high point for which the rest of the Gospel has prepared and to which it points, it stands out in sharp contrast to all that has
come before. The Jesus who lived and spoke throughout the Gospels as if
God were close, who entered Gethsemane seeking the narcissistic hope of
relief from suffering, is now changed and on Golgotha faces God's
absence, the necessary precondition for his own coming of age.[7] These
twin experiences, the loss of God and the gaining of a new sense of self,
illumine the isolation, aloneness and Godforsakenness characteristic of

modern life. At Jesus' time of greatest need, 'God was silent as so often in history'.[8] Jesus' cry of forsakenness, which dramatically expresses living and suffering without God, is interpreted existentially as a paradigm for our modern world. Whereas we have approached Mark's Gospel with the help of narrative criticism, for Sölle it is modern experience which provides the hermeneutical key.

### b. Taking suffering seriously

Within this mythological framework, Sölle seems to treat Jesus' suffering and forsakenness with utter seriousness. She compares Jesus' experience with those who suffer today – 'a fifty-year-old woman piece worker hangs on the cross no less than Jesus, only longer'[9] – but in order to uphold the dignity and significance of all suffering. Furthermore, she specifically rejects Augustine's traditional solution, that it was not Jesus who was crying out, but Adam (humanity) crying out in Jesus.[10] However, we must observe that Sölle's positive interpretation of Jesus' cry seems at odds with the utter forsakenness implicit in the cross. Thus, 'we must ask whether in fact this does justice to the story of the cross as one of deepest desolation and abandonment'.[11] For Sölle, the absence of God, far from being a matter of despair, becomes a reason for celebration; Jesus' cry loses its essential starkness and becomes a victory shout.[12]

In later books Sölle departs from the liberal tradition of her upbringing. As a result, talk of God's absence is left to one side, the specific 'growing up' experience of the cross is no longer explored and, increasingly, a new paradigm of liberation is explored. This provides greater opportunity to stress the starkness of the cross; it is not a symbol but a realistic event.[13] But even here this loss of the very depths of abandonment is compounded:

> he knew himself to be so borne up by God that he did not fall out of God, not even when he felt himself abandoned by God.[14]

> 'The consequence [of living in a relationship to God] – suffering, the cross – certainly clouds Jesus' certainty of God, as can be seen in his cry of despair on the cross. But this night of faith, the 'My God, my God,

why have you forsaken me?' at the same time contains light from Easter morning.[15]

Two factors influence Sölle's reluctance to attribute this full sense of forsakenness to the cross. On the one hand, theologically, the resurrection is understood as an interpretation of the cross; Friday and Sunday are condensed into one event. As the foundation for understanding our own suffering and as an example of active discipleship, the cross is only significant if it is an account of real suffering, a historical event. By contrast the resurrection means 'they could not do away with him. They could not succeed in destroying him . . . this "yes" to God's will lived, and lives today, and this life appears in the cross'.[16] If the resurrection is not a distinct and subsequent event, but only an interpretation of the cross then we can only glimpse Easter morning in the very forsakenness of the cross. By condensing the resurrection into the cross, the extremity of this forsakenness is thus necessarily played down.

On the other hand, existentially, Sölle attempts to find meaning in suffering and draws on the mystical tradition which sought to convert all suffering into birth-pangs. The night of abandonment by God becomes a necessary and productive experience[17] in which the light of Easter in the cross provides meaning in the isolation of suffering. Yet the repeated problem with Sölle's interpretation will be that, according to her, Jesus does not find meaning and strength *in* the suffering of the cross, but the suffering itself *produces* that meaning. By converting profound suffering and abandonment into the path towards freedom, Sölle is in danger of the very thing she opposes, justifying suffering. There is, at times, a profound and creative tension in Sölle's work between embracing suffering and struggling for change, but it is still questionable whether Sölle's basic understanding of the cross treats all suffering with full seriousness. Sölle is acutely aware of those who suffer without hope and find no meaning in their suffering.[18] While the atheism which springs from such suffering is no more a satisfactory answer than theistic religion, turning again to the mystical tradition which sought to make *all* suffering into labour pains undermines the reality of such experience; in my view, Sölle verges in this direction, despite an awareness of the inherent dangers.[19] Surely some suffering, in a profound sense, is not to be accepted; deliberate and inhuman evil remains meaningless. Before the light of Easter is glimpsed the hell of the cross must be encountered.

At this point it must be recognized that an interpretation of the cross as myth is itself part of the problem, since the whole category of myth contains much room for slippage. Myth may be interpreted within a wide spectrum of meaning, from being simply equivalent to analogy (in which case, if all talk of God is analogy it must all be 'myth'), to being a term for a fictional account which transmits a deeper meaning. In her earlier books, Sölle offers no explanation and her use of the term 'myth' seems intentionally vague – the 'myth of cross and resurrection' draws on two different concepts simultaneously, resulting in a weakened understanding of Jesus' sufferings. Later, Sölle examines the concept of 'myth' itself, prompted by its importance in liberation theology and in the light of a more general resurgence of interest, and now it becomes equivalent to narrative.[20] In contrast to the language of science, the telling of stories is necessary, and thus the use of 'a post-naïve concept of myth', so that 'the action of God for the world, which otherwise would remain hidden... shines forth'.[21]

Although there is this changing meaning of the word myth, Sölle's consistent approach is to demythologize the event in Mark 15:34. This renders unnecessary any historical-critical considerations, and thus they are completely lacking in Sölle's work. It is modern experience which provides the basis for Sölle's interpretation. It is the concept of Godforsakenness which becomes an important feature of Sölle's thinking, overshadowing Jesus' cry itself, although this concept is still derived from the text, understood in a demythologized way.

## 2. The 'myth' of God's death: the absence of God

The essence of Jesus' passion history is the assertion that this one whom God forsook himself becomes God. Jesus does not die like a child who keeps waiting for his father. His 'Eli, Eli' is a scream of growing up . . [22]

*a. The modern loss of God*

One central thread of Sölle's interpretation is that Jesus' cry indicates his experience of the absence of God. Despite all that he had hitherto known, now he is alone, without friends and without God. There is an important connection here between this cry of Jesus and the modern phenomenon of a similar loss of the immediacy of God's presence, which Sölle considers to be now almost a universal human experience. She registers a widespread sense that God is no longer a given of life and the experience of 'God-with-us' is no longer available. It seems that it is not possible simply to posit God and affirm God is alive.[23] In the wake of the theology of the 1960s Sölle describes this experience as the 'death of God', an event, she claims, 'which has taken place within the last two centuries of European history and which conditions every aspect of life'.[24] We have already noted an alternative use of the phrase 'death of God' in Moltmann's thought, based on Luther's original christocentric interpretation. The whole 'death of God' movement, however, engineered a fundamental shift in meaning and Sölle's usage is mediated mainly from Hegel through Nietzsche, although for Sölle it is less an intellectual conclusion and more an existential experience. Eberhard Jüngel traces the various twists and turns in the history of this phrase, and concludes that for those who use the phrase as Sölle does,

> the talk is theologically insignificant . . . For this use of the expression 'death of God' says nothing at all with regard to God, but says on the contrary only something about our conceptions of God.[25]

Jüngel contends that Sölle and others have not been theological enough, for it is precisely by encountering death that God reveals God's relevance to human life. Yet his criticisms of Sölle are too sweeping, for her work is only theologically insignificant in the very strictest sense of the word, in that Sölle consciously refers to the experience of humanity rather than the being of God. For her the 'death of God' is 'in fact only the death of God's immediacy – the death of his unmediated first form, the dissolving of a particular conception of God in the consciousness'.[26] Sölle argues that it is not possible to speak with any certainty about the being of God and that all significant theology is precisely about human experience.[27] Whereas for Luther and Jüngel the 'death of God' referred to the event of the cross, Sölle uses the phrase mythologically. 'God-language', here a particular catch-phrase, is being used as a description for a human experience. The myth of God's death expresses our experience of God's absence, living without the certainty of God's presence, waiting for God. It is our understanding that has changed, not the being of God. We notice at once an important distinction with Moltmann. Moltmann affirms that God experiences death *in* Jesus' death on the cross. For Sölle, God is dead *for* Jesus, as he dies on the cross.

Throughout Sölle's work there is an explicit and implicit interplay between Jesus' cry of forsakenness and our own lives, which goes to the heart of her understanding of the cross. Although Sölle in fact never uses this phrase about Jesus on the cross, this also could be described as an experience of the 'death of God'. Sölle's assessment of modernity is not dependent on her understanding of Jesus' cry – she is convinced of this modern loss of God, whatever Jesus may have experienced on the cross – but she finds in Jesus' death a profound myth which illumines her own experience. Jesus' cry and our cries are thus interpreted within a matrix of mutual influence. It is Sölle's own experiences which lead her to understand Jesus' cry in this way, but she then finds in Jesus' cry a greater understanding of her own life.[28] There are two important and contrasting aspects of this mutuality. On the one hand, the story of the cross is a mirror in which Sölle sees her own experiences reflected back, irrespective of any meaning intended by the Gospel author. The emphasis is on the modern enlightenment experience during the last two hundred years, and Jesus' cry of forsakenness illuminates this. On the other hand, far from being a mirror, the cross is itself the defining act which brings about existential change.

## b. Loss and the being of God

The God whom men believed in, and for centuries worshipped as the God who sits on his heavenly throne, comes to be regarded instead, from a definite date onwards, from the time of the man Jesus of Nazareth, as a disinherited and homeless being.[29]

'We may say', Sölle continues, using mythological language, 'that God himself is changed when he allowed Christ to play his role'.[30] By asserting that God is changed by the cross, Sölle is of course affirming the change in our perception of God, from the omnipotent ruler to the suffering servant. What is significant is that the story of the cross itself *creates* a changed perspective in our understanding of God. At the same time the details of the story of Jesus – the love, service and vulnerability, which led Jesus to the cross and its Godforsakenness – gain a renewed significance in the light of our new sense of loss. At the end of *Christ the Representative* Sölle combines both ideas: 'Christ took over God's role in the world, but in the process it was changed into the role of the helpless God'. Although some people in all ages have understood this helplessness of the absent God, 'it was only after the death of God that this experience became the decisive factor'. The decisive change was caused by the 'death of God', that is, by modern existential experience, and this experience is not only illuminated *by* the cross but also brings into the open the implicit revolution essentially contained *in* Jesus' cry.

These two different directions of thought are held in tension. It may be that Sölle thinks a complete understanding of the cross requires both aspects and that the tension is partly caused by the distortion of the radical message of the cross in a framework of omnipotence and impassibility, which was only corrected by the 'death of God'. But they do not always sit easily together, due in part to Sölle's diverse usage of the category of myth, which in turn affects the scope of Sölle's theology. First, as a mirror, Jesus' cry is a universal myth of change through suffering, the specific details of which are insignificant because it is the modern experience which takes centre stage. Jesus' cry reveals that God is absent and that we, like Jesus, must 'grow up'. Sölle is reluctant to invest any greater significance than this in the cross. Yet, second, Jesus' cry is also a myth in the sense of a narrative, significant in its own right and active in changing modern perspectives. There are, therefore, occasions when Sölle's discussion of God does move into the ontological dimension: God is not omnipotent, but helpless; God is not independent of creation, but representable; God is absent, but God still concerns us. Although the cross is not revelatory in any kind of unique way, Sölle does draw some insights into the nature of God's being from Jesus' Godforsaken death.

The cross repeatedly breaks through the restrictions imposed by the framework of universal myth.[31]

The 'death of God' movement of the 1960s itself died out and in Sölle's later books the phrase no longer appears, apart from references back to earlier work. This parallels some important changes in Sölle's own outlook. Sölle's own intense phase of nihilism, the prelude to *Christ the Representative*, gives way to more positive affirmations, and a strict Christocentricism – the one positive aspect of her early theology – broadens to a wider reflection on God.[32]

> I do not mean that people experience God less today than in earlier times. God's presence and absence are given to us, too, in jubilation and desperation and sometimes even in a puzzling mixture of both.[33]

The earlier language of the absence of God is now redefined in two specific ways. First, there is the absence of language with which to articulate our encounter with the divine, for we 'lack the language to name God'.[34] The word 'God' itself is problematic, not only because God is always greater than the language we use but because two thousand years of Christian theology has distorted all 'God language'. God, for example, is experienced among the women at Greenham Common but is not named. 'We cannot conceive of God and have no language for God because our concepts of power, mastery, strength and energy, now as before, form the Babylon in which we live'.[35]

Second, Sölle is more specific about the kind of God she believes to be absent. She narrates one experience of her involvement in the peace movement's non-violent protest against stationing nuclear weapons in Germany, in which, soaked by police water cannons, she inwardly echoes Jesus' cry. 'In our godforsaken state we lacked God'. Her conclusion was that she offered no prayer to an authoritarian power who could have forced a different outcome. 'The Regent, Sovereign, All-powerful Potentate did not, indeed could not, help us. But the God of defeat and of pain, the God of Golgotha, was with us'.[36] Whereas in Sölle's earlier appropriation of the 'death of God' tradition the absence of God pointed to the *total* disabling of the human experience of God (although, as we have seen, hints of an alternative ontology did peep through), in more recent work the God they lacked is identified more specifically as the omnipotent God of the theistic tradition.

Such a reflection has always been central to Sölle's desire, but now a positive divine ontology is presented, it would seem without embarrassment. There are genuine encounters with a God who is present in the world, indeed these are 'foundational experiences',[37] but only when God is properly understood, as a God of pain and defeat. Although Sölle is sometimes only known and judged on her early books, her own thinking develops and the myth of Jesus' forsaken cry comes to be definitively understood in narrative rather than universal terms. Jesus' cry of abandonment points us towards this God. The revelatory nature of Jesus' cry wins through: 'Christ is the exegesis of God'[38], although not in an imperialist or exclusive way, but as one who calls forth involvement, a new understanding of God and a new language with which to express it.

### 3. The 'myth' of God's suffering: the example of Christ

Jesus' Godforsakenness, then, points us towards the God of the cross, the God of defeat and pain, a God at odds with the theistic tradition. Despite her hesitancy, Sölle had begun to grasp this from the very beginning. While all religions question divine omnipotence, 'only in Christ does the concept of a suffering God appear . . . That God in the world has been, and still is, mocked and tortured, burnt and gassed: that is the rock of the Christian faith which rests all its hope on God attaining his identity'.[39] A second strand of interpretation of Jesus' cry is thus revealed: God is absent, but God also suffers, for 'the story of Jesus' passion is . . . a narrative about suffering'.[40]

To cry out in abandonment not only declares the absence of God but also indicates a life in which meaning is destroyed and emptiness reigns. 'That which gave life its meaning has become empty and void; it turned out to be an error, an illusion that is shattered, a guilt that cannot be rectified, a void'.[41] Physically, this suffering is the blood, sweat and tears; socially, the disintegration of his company of followers, as Jesus is denied, betrayed and abandoned by his friends, in which the sleeping of the disciples in Gethsemane is 'one more link in Jesus' chain of experiences';[42] spiritually the Gospel is 'the story of a man whose goal is shattered'.[43] Jesus' experiences are the same as many others – the agony of waiting is compared to letters of twentieth century sufferers and the abandonment of Jesus is compared to the experiences of German Jews under the Nazis who found that their friends no longer wished to know them.[44]

There is here a clear link between Jesus' Godforsakenness and divine suffering, although its exact nature is left uncertain. Jesus' whole experience of suffering is exemplary, that is, he lived out of vulnerability and love and gave himself for others; thus there was clearly something of God in him,[45] but this must not be misinterpreted in an exclusive way. Jesus' dignity is not upheld by protection from suffering, but is protected by the very *humanness* of the experience, which 'makes him one with all people and their indifferent neighbours'.[46] Equally, then, this difference between Jesus and all other people is existential and not metaphysical. There can be no 'simple' conclusion, based on a belief in the self-evident divinity of Jesus, that the very fact of the suffering of Jesus expresses God's participation in our suffering. The centurion's assertion at the cross does not convey an exclusive meaning but is demythologized to point to the superiority of all those who die for a just cause.[47] Sölle must thus explain *how* she can speak of the suffering of God.

### a. God's suffering as God's absence

In *Christ the Representative* Sölle speaks of how 'God suffers by reason of his unrealized or only partly realized existence in the world. He suffers by reason of his defeats'.[48] The two parallel affirmations of absence and suffering are brought together: it is because God is absent that he suffers. Jesus' suffering in Godforsakenness is seemingly mirrored by God's suffering in absence. God's absence, however, describes the human phenomenon of the loss of certainty of God and therefore the suffering of this absent God must also be an attempt to describe a human situation.[49] Divine suffering becomes a sign for a *human* attitude that is loving and vulnerable and which accepts the suffering of love.

Yet, once again, Sölle breaks out of her own mythological framework. Her impassioned language speaks so movingly of God that its beauty and power are lost in any reduction to the merely human level, and

despite her 'death of God' experience Sölle still insists, somewhat paradoxically, that this absent God is still for us, for 'the absence of God can
be interpreted as one mode of his being-for-us'.[50] How this can be so is
not made clear. It may be that God's absence provides the space for
human freedom, or that God's absence demands representation, requiring
us to take responsibility and act like Christ. If we represent God to others,
then the absent God is present. But human freedom and human representation of God requires only the absence of a God who is conceived of in
terms of authority and omnipotence, and such a God quite clearly could
not suffer, even when absent. Ultimately, to interpret divine suffering as
an aspect of God's absence, as Sölle does, confuses human experience
and divine ontology and can make no sense.[51]

### b. God's suffering as an expression of human dignity

In her later book, *Suffering*, divine suffering is understood mythologically, through a universalizing of Jesus' sufferings. 'All extreme
suffering', Sölle insists, 'evokes the experience of being forsaken by God.
In the depth of suffering people see themselves as abandoned by every-
one'.[52] These two sentences seem a modern example of biblical
parallelism. To be forsaken by God is a forceful expression for being
alone, abandoned by all others and in the same way that *God*-forsaken-
ness describes the extremity of human abandonment, so divine suffering
points to the heights of dignity in human suffering. 'Jesus continues to die
before our eyes; his death has not ended. He suffers wherever people are
tormented'.[53] When people suffer and die today they are following Jesus'
example; the love for others that suffered in Jesus, suffers in them as well.
This is not to negate the historical and human sufferings of Jesus of
Nazareth, for 'Jesus', here, is a symbol for something that transcends
individual human life and is an attempt to point to the transcendent, the
divine, within our own suffering. All suffering can be declared to be
divine suffering not on any metaphysical basis but on account of a common humanity.

Sölle retells Wiesel's story of the boy who hangs on the gallows,[54]
and her conclusion is twofold: God is 'here on this gallows' means both
that God 'is on the side of the sufferer, is on the side of the victim, he is

hanged', that is God suffers with the boy, but also that this boy 'truly was God's son', in fact 'every single one of the six million was God's beloved son'.[55] The conclusion that, in any particular situation, God suffers, is an assertion about the value and dignity of the victim. Once again Jesus' Godforsaken cry illuminates modern experience, both in the pain of isolation and in the dignity accorded to the individual sufferer. In this way Sölle adds greater emphasis to the uniqueness of Jesus' own abandonment, in that in some way it continues and is not just copied in the experiences of others. But at the same time she is in danger of making divine suffering simply a description of human experience. God becomes a symbol 'for this affirmed and loved totality'[56], 'for our unending capacity to love'[57], and for the object of our love 'in the night of despair . . . in the void'.[58] Sölle wants to speak to a student in despair about 'God', although '"God" should be replaced in a meaningful way by words such as "love" or "justice."' Kenneth Surin, for example, concludes:

> In repudiating what she regards as the apathetic and impartial God of 'traditional' theism Sölle virtually identifies God with the emancipatory aspirations of marginalized groups. 'God . . . exists only where the oppressed take action'. Sölle, it seems, views God as a grounding principle of human endeavour, as a deity whose 'reality' is exhausted by the totality of human transformative practices.[59]

There are certainly some occasions when Sölle's use of 'God' has collapsed into a symbol for human love and nothing more. Although Sölle does not take the Marxist critique of religion as far as insisting that God cannot exist, there are phases when her theology follows Ernst Bloch's philosophy, to the extent that for all practical purposes it may have eliminated God altogether.[60] Yet, as we have already seen, early hints of a divine ontology that goes beyond the merely symbolic[61] are filled out in later books. The criticism that is valid for some of Sölle's earlier work becomes increasingly misplaced as she continues her theological reflections. In *Thinking about God* Sölle seeks to replace the traditional and neo-orthodox stress on God's 'aseity', or being-from-and in-itself, with a new understanding of God as being-in-relationship.

Earlier on, Sölle did refer to God as simply 'that which occurs between people'[62], but here she asserts that although God can only be thought of as relationship and is only found within the experience of relationships, God is something *more* than those relationships themselves.[63] She claims she has not sacrificed the vertical for the horizontal, 'rather, we must find the point where the horizontal and vertical touch'.[64] Sölle has always turned back the question about God's existence as a detached, superficial enquiry[65] – what matters is our relationship to God, how our faith changes our own lives and whether we live out God – and this has added to the uncertainty fostered in those reading Sölle. Yet we might summarize Sölle in her later work as believing that God, who exists, is only *experienced* in relationships, and when the oppressed take action.

*c. God's suffering as an existential necessity*

Although Sölle has recently articulated a divine ontology more strongly than before, she has not explored how this might influence and modify her earlier thinking on divine suffering. Instead her third attempt to tackle this issue, in 'God's Pain and Our Pain',[66] develops an understanding of divine suffering from first principles. 'Between the victors and the victims, God is only credible if God stands on the side of the victims and is thought to be capable of suffering'[67] and it is this 'suffering God, who alone answers the question of the suffering of the innocent'.[68] God is not like a president who occasionally turns up and visits the people, rather 'God suffers with us'.[69] What is notable in this article is the lack of any reference to the cross and only the briefest of references to Jesus.

Sölle has moved away from Jesus' forsaken cry on the cross as a basis for belief in the suffering of God, and turned instead to the guiding principles of feminist theology. The 'male' God, characterized by power and authority, the subject of the majority of theology, no longer has any validity. The only alternative is to feminize the question,[70] to focus on God's pain, God's motherly sorrow and comfort.[71] If Christians wish to continue worshipping God, then the only credible faith in a suffering world is a suffering God. There is no alternative. Linguistically at least, Sölle revisits her earlier work, for she declares that 'the most important image which the Bible uses for God's pain is . . . an image of giving birth'.[72] It is this experience of joy in pain contained in the language of birth-pangs, which justifies defining our pain as 'God's' pain. But theologically, the emphasis on the cross is no longer explicit. It is no longer Jesus' Godforsaken death which fashions Sölle's doctrine of God, but rather a more general religious conception. As before, I suggest that this is a development of emphasis rather than a new departure. Kenneth Surin, commenting only on Sölle's earlier books, had already concluded that 'the proposition that the pain of Christ and that of all human beings is God's pain is virtually an axiom in Sölle's treatment of the theodicy-problem'.[73] In the earlier books more thought is given to explain and defend this 'axiom', whereas more recently it has simply been assumed.

In the end, however, Sölle fails to justify why 'only in Christ does a suffering God appear'. Stylistically, Sölle 'mediates, often impressionistically'[74] rather than offers closely reasoned argument. The reader must constantly ask what Sölle actually means by her use of this word or phrase in that context. There are times that this seems to be to Sölle's advantage, not wanting to tie herself down to one particular meaning, but this can make reading her work a frustrating experience. Theologically, Sölle has moved away from her original concentration on Jesus' Godforsakenness. 'God's Pain and Our Pain' is essentially an argument from the philosophy of religion, articulated here through the Christian tradition, but equally applicable to all faiths. The lack of that which is specifically Christian, the life and death of Jesus, and in the context of a suffering world, Jesus' Godforsaken cry, weakens rather than strengthens her case for Christianity's faith in a suffering God.

#### 4. The 'myth' of God: true divinity

Characterizing Jesus' cry as a 'scream of growing up' emphasized Sölle's practical and human concerns. We have already seen how, unlike Moltmann, she avoids any metaphysical account of God, concentrating instead on the reality of human life, whether lived in God's absence or presence. What matters is whether belief in God would change the way we lived.[75] Faith is human life lived in the light of a relationship to God. Properly speaking then, as a theologian, Sölle does not aim to speak *about* God, as if God were an object that can be comprehended by the human mind, but aims to speak *to* God and *from* God, about a human relationship with God.[76] Yet any attempt to speak to God must imply some concept of the Thou in the relationship and, with increasing frequency, Sölle is forced to grapple with the concept of divine ontology, or the nature of the *being* of God.

Even in her earliest work, when declaring God's absence, Sölle could not avoid ontology altogether, for Christ, the representative of God, still revealed something of this absent God. Although Sölle sought to establish that this representation was based on identity in difference,[77] there must be some correlation between the representative and the represented. Christ does not replace a dead God as a substitute, but represents a living, though absent God.[78] Therefore, as God's Representative, Christ must point beyond himself to that which he represents, and this very act of representation must convey some element of revelation. Why is it Christ who represents God, who is 'God's leading player,'[79] rather than some other figure? Christ's representation involves dependence and this presupposes suffering;[80] the qualifications for this task are his love and suffering, for 'having left behind the life of security, [he] claimed God for this new mode of existence – powerless, homeless, in alienation'.[81] On the other hand, a self-important, power-crazy leader could not act as God's representative! If Sölle contends that God is absent and is able to be represented by another, then there must be some revelatory aspect of this representation. Although there is no complete identity between the one who represents and the one who is represented, the life of Jesus must be an indication of the nature of this absent God. Indeed, 'to this dying God anyone can turn. He bears a definite, historically recognisable face'.[82]

Representation thus provides a context for Sölle's interest in Jesus' forsaken cry, for this tortured figure opposes the human fixation on power and the male fascination with the true omnipotence of God.[83] Even when Jesus' cry is no longer explicit, it is still heard in its implicit influence on the divine ontology which Sölle tentatively proposes. Reflecting recently, Sölle concedes that preaching the 'death of God' while still using the word 'God', in a positive sense, left her easy prey for her critics. But it was always a particular concept of divinity which Sölle was rejecting, balanced by her continuing yearning for God.[84]

## a. Rejecting an authoritarian God

In the first chapter of *Suffering* Sölle launches a fierce attack on all those theologians whose writings have either supported an attitude of Christian masochism or presented a picture of a sadistic God. Calvin is at the forefront of her criticism and it is in response particularly to his prayers that Sölle concludes that 'any attempt to look upon suffering as caused directly or indirectly by God stands in danger of regarding him as sadistic'.[85] But we noted in the previous chapter how Moltmann too is specifically in Sölle's sights, and especially his understanding of Jesus' Godforsakenness. Although Moltmann presents a very different picture of God from Calvin, and despite his desire to understand God only as the Crucified God, in Sölle's opinion 'this passion is weakened by the theological system that transmits it'.[86] Jesus suffers 'at God's hands', so that the Father is the cause of the suffering of the Son. 'Moltmann attempts to develop a 'theology of the cross' from the perspective of the one who originates and causes'.[87] An authoritarian, almighty Father still casts a long shadow over the Crucified God.[88]

Sölle's basic criticism is valid, and we have already noted how Moltmann fails, even in later books, completely to resolve the issue of the Father's direct involvement in the suffering of the Son. Any understanding of God as sadistically sending suffering simply will not do. Yet Sölle weakens her own case by the language in which she encapsulates it! In the midst of her own argument she quotes the passage from Wiard Popkes, which Moltmann himself uses and concludes, 'the author is fascinated by his God's brutality', even to the point of comparing the offending quotation to a speech by Himmler to SS leaders.[89] Sölle can easily be misunderstood here. In the corresponding footnote the quotation is correctly assigned originally to Popkes and quoted by Moltmann, but her comments are vague, perhaps intentionally so, and there may be for Sölle a merging of Popkes and Moltmann.[90] Although Moltmann is justified in pointing out that a number of feminist writers, on the basis of Sölle's book, make Moltmann the author of the quotation,[91] we have seen that Moltmann still quotes Popkes approvingly. Further, Sölle's style can best be described as polemical. The accusation that 'the author is fascinated by God's brutality' is surely misplaced, for it is a description that

certainly does not fit either Popkes or Moltmann. They do not, to quote
Sölle's introduction to her theme of theological sadism, 'make the wrath
of God their essential motif'.[92] Moltmann does not show an 'insensitivity
to human misery and a contempt for humanity,'[93] as Sölle herself admits,
and Moltmann's theology is much more akin to Sölle than to Calvin's theism.

But the force of these comments do indicate the strength of Sölle's
feelings, and this desire to overcome an authoritarian concept of God is a
constantly distinctive feature of all her feminist theology. She sees her
own involvement in the feminist movement not merely in order to win
half a pie – that women have an equal share economically, academically,
structurally – but in order to make a whole new pie![94] For so long theology has been done by men, and it is not enough for women to become
professors and continue to teach and think in the same masculine categories. A whole new approach to our understanding of God is needed, one
which dispenses with the projection of male power and isolation and
instead understands theology in relational terms. Jesus' Godforsaken cry
and his whole experience of the cross again provides a springboard for
Sölle's reflection. If God is revealed in Jesus then it is in the forsakenness
which endures suffering that we see God and not in the power and authority which sends suffering. Thus Sölle insists that Christ is God's
Representative to us as well as our representative before God, because it
is only the Godforsaken Christ who offers a true understanding of divine
nature. This insight is then placed alongside her own experience as a
German female Christian.[95] In the light of Auschwitz she had always
rejected the Christian tradition of omnipotence, the so-called God of the
philosophers, distinguishing between authoritarian and humanistic religion,[96] but with the gradual dawning of her feminine consciousness, Sölle
has recognized the need to discover the God of Sarah as well as of
Abraham.[97] This leads to a heightened awareness of the inadequacy of
much traditional Christian language and a search for a new and authentic
Christian lifestyle.

*b. Rejecting an apathetic God*

Sölle's second concern is that the picture of Christ presented in the Gospels has been subsumed within a doctrine of God's impassibility and omnipotence, which owes its formulation to Greek philosophy. This theological heritage is further strengthened by the modern desire for a pain-free life, the masculine theology of individuality and the inability to sympathize caused by increasing isolation, to the point that Sölle sees apathy rather than masochism as the greatest reproach to modern Christianity.[98] Here the older, literal meaning of 'apathy' as inability to feel passion or suffering (*pathos*) leads to the more modern sense of the word as 'indifference'. Such an understanding of God is in sharp contrast to the Jesus presented in the Gospels who lived out of vulnerability and suffering love, giving himself fully to the point of Godforsakenness.

Even so, early on in Christian doctrine attempts were made to recast the Gethsemane story from the perspective of the apathy-ideal. Jesus was portrayed as invulnerable and unafraid, a picture reaching its sharpest lines in Augustine's refusal to take seriously Jesus' Godforsaken cry. By contrast, Sölle has always insisted that Jesus' cry does not set him apart from others, but is a sign of solidarity, of involvement in the world, thus revealing not an omnipotent and apathetic God, Being-in-itself, a God who has no need of friends,[99] but a suffering God who is Being-in-relationship.

*c. Affirming a helpless God*

The climax of Jesus' life was that he died abandoned by human beings and by God, and it is starting from this experience of helplessness that, in *Christ the Representative*, Sölle presents her alternative conception of the helpless God.

> The absent God whom Christ represents is the God who is helpless in this world . . . Christ, by his teaching, life and death, made plain the helplessness of God in the world; the suffering of unrequited and unsuccessful love.[100]

Sölle concludes that helplessness is also the essential message of
Bonhoeffer's famous dictum, 'only a suffering God can help'. God stands
with the victims of the world and not the oppressors, and therefore, as a
victim, is helpless. Reflecting on Wiesel's story of the boy hanging on the
gallows, Sölle concludes that in the face of that experience God must be
either the victim or the executioner.[101] There is no 'Pilate standpoint'[102] in
which even God can stand outside the situation and be a mere spectator,
for 'in the face of suffering you are either with the victim or the executioner – there is no other option'.[103] As Sölle stands with other peace
campaigners, victims both of police water cannons and militaristic politics, feeling that they had been abandoned by God and crying out 'why?',
she concludes that 'God was sad like us, small like us, without bank
accounts or bombs as backing, exactly like us'.[104] This God needs us as
much as we need God; this God waits on us as much as we wait on
God.[105] God has no ears and hands apart from ours and God has become
completely dependent on us.[106]

Once again Sölle writes within the context of her understanding of
her own German-ness. She values much of Rudolph Bultmann's teaching,
for example, but concludes that one word summarizes the difference
between her political theology at the end of the twentieth century and
Bultmann's earlier bourgeois existentialism: Auschwitz.[107] If God willed
Auschwitz to happen then God is a sadistic executioner and the only
response is atheistic rebellion. If God were the heavenly spectator, who
could have intervened but chose not to, then God's goodness is fatally
undermined and God is no different from an executioner. The only
morally acceptable answer to the despairing Jew who cries out 'where is
God?' is that he is 'on the gallows', in the sense that God is a helpless victim.[108] Sölle offers this same response to all instances of suffering,
including Jesus' death on the cross, where God has an entirely passive
role; God is always powerless and unable to help. We saw how Sölle's
initial interpretation of Jesus' forsakenness was to cast it as a cry of growing up in the face of the absence of God, and the influence of this
interpretation persists. God does nothing to forsake Jesus, there is no
inner-trinitarian struggle, because God can only be thought of as a helpless victim.

We have seen that Moltmann's Achilles' heel has been his insistence that the cross must be seen as primarily God's action; Sölle's difficulty is that God is entirely passive. Like the prisoners of Auschwitz, God is trapped in a suffering world, unable to do anything but endure the pain. This is partly because Sölle is adamant about avoiding any suggestion of an authoritarian God and the excesses she finds in Moltmann and others, but also because her vision for a hopeful future is based on a clear distinction between victims and executioners. What is required in a suffering world is solidarity with the victims, adequately provided for by a theology of God's helplessness.

Sölle's laudable desire to remove any hint of sadism in her concept of God has actually led to a blinkered view of the world and subsequently God's role within it. Kenneth Surin points out that Sölle's doctrine of solidarity is based on an ill-conceived anthropological model that claims to be able clearly and decisively to separate the victims from the executioners. He retells Wiesel's account, also in *Night*, of the Jewish prisoner killed by his own son in a fight for a crumb of bread. The boundaries have become blurred, and in a later book Wiesel himself comments, 'deep down, I thought, man is not only an executioner, not only a victim, not only a spectator: he is all three at once'.[109] If human beings are more complex than just victims, something in addition to solidarity is needed to tackle the 'executioner' in all of us. This, concludes Surin, is a doctrine of prevenient grace. Although this is not incompatible with the doctrine of divine co-suffering, it is doubtful whether Sölle's theology could accommodate this idea.[110] Even Bonhoeffer, who is quoted as a proponent of a helpless God, actually believed something subtly different. Fiddes comments that Bonhoeffer speaks neither of a helpless God nor an absent God, but of a powerless and suffering God, who precisely because of suffering is *able* to help.[111] Later in this same letter which Sölle quotes, Bonhoeffer himself goes on to reject a false conception of God in order to see 'the God of the Bible, who wins power and space in the world by his weakness'.[112] Bonhoeffer, also determined to do away with theological sadism, sees God's suffering as the essence of God's saving *activity* in the world.

Once again, however, there has been a decisive development within Sölle's own thinking and although she makes no specific acknowledge-

ment of the criticism of others, her current search for a positive understanding of 'good power', focuses her attention on the inadequacies of her
own earlier theology.

> It is possible to understand the cross of Christ in the language of power-
> less love, but it is impossible to articulate the resurrection as long as we
> regard all power as 'evil', as tyrannical, as split off and masculine. I
> note that tendency in a critical attitude to my own theology.[113]

Her immersion in liberation theology has moved her on from the 'death of
God' through the impotence of love and onto a new search for good
power, power that is inclusive and shared, the powerfulness as well as the
powerlessness of love.[114] God is no longer helpless, but is defined in a
phrase borrowed from Goethe as 'voluntary dependent'.[115] Sölle is moving towards an understanding of God based on vulnerability, on the
intentional and deliberate opening of oneself to the suffering that others
might inflict. This includes a profound sense of solidarity, for the sharing
of the pain of others entails the opening of one's life, but goes beyond it.
If the cross reveals the vulnerability of God, then God is not entirely passive, not simply a victim of injustice inflicted by others, but has acted in
love. In *The Window of Vulnerability*, written in the same period, Sölle
expresses this development most clearly, in language which holds significant echoes of Moltmann:

> In Christ, God makes Godself vulnerable; in Christ God defines God as
> non-violent. The manly idea of invulnerability is opposed, in fact cari-
> catured, by the Crucified, who was and is experienced as Son of God...
> Christ is God's wound in the world.[116]

Such sentiments echo what Sölle has fought for throughout her
career: the masculine theology of power is stripped bare in favour of a
new understanding of the suffering God. But the context gives few clues
as to exactly how the language is to be understood, beyond identifying
God's wound with Christ as he is found in the hungry and imprisoned. It
would seem that the crucified Jesus is both decisive for God's own nature
– God *makes* God's self vulnerable – and for God's self-revelation – God

*defines* God as non-violent. The utter vulnerability of Jesus' Godforsaken cry is now the crucial determinant for the nature of divine being (ontology).

## 5. The 'myth' of Christ: true humanity

'Tell me how you act politically, and I will tell you what God you believe in'.[117] For Sölle, discipleship is not linked to doctrine in a pedagogic fashion, but our action or inaction reveals our actual inner beliefs. Doctrine and discipleship are two sides of the same coin. Thus we notice Sölle's rejection of Bultmann's individualistic interpretation of sin in favour of a growing affinity with liberation theology. Any understanding of what it means to live as a Christian must be centred on the political and social spheres, moving from 'faith' and 'understanding' to faith and action.[118] It was only a radical Christianity, and particularly one which engaged with Auschwitz, which Sölle experienced in both her early teachers and authors of the past that tempted her to abandon her sceptical nihilism and embrace this life of faith. Any discussion of the absence, suffering and helplessness of God necessarily involves an intertwined Christian discipleship, for 'every theological statement has to be at the same time a political one'[119]. Although Sölle prefers now to describe her work as 'a theology of liberation' rather than 'political theology,'[120] Sölle's interest in Vietnam, her involvement in the peace-movement and her developing links with Latin America were an essential element in this theologizing.

### a. Growing Up

Sölle's positive interpretation of Jesus' cry of forsakenness, that 'the essence of the passion is that the one whom God forsook himself becomes God',[121] craves a mature Christian faith. So often people have been imprisoned as children by a belief in an authoritarian God; instead they need to grow up, to become more human, recognizing that 'naïve theism, a direct childlike relationship to the father above the starry sky has become impossible'.[122] Sölle urges that, in the same way as Jesus' cry proclaimed the absence of God, we too, following his example in our experiences of isolation and suffering, must learn to live without God.

Then we too become God's representatives. In the same way that Christ represents us, we can then represent the world, giving it time so that it too might attain its true identity,[123] for wherever anyone acts or suffers in God's stead there Christ is implicit.[124]

Even when the language of God's absence fades, Sölle still emphasizes our continual need to free ourselves from authoritarian language and belief. Obedience to a heavenly master is no longer a valid understanding of the Christian life, especially in the light of the history of obedience in twentieth century Germany.[125] Obedience has too strong a masochistic aspect, as if submission to suffering were the path to God.[126] Christianity's patriarchal tradition has left a legacy of deep-rooted pessimism about human ability, which has given room only for suffering and submission.[127] Like Jesus we must grow up and discover ourselves. No longer are we subjected like children to whatever God ordains, as if to some impersonal fate, but we take a renewed responsibility for our own lives and find a new freedom.[128]

This interpretation of Jesus' cry brings Sölle's soteriology in line with much of liberation theology. We cannot expect God to break in, that is still to look for a heavenly Father to sort out his children's problems. We must grow up and break out.[129] It is the 'poor' – understood in its widest possible meaning – who must free themselves. Salvation is only to be found in cooperation with God.[130]

*b. Being involved*

While Jesus' cry loudly proclaims the absence of God, it also resounds with solidarity for humankind.

> Only here on the cross does Christ identify himself with the fears and
> sufferings of those whom God has forgotten, with the sin of those who
> have forgotten God and the destruction of the world which is the inner
> logic of this sin.[131]

As the climax of a life lived for others, the priority of love and the acceptance of suffering become hallmarks of true discipleship. Again we are to follow Jesus' example. 'To meditate on the cross means to say good-bye to the narcissistic hope of being free of sickness, deformity and death;'[132] it means to turn away from the modern apathetic drive for a pain-free existence, the desire to be in the image of God without accepting the image of Christ, and instead to live a life of solidarity with those who suffer and to continue the transformation of suffering. At the end of her book *Suffering*, Sölle recasts Alyosha, from Dostoevsky's *Brothers Karamazov*, not as a submissive masochistic novice monk, but as an example of true solidarity, genuinely feeling for all the examples of suffering with which Ivan harangues God. To live as a Christian is to be involved in a suffering world, to act politically and to take sides, even when it means admitting that in the West we are not spectators or victims but the culprits, the executioners.[133]

An apathetic God leads to apathetic disciples, isolated and unaffected by the suffering of those around them. Jesus of Nazareth, on the other hand, and especially when he cries out in forsakenness, exemplifies beyond all others this lifestyle of solidarity. An essential part of discipleship is then to stand with those who echo Jesus' cry today, to the point that Ernesto Cardenal is justified in saying 'we' of those in Auschwitz. This solidarity 'cannot be historically substantiated, empirically demonstrated and racially or ethnically rooted. It is a mystical category in the strict sense of the word. The solidarity of the suffering is grasped in and by faith'.[134] For this reason Sölle refuses to interpret Jesus' sufferings in an exclusive way, as if he suffered more than any others or had experiences denied to us. Luke's interpretation of Gethsemane in which an angel appears to strengthen Jesus could be misleading, for it 'entails the danger of separating Jesus from us, assigning privileges to him and ascribing to him a special status he did not possess'.[135] Sölle specifically criticizes Moltmann for continuing this exclusive tendency: the whole point of Jesus' passion is its repeatability.[136] Sölle is concerned that any exclusive or final interpretation of the cross leads to a suffering-free Christianity, what Thomas Müntzer described as 'the honey-sweet Christ', rather than the 'bitter Christ' experienced in costly discipleship and solidarity.[137] There is another consequence too, as Surin has noted: the wider view of salvation which is needed to embrace such an interpretation squeezes out any place for the active grace of God here and now.

## c. Suffering

Ultimately Jesus' cry – 'why?' – knows no answer, for it does not express a search for a cause or a reason, but for an end, for purpose and finality.[138] It is a cry which questions the very meaning of existence, and in the face of this 'why', experiencing the absence of God, the possibility of loving is destroyed. The only answer, the only possible salvation, is to do as Jesus did, to go on loving in the void. Thus Sölle establishes a creative though difficult tension between accepting one's own suffering and changing the causes of suffering.[139] At an individual level the impetus to be free from pain is both selfish, in that it isolates me from other people, and unrealistic, treating the world as if it were somehow different. 'Not to accept an event which happens in the world is to wish that the world did not exist'.[140] Jesus epitomized a different relationship to suffering, one which affirmed life and accepted the suffering which a life lived with and for others entailed. Instead of regarding suffering as something outside, alien, fated, we must make our suffering our own, which means more than simply to tolerate, put up with or bear it.[141] This does not ask after the ultimate cause of suffering, but accepts reality as it is.

This is the beginning of loving in the void. Sölle draws here both on Kitamori's evocative call to 'serve the pain of God by our own pain'[142] as well as the similar thought in mystical theology epitomized by Thomas Müntzer and Meister Eckhart, encouraging us to affirm and embrace and even long for our suffering, so that accepting the cross means loving the cross.[143] What is significant about suffering is not whether it is biologically or socially derived, whether it is thought to be 'right' or 'wrong', but the attitude with which we face it; what finally matters is not its cause, but its effect. If we embrace it, then suffering becomes meaningful and leads to change; if we regard it as fate, it destroys our power; suffering becomes meaningless and we can no longer work on it.[144] This reminds us of Sölle's initial description of Jesus' God- forsakenness as a birth pang,[145] which in turn becomes the most evocative image for the suffering of God.[146]

When suffering is the pain of giving birth it becomes something creative, leading to meaning and resulting in joy. What is necessary is the ability to move from experiencing stomach pains to labour pains, so together with the mystics of the past we experience suffering as a giving birth.[147] A realistic view of life recognizes that all will endure some measure of suffering, however much we may attempt to shield and protect ourselves; the pain-free life is not an option. Therefore all must face the question of what we *do* with our suffering. Sölle insists there is no neutral suffering; we must choose between the cross of meaninglessness and the cross of Christ,[148] being the 'devil's martyrs' (Müntzer) or suffering for God.[149] This 'leads suffering out of its primitive little corner to achieve human solidarity'.[150]

We saw at the beginning of this chapter that it is doubtful whether Sölle's theological system can understand Jesus' cry in its full seriousness, since, for her, the suffering involved *provides* the meaning of the cross. It seems equally uncertain whether Sölle's creative tension is an adequate response to the occasions of human evil. Sölle is aware of the dangers of the mystical approach she embraces. It could be seen to justify the status quo[151] or appear to be masochistic,[152] especially the language of 'longing for' suffering. But it is not quietistic endurance she seeks;[153] rather, it is suffering that becomes passion in the double sense of the word.[154] 'It is paradoxical but true, that unconditional love for reality does not in the least defuse the passionate desire to change reality'.[155] This is indeed a delicate tightrope, especially in the light of her scathing criticism of masochistic Christianity.

Sölle attempts to strengthen her case by suggesting that those who suffer in vain 'depend on those who suffer in accord with justice'.[156] That some have lived differently and found meaning in suffering, this 'history of resurrections',[157] is the ground of hope for others. Sölle, however, is not clear as to the nature of this dependence. Do those who find meaning in suffering offer the hope that all can find such meaning whatever the circumstances, or do they offer hope because they were working to change the very structures that produce suffering for others? Sölle treats all experiences of suffering as essentially the same, yet surely a greater differentiation is needed. It would seem almost blasphemous to ask those Jews, who were treated more brutally than animals, to find meaning in their suffering. Some may have found meaning in their faith even when surrounded by such suffering, but that is quite different from meaning in the suffering itself.

Once again Sölle herself highlights a change in emphasis in her own thinking. In *Theology for Sceptics*, Sölle recounts the story of Father Alfredo, a Guatemalan Priest, who damages his back carrying containers of water. His response is to offer his own suffering in sacrifice to Christ, and Sölle comments:

> Earlier, in my enlightened Protestantism, I used to smile at this custom and the theology that lies behind it. Later, I criticized its awful abuse, by which the poor and especially women are supposed to be held in eternal submissiveness. Today, as I try to overcome the bourgeois-individualistic understanding of suffering, I am much closer to this thought. I understand Alfredo better. It is not technology, he seems to say to me, which makes life bearable, but rather a changed attitude toward suffering.[158]

Father Alfredo is only in the position of carrying water containers because he lives in a base community, working for better conditions and healthcare for the people. His individual acceptance is balanced by his political action. But, although Sölle presents the same essential idea here as thirty years earlier, the balance has changed. Now there is a greater stress on acceptance, and consequently a lesser stress on transforming action. Sölle's discussion here of God's pain and ours is, as always, grounded in concrete instances of suffering, but it is notable that the examples chosen, although deplorable suffering in their own right, do not challenge our theology in the same way as the radical 'evil' of the Holocaust. Despite Sölle's own commitment to the overcoming of suffering, there seems to be a need to explore further the theological connection between contemporary events of suffering and Jesus' own cry of forsakenness.

## 6. Conclusion

By drawing on the variegated category of 'myth', Sölle has sought to relate Jesus' cry intimately to real human experience, neither leaving it in the past nor transferring it to some eternal realm. It is in relationship to contemporary forsakenness that Jesus' own cry receives its true significance. The twin themes that have emerged most strongly are divine suffering and human forsakenness and both are imbued with real personal significance. Whatever tensions may remain there is no doubting Dorothee Sölle's own commitment to a suffering world through her non-violent protest, experiencing weakness and isolation, becoming the victim of those who have power. In the face of such experiences she has always invoked a discipleship not of passive helplessness but of active and vulnerable love. If political action does reveal inner belief, then Sölle has always championed an active and vulnerable God. More than anyone else Sölle has attempted radically to live out her own understanding of Jesus' forsaken cry.

## Notes to Chapter 7

[1] Dorothee Sölle, *Christ the Representative. An Essay in Theology after the 'Death of God'*, trans. D. Lewis (London: SCM, 1967), p. 152.

[2] Sölle, *Suffering*, p. 147.

[3] Sölle's deliberate avoidance of trinitarian categories to describe the cross is brought into sharp focus, for example, by the way Fiddes uses the term 'Father' in place of Sölle's use of 'God', *The Creative Suffering of God*, pp. 186-7, adding trinitarian overtones not present in Sölle's own account.

[4] Sölle, *Suffering*, p. 163.

[5] Ibid., p. 147.

[6] Dietrich Bonhoeffer, *Letters and Papers from Prison*, p. 121.

[7] Sölle sees this, in her *The Inward Road and the Way Back*, trans. D. L. Scheidt (London: Darton, Longman and Todd, 1979), p. 102, as a necessary path for all to tread. A letter from a student pleads for someone to help and tear down the walls he has built: 'but this fearful child must die. Each must give up this kind of seeking, waiting, hoping and crying out'.

[8] Sölle, *Suffering*, p. 79.

[9] Ibid., p. 146.

[10] Ibid., p. 81; cf. Dorothee Sölle, *Thinking about God*, trans. J. Bowden (London: SCM, 1990), p. 112. Sölle compares the different theological approaches to a contrast between Handel's *Messiah* and Bach's *St Matthew's Passion*.

[11] Fiddes, *The Creative Suffering of God*, p. 149.

[12] Sölle's interpretation of another myth, the Fall, *Thinking about God*, p. 47, bears important similarities to her treatment of Jesus' cry. That too recounts a growing up, a desire for human freedom in place of a Father God and can even be considered 'the happiest event in human history' (Schiller). Cf. Dorothee Sölle, *The Strength of the Weak,* trans. R. and B. Kimber (Philadelphia: Westminster, 1984), pp. 123, 126.

[13] Sölle, *Thinking about God*, p. 123.

[14] Dorothee Sölle, *Theology for Sceptics*, trans. J. Irwin (London: Mowbray, 1995), p. 96.

[15] Sölle, *Thinking about God*, p. 130.

[16] Sölle, *Thinking about God*, pp. 131-2.

[17] Sölle, *Suffering*, p. 100. Sölle turns to mysticism for its narrative basis and opposition to philosophical metaphysics; cf. Sölle, *Against the Wind*, p. 33.

[18] Ibid., pp. 140-44.

[19] Ibid., p. 95.

[20] Dorothee Sölle, *The Window of Vulnerability*, trans. L. Maloney (Minneapolis: Fortress, 1990), pp. 129-155.

[21] Ibid., p. 131.

[22] Sölle, *Suffering*, p. 147.

[23] Sölle, *Christ the Representative* p. 131; cf.. Dorothee Sölle, *Creative Disobedience* (Cleveland, Ohio: Pilgrim Press, 1995), p. xvii, where Sölle summarizes the essence of *Christ the Representative*.

[24] Sölle, *Christ the Representative*, p. 10.

[25] Jüngel, 'Vom Tod des Lebendigen Gottes. Ein Plakat', p. 108, from an unpublished translation by Paul S. Fiddes.

[26] Sölle, *Christ the Representative*, p. 133. Sölle echoes this same point recently, *Thinking about God*, p. 171, 'The conception of a Supreme Being is no longer possible'.

[27] Sölle, *Christ the Representative*, p. 141.

[28] James Bentley, *Between Marx and Christ* (London: NLB, 1982), p. 135, finds this mutuality to be at the heart of Sölle's theology, especially her understanding of divine-human relationships: 'Jesus, breaking into the cry of dereliction on Golgotha, was given meaning and also gave meaning to the crucifixion'.

[29] Sölle, *Christ the Representative*, p. 138.

[30] Ibid., p. 140.

31 Ibid., pp. 141, 150-1.

32 Sölle, *Thinking about God*, pp. 184, 188. Sölle reflects later, *Against the Wind*, pp. 32, 34, that *Christ the Representative* was written in the 'gloomy years of separation from my first partner in marriage', which seems connected with her nihilistic outlook.

33 Sölle, *Theology for Sceptics*, p. 40; cf. Sölle, *Thinking about God*, p. 138, 'The hidden God becomes visible, tangible, audible. He does not remain hidden, but becomes knowable; it is possible to taste the goodness of God'.

34 Sölle, *Theology for Sceptics*, p. 41.

35 Sölle, *Thinking about God*, p. 48.

36 Sölle, *Theology for Sceptics*, p. 45.

37 Ibid.

38 Sölle, *The Window of Vulnerability*, p. 12.

39 Sölle, *Christ the Representative*, p. 151.

40 Sölle, *Suffering*, p. 16.

41 Ibid., p. 85.

42 Ibid., p. 79.

43 Ibid., p. 16. This description of Jesus' passion experience echoes Simone Weil's assessment of affliction, containing physical, psychological and social dimensions, discussed earlier; cf. ibid. p. 13.

44 Ibid., pp. 135-40, 79.

45 Sölle, *Thinking about God*, pp. 116-7.

46 Sölle, *Suffering*, p. 81.

47 Ibid., pp. 138-139; cf. *Theology for Sceptics*, pp. 88, 94-5.

48 Sölle, *Christ the Representative*, p. 149

49 See Fiddes, *The Creative Suffering of God*, p. 187.

50 Sölle, *Christ the Representative*, p. 132.

51 Paul Fiddes draws a similar conclusion, in *The Creative Suffering of God*, pp. 191-2.

52 Sölle, *Suffering*, p. 85.

53 Ibid., pp. 139-40; cf. p. 79. This symbolic understanding is already present in *Christ the Representative*, pp. 124-5, but developed more fully here.

54 See above, p. 3-4.

55 Sölle, *Suffering*, p. 148.

56 Ibid., p. 91.

57 Ibid., p. 92.

58 Ibid., p. 157.

59 Kenneth Surin, *Theology and the Problem of Evil* (Oxford: Blackwell, 1986), p. 122. Sölle's own comment, 'God exists only where the oppressed take action', quoted in Bentley, *Between Marx and Christ*, p. 130, is originally from a paper given at Melum, France, 1972 and reproduced in B. L. Cordingley, 'An Essay in Faith and Radical Politics' in *Theology and Politics* (Manchester: Industrial Mission Association, 1978), p.6. Bentley himself introduced this quote with a similar assessment, 'For them [Cardenal and Sölle] God was virtually identified with the creative proletariat and revolutionary peasantry'.

60 Bentley, *Between Marx and Christ*, p. 131.

61 See, for example, Sölle, *Christ the Representative*, p. 150-52; *Suffering*, p. 146.

62 Sölle, *Suffering*, p. 173.

63 Sölle, *Thinking about God*, pp. 180-81.

64 Ibid., p. 192. Transcendence is always found in immanence and 'my experience in many committed groups tells me that those who lack transcendence also fall short on immanence'.

65 Sölle, *Christ the Representative*, p. 141; *Thinking about God*, p. 186.

66 This article first appeared in Marc Ellis and Otto Maduro (eds.), T*he Future of Liberation Theology*, (Maryknoll: Orbis, 1989), pp. 326-33, and again with some changes in Sölle, *Theology for Sceptics*.

67 Sölle, *Theology for Sceptics*, p. 65.

68 Ibid., p. 66.

69 Ibid., p. 72.

70 Sölle, *Against the Wind*, p. 78.

71 Sölle, *Theology for Sceptics*, p. 72

72 Ibid., p. 76.

73 Surin, *Theology and the Problem of Evil*, p. 115.

74 Ibid., p. 113.

75 Sölle frequently refers to one of Brecht's Keuner stories in which Herr K. answers the question of God's existence by asking what would change thereby. See Sölle, *The Inward Road*, p. 66, *Thinking about God*, pp. 103, 182-3, *Theology for Sceptics*, p. 49.

76 See, for example, Sölle, *Thinking about God*, pp. 184-5.

77 Sölle, *Christ the Representative*, p. 137.

78 Ibid., p. 134.

[79] Ibid., p. 140.

[80] Ibid., pp. 123-24.

[81] Ibid., p. 141.

[82] Sölle, *Christ the Representative*, p. 71.

[83] Sölle, *Thinking about God*, pp. 180-1.

[84] Sölle, *Against the Wind*, p. 33.

[85] Sölle, *Suffering*, p. 26; cf.. *The Strength of the Weak*, p. 29; *Theology for Sceptics*, p. 24.

[86] Sölle, *Suffering*, pp. 26-7

[87] Ibid., p. 26.

[88] For an assessment of Moltmann's treatment see above, pp. 85-9.

[89] Sölle, *Suffering*, pp. 27-8.

[90] Moltmann's defence, that the offending passage is not his original work and thus he is not subject to Sölle's criticisms, is unconvincing. To quote Popkes twice in the flow of his argument is clearly indicating an agreement with its content.

[91] Moltmann cites, in his *The Way of Jesus Christ*, pp. 175-6, the work of E. Sorge and D. Stahm as examples. From another perspective, Francis Fiorenza, 'Joy and Pain as paradigmatic for language about God', *Concilium* 5 (1974), pp. 72-3, makes what is in effect an oblique reference to Popkes' quotation the starting point of Moltmann's theology.

[92] Sölle, *Suffering*, p. 22.

[93] Sölle, *Suffering*, p. 26.

[94] Sölle, *The Window of Vulnerability*, p. 79.

[95] See Sölle, *Creative Disobedience*, pp. ix-xvi; *Thinking about God*, p. 108; Dorothee Sölle, *Hope for Faith* (Geneva: WCC, 1986), pp. 7-8; Sölle, in Moltmann (ed.), *How I have Changed*, pp. 22-28.

[96] Sölle, *The Inward Road*, pp. 67-8, *Strength of the Weak* pp. 111-14, *Thinking about God*, pp. 181-2, 188-9; see particularly the new preface to Sölle, *Creative Disobedience*, pp. ix-xx.

[97] Sölle, *The Window of Vulnerability*, p. 86, *Creative Disobedience*, pp. xv-xvi; cf. *Theology for Sceptics*, pp. 26-8. Although the critique of the omnipotent God in *Christ the Representative* did not derive from a conscious feminism, Sölle now sees this as actually already present: Sölle, *Against the Wind*, p. 72.

[98] Sölle, *Suffering*, p. 41; c.f. Sölle, *The Strength of the Weak*, p. 26.

[99] Sölle, *The Window of Vulnerability*, p. 65.

[100] Sölle, *Christ the Representative*, pp. 150-51.

[101] Sölle, *Suffering*, p. 148.

[102] Ibid., p. 173.

[103] Ibid., p. 32.

[104] Sölle, *Theology for Sceptics*, p. 44.

[105] Sölle, *Thinking about God*, p. 182.

[106] Sölle, *The Inward Road*, p. 99.

[107] Sölle, *Against the Wind*, p. 30; *The Window of Vulnerability*, p. 129.

[108] Surin, *Theology and the Problem of Evil*, p. 118.

[109] Elie Wiesel, *The Town Beyond the Wall* (New York: Avon, 1970), p. 174, quoted by Surin, *Theology and the Problem of Evil*, p. 120.

[110] Surin, *Theology and the Problem of Evil*, p. 122. Bentley, *Between Marx and Christ*, p. 134, comments that Sölle fears any doctrine of grace keeps us as children.

[111] Fiddes, *The Creative Suffering of God*, pp. 2, 191.

[112] Dietrich Bonhoeffer, *Letters and Papers from Prison*, p. 361.

[113] Sölle, *Thinking about God*, p. 187.

[114] Ibid., pp. 187-8

[115] Ibid., p. 189.

[116] Sölle, *The Window of Vulnerability*, p. xi.

[117] Sölle, *Thinking about God*, p. 8; *The Window of Vulnerability*, p. 106.

[118] Dorothee Sölle, *Political Theology*, trans. J. Shelley (London: SCM, 1974), p. 3; cf. Bentley, *Between Marx and Christ*, p. 122. This word play changes the title of Bultmann's famous book.

[119] Sölle, *Against the Wind*, p. 38.

[120] Ibid., p. 98.

[121] Sölle, *Suffering*, p. 147.

[122] Sölle, *Christ the Representative*, p. 131.

[123] Ibid., pp. 112, 140.

[124] Ibid., p. 134.

[125] Sölle, *Creative Disobedience*, p. 10.

[126] Ibid., pp. 37-9.

[127] Ibid., p. xii.

[128] Sölle, *Theology for Sceptics*, p. 15.

[129] Sölle, *The Inward Road*, p. 101.

[130] For a fuller treatment of these soteriological implications see ch. 11 below.

[131] Sölle, *Christ the Representative*, p. 126.

[132] Sölle, *Suffering*, p. 131.

[133] Sölle, *The Window of Vulnerability*, p. 114.

[134] Sölle, *Against the Wind*, p.110.

[135] Sölle, *Suffering*, p. 79; cf. *Christ the Representative*, pp. 85-6.

[136] Sölle, *Suffering*, p. 81.

[137] Ibid., pp. 128-130; cf. Sölle, *The Inward Road*, p. 10.

[138] Sölle, *Suffering*, p. 155.

[139] Sölle, *Suffering*, p. 5, sets out two questions that guide this tension throughout the book: what are the causes of suffering and how can these conditions be eliminated? What is the meaning of suffering and under what conditions can it make us more human?

[140] Sölle, *Suffering*, p. 107, quoting Simone Weil, *Gravity and Grace*, trans. A. Wills (New York: G P Putnam and Sons, 1952), p. 197.

[141] Sölle, *Suffering*, p. 103.

[142] Ibid., p. 44.

[143] Sölle, *Thinking about God*, p. 130.

[144] Sölle, *Suffering*, p. 107.

[145] Ibid. p. 147.

[146] Sölle, *Theology for Sceptics*, p. 76; cf. *Thinking about God*, p. 140. See Sölle, *Against the Wind*, for Sölle's most recent reflections on the experience and image of child-birth.

[147] Sölle, *Theology for* Sceptics, p. 77; cf. *Suffering*, pp. 97-8.

[148] Sölle, *Suffering*, p. 157.

[149] Ibid., p. 133.

[150] Ibid., p. 45.

[151] Ibid., p. 103.

[152] Ibid., p. 95; Sölle, *Against the Wind*, p. 75.

[153] Sölle, *Suffering*, pp. 97-8.

[154] Ibid., p. 125.

[155] Ibid., p. 94.

[156] Ibid., p. 150.

[157] Ibid.

[158] Sölle, *Theology for Sceptics*, pp. 80-81.

# 8
# Eberhard Jüngel:
# Receiving the Revelation

'God is dead' was Sölle's initial conclusion from her own experience of the modern world. Jüngel in no way denies the reality of this kind of experience, judging that 'a theologically responsible use of the word 'God' which fails to come to terms with this dubiousness is difficult to conceive of'; but his response is distinctly different – 'nevertheless, this dubiousness need not lead to a state of theological mourning.'[1] Jüngel hears this characteristic modern uncertainty, and recognizes an accompanying perplexity about thinking and speaking of God, since God, as a necessary hypothesis, has indeed been declared redundant. Jüngel is sensitive to Bultmann's question, 'what *sense* is there in speaking of God?' What is there for a theologian to say as a *theo*logian in the modern world?[2] Whereas Sölle increasingly turns to liberation theology in her search for meaning, Jüngel finds his answer to this modern bewilderment chiefly in the work of Karl Barth. Theology is only possible in the midst of such uncertainty when it is a response to God's own revelation. In this case it is not only truly possible, but indeed necessary, to think and speak of God. Barth therefore asks, 'in what sense *must* we speak of God, so that the speaking is of *God*?'[3]

## 1. Jesus' forsakenness as a word of revelation

> Jesus died crying out in a loud voice. This loud voice – *phōnēi megalēi* – is to be taken as the voice of God – *phōnēi theou*. But then the voice with which Jesus cried out as he died would be God's own voice. Jesus' last words and his human death cry would have been *the word of God*.[4]

That it is Jesus' forsaken cry in which Jüngel finds such profound revelation links in well with his sensitivity to modern concerns, resonating deeply with the modern search for God in the midst of uncertainty. Thus in *God as the Mystery of the World*, Jüngel's attempt at a theology of the crucified Jesus that relevantly addresses the contemporary philosophical setting, Jesus' cry of forsakenness is initially set within the wider Old Testament tradition of searching for God, for it is 'the most agonizing variant of the biblical question "where is God?"'[5] From this point of cultural intersection Jüngel proceeds to discuss the revelatory significance of Jesus' cry – what it tells us about God – but more than that he also builds on this foundation a whole understanding of divine ontology. Following this pattern, we too will consider first the kind of God revealed in Jesus' cry and then the significance of Jesus' Godforsaken death for the very being of God.

*a. The coming of God in language*

Underlying Jüngel's discourse on both revelation and ontology is the concept of the coming of God in language. We speak of God, and can speak of God in the right kind of way so that God is not talked to death or silenced,[6] because God has spoken first, God has come to human language. 'The necessity to speak of God is grounded in the fact that God brings his being into appearance as word, that in speaking he introduces himself.'[7] Jüngel moves beyond the Augustinian approach to language as signs, which created a distinction between the word and the thing referred to, between the linguistic *res significantes* ('thing signifying') and the absent *res significatae* ('thing signified'), to an inclusive understanding that unites word and reality together.[8] While human language has no inherent ability with which to grasp the divine reality, Jüngel follows Karl Barth in affirming that 'God is known through his word',[9] and so God 'comes to human speech';[10] the coming of God commandeers or captures human language for the purpose of self-revelation, and it is these 'captures' which become the biblical texts.[11] The word of God is not, then, something separate behind the text to which the text simply points, nor are the words of the Bible the word of God in an over-simplified way, for 'the Word of God . . . is not a priori identical with any linguistic context', but the Word of God is present in the language and text of the Bible and can be 'encountered only . . . within the context of human language as such.'[12]

What is crucial for Jüngel is that language becomes a place of encounter between speaker and the one addressed: the word *interrupts* us. He borrows Ernst Fuch's description of this as a 'language event', an idea Jüngel had already developed more fully in his doctoral dissertation, *Jesus und Paulus*. Barth had also, earlier on, spoken of revelation as an 'event' or 'happening'. Jüngel stresses that in such an event it is *God* who comes to language, and therefore if God comes to human speech in Jesus' cry, it has to do with the *being* of God. In the far country of death God comes, definitively, to humanity, but at the same time God also comes to God, the Father to the Son.[13] In the language of Jesus' death-cry we encounter the coming of God to God, and therefore we are dealing with the very being of God. Jesus' forsaken cry is thus an implicit foundation for much of Jüngel's work; this is because it is the supreme example of the word addressing, indeed interrupting, humankind in its current condition, and also because Jesus' death is the 'seal' of that event in which God comes both to God and man.[14]

Theology is the human response to the self-revelation of God in Jesus, and John Webster suggests that Jüngel attempts this by uniting historical-critical investigations and doctrinal thought.[15] We respond to that which revelation has 'captured'; we must do this critically, using carefully the tools of enquiry we have, so that revelation might be *revelation*; we must also respond in doctrinal thinking, so that it might be revelation *for us today*. In one article, Jüngel begins by linking Jesus' death, the centurion's confession and the resurrection. Because Jesus' death elicited the centurion's response, and believing that the confession '"truly, this is the Son of God" can be made on good grounds', we must think of God as the unity of life and death in favour of life, a proposition that is confirmed by the resurrection.[16] It is both surprising and unfortunate, therefore, that in the case of Mark 15:33-39 Jüngel limits his comments of a historical-critical kind, and moves on quickly to the doctrinal significance of the event.

*b. The coming of God in Jesus' cry*

In his book *Death*, Jüngel establishes a context for interpreting Jesus' cry by suggesting that we know little or nothing of Jesus' attitude to his own death, since the Gospel prophecies of suffering, death and resurrection have been projected backwards. Therefore, 'it is quite likely that the words of the Crucified One were only later attributed to the dying Jesus',[17] for 'the words from the cross have been affected by the way in which the Christian community interpreted this death.'[18] Conversely and at the same time, Jüngel suggests that 'the tradition that Jesus cried out when he died is quite firmly established'[19] and 'the one saying which most probably goes back to Jesus himself is the prayer "My God, my God, why have you forsaken me?"'[20] But at this point Jüngel, like Moltmann, equivocates and immediately adds, 'the words are from Psalm 22 [and] in the knowledge that this same psalm ends in triumphant trust in God, these words could have been put in Jesus' mouth after the event.'[21] But the matter is still not settled, for Jüngel continues, 'we cannot exclude the possibility that his death was one of utter despair . . . . And it may well be that his final cry was a cry of despair at this divine absurdity.'[22]

This somewhat conflicting account, a curious blend of historical scepticism and theological speculation, is difficult to decipher. On balance, Jüngel here doubts the historicity of Jesus' cry, which he thinks to have been most likely added by the church. Further, it would seem that, without further elucidation, Jüngel links the possible historicity of the cry to an expression of despair, whereas its addition by the church would have been due to the positive ending of Psalm 22. Not only are these undefended hypotheses confusing, they stand in sharp contrast to his introductory comments on this verse in his book *God as the Mystery of the World*. Considering this cry as the climax of the biblical question 'where is God?' Jüngel implies that this cry does not result from a loss of faith or from despair but rather, 'right faith cries with its questions for the right God.'[23] On this occasion the brevity of Jüngel's comments subsume Jesus' cry under the general category 'where is God?' rather than consider the specific situation of the cross, and the description here of Jesus' cry as 'interpreted with Psalm 22:1'[24] leaves the exact influence of that psalm on the Gospel open to question.

Later in this book Jüngel does offer some limited exegesis of the text. He implicitly offers one interpretation of *houtōs* ('thus'),[25] that the confession of the centurion was a direct response to Jesus' agonizing death, for Jesus' death-cry 'apparently *was understood* by this Gentile as a cry inspired in the dying man by God. At least that is how it is to be understood in Mark.'[26] This condensed sentence seems to imply that the centurion's declaration has a particular function in Mark's Gospel, which may be different from the centurion's original intention, and Jüngel's notion of the divine inspiration of Jesus' cry seems to strengthen the validity of the centurion's confession. In general terms Jüngel is in agreement with the kind of interpretation presented in earlier chapters, although there remains a lack of clarity and detail in Jüngel's account. Jüngel also contrasts Jesus' Godforsaken death with the closeness to God he knew in his life, and relates Godforsakenness to the verdict of the law.[27] These combine to indicate the uniqueness of Jesus' Godforsaken death, such that the 'loud voice' (*phōnēi megalei*) is seen to be the voice of God (*phōnēi theou*). Jüngel's aim throughout is to show that Jesus' humanity is the only true vestige of the Trinity, and supremely so in his death. Yet at this crucial point there is limited critical content, which is interspersed with doctrinal statements, such as the claim that Jesus' Godforsakenness had a 'special severity' and was intensified to 'an extreme degree'.[28] Such exegesis is even more surprising given that the life and ministry of Jesus is played down – possible indications of divinity are described as a 'human humanity'[29] – in favour of a doctrinal stress on the revelation of Jesus' divinity on the cross and the retroactive force of the resurrection.[30]

Given the significance for Jüngel that Jesus died a Godforsaken death, which in turn inspired the confession of the centurion, decisive historical-critical comment is notable by its absence. The text of Mark 15:34 itself is of great importance, for Jüngel's conviction that the 'loud voice' is the 'voice of God' is at the heart of his understanding of Godforsakenness. Yet, although there is some limited attempt to grapple with the text, the impression remains that equating Jesus' cry with the word of God is a conviction Jüngel brings to the text rather than a conclusion he draws out of it. Jüngel's general approach is to start from a position of conviction, approaching theology from within the Lutheran tradition, and bringing with it many presuppositions. That the Gospel declares Jesus' divinity as a response to his Godforsaken death suffices for Jüngel as a foundation on which to build. Once again the concept of Godforsakenness predominates, and it is related by Jüngel to Jesus' unique cry, but in such a way that doctrine overshadows exegesis.

## 2. Jesus' forsakenness as the revelation of God's being

Jüngel's expressed aim in *God as the Mystery of the World* is to show that we *can* think and speak of God, on the basis that 'God has defined himself through identification with the Crucified Jesus.'[31] Therefore, despite a lack of exegesis, forsakenness is at the heart of the revelation of God in our encounter with Jesus.

### a. God and death

> Was not the confession of the Roman Centurion: 'Truly this man was the Son of God!' elicited by Jesus crying with a loud voice as he died – nay, by the Jesus who was already *dead*?[32]

When the response to Jesus' Godforsaken death is the centurion's confession, Jüngel concludes that 'it means that in the event of this death the divinity of the Son of God was the phenomenon.'[33] It is because Jesus' life ended in this Godforsaken death and because 'in the person of Jesus Christ is revealed what God as the one who speaks is all about'[34] that God must be spoken of and understood in the context of death and not in contradistinction from it. More than that, the connection between the declaration of Jesus' divinity and his Godforsakenness is the essence and the identity of Christianity[35] making Jesus' cry of forsakenness, 'the first and last word which points to the meaning of Jesus' death',[36] itself a moment of supreme divine self-revelation.

Jesus' forsakenness is not the only occasion that brings God and death together – any relationship between God and the world necessitates this same connection – but, for Jüngel, the cross is a unique revelation of the place of God in death, on account of God's identification with Jesus.[37] Confession and resurrection declare that the cross was not another human tragedy but that God identified with the dying, dead and Godforsaken Jesus, therefore compelling us to think of God and death together. In fact, Jüngel understands the resurrection not as a separate and subsequent event, but as the revelation of the meaning of the cross[38]: God and death are brought together.

Paradoxically, this cry is indicative, not of a total separation of God from Jesus, but of his identification with the dead Jesus in a way which takes human sin and death, seen as non-being, into the being of God and overcomes them.[39]

But this divine encounter with death is not necessary for God, and Jüngel seeks, generally successfully, to base God's encounter with death on God's intrinsic freedom.[40] God is under no compulsion, but always acts freely out of love, in such a way as to be supremely God. The poet Goethe's 'mysterious statement' that 'noone is against God, but God himself'[41] is called upon to reject any sense of external coercion. Here, again, Jüngel depends on Barth, who had insisted that we must learn from the cross that God *can* do this as God,[42] and he finds an expression for this freedom in affirming that 'God's being is in becoming'. With such a concept, Jüngel seeks a renewed understanding of the nature of God that moves beyond the modern impasse of both theism and its atheistic shadow. This is the significance of Jüngel's recasting of Jesus' cry into the alternative question 'where?' Jesus' cry was a search for the *right* God. It stood in the biblical tradition which asked *where* God can be encountered, and thus was asking after the nature of God's being. Jesus' cry of forsakenness, uniting divinity and death, thus offers an insight into what God is like.

Whereas Jüngel understands Jesus' cry as having a place within the biblical quest for the essence of God – *which* was the right God and *where* could this God be found and encountered? – the modern 'where?' places a question mark against the very *existence* of God. When God is understood in a theistic way as the totally Other who controls all things, one real possibility in the light of human history is that this kind of God is nowhere, so that there is no God. This, as we have seen, came to one form of expression in the modern 'death of God' movement.[43] We have already noted Jüngel's criticism of Sölle's use of the phrase 'death of God' on the grounds that it is being used in a philosophical sense, initiated by Hegel and mediated through Nietzsche. Such philosophy only rejects the *existence* of God because it has misunderstood the *essence* of God, for although atheism rightly rejects classical theism it says nothing of the true nature of God. Marxist atheism had been a dominant feature in Jüngel's

East German upbringing and this prompted him to take atheism seriously and find in it a moment of truth, in its critical function.[44] Despite this, we must say that Jüngel defines atheism solely in terms of its relation to and rejection of philosophical theism, and his work lacks a sustained critique of a more broadly defined atheism.[45]

Jüngel thus takes the philosophical usage of the phrase 'death of God', which questions God's existence, and makes it a foil to the proper *theological* term that establishes God's true essence. By questioning the basis for the notion of 'the death of God', Jüngel turns it into a highly significant positive statement in his theology. For Jüngel, God has encountered death, though God is not 'dead' but very much alive.[46] Death is fundamentally eventless, but both the confession and the resurrection confirm that something happened in the death of Jesus, that somehow God happened there.[47] The natural reaction of the disciples was to flee, but the resurrection revealed that 'God has not forsaken this man who had been executed.'[48] The cross reveals a God who can encounter death and still be God, whose essence is such that God can be present in the very Godforsakenness of Jesus. In a favourite and oft repeated phrase, 'God is the unity of life and death in favour of life.'[49]

### b. God and 'perishing'

In order to challenge the underlying metaphysics of the philosophical tradition, and to speak positively of the 'death of God', Jüngel searches for new categories with which to explain the possibility of God's involvement in the cross. He suggests, therefore, that God's engagement with death can be understood as a kind of 'perishing'. Traditionally God had been thought of as 'pure actuality', in terms deriving from the thought of Aristotle; by definition, such a God could not be associated with death.[50] But on the cross God has revealed God to be otherwise, and so Jüngel, acting in response to God's self-revelation, redefines both perishability and God. First, he inverts the Aristotelian primacy of actuality in favour of *possibility*. What is possible takes priority over what is actual. God as eternal being can therefore be characterized not simply by pure actuality without any potentiality; instead possibility, what God *can do*, becomes a genuinely divine characteristic.

The God who is in heaven *because* he cannot be on earth is replaced by the . . . God who is in heaven in *such a way* that he can *identify himself* with the poverty of the man Jesus, with the existence of a man brought from life to death on the cross.[51]

Second, Jüngel rejects the entirely negative view of 'perishing' as annihilation,[52] since 'that which is ontologically positive about perishability is the possibility.'[53] Jüngel describes perishing as a tendency towards non-being, and building on his reforming of the relationship between actuality and potentiality, this means that it is a struggle between nothingness and *possibility*, between non-being and being.[54] By identifying with the forsaken Jesus God encounters not only the tendency towards nothingness but nothingness itself, hostile non-being, something which both is alien to God and alienates from God.[55] This encounter with non-being with all its negativity is for God an experience of 'perishing' in that it is a struggle which has possibility at its heart, because God is not ended by the experience. Underlying this reversal of the metaphysical tradition is, however, an understanding of human perishing which is considered to be analogous to God's own experience, and this is where the potential weakness of Jüngel's approach can be found. Jüngel seems to take little account of the discontinuity of the analogy, for undoubtedly there are significant differences between the divine and human encounters with non-being.

The 'death' of God can thus, according to Jüngel, be interpreted positively because it is a shorthand description for an encounter with perishing from which new possibilities emerge, and as such it is the answer to Jesus' searching cry 'where?'[56] The identification of God with the Godforsaken Jesus reveals the true essence of God. The cross is not to be understood as an event which is to be interpreted on the basis of some prior conception of God, but 'God's divine being is to be understood from the event of this death.'[57] Jüngel rejects the attempt of Wolfhart Pannenberg to do theology in the contemporary setting by beginning with a universal idea of divinity, and insists instead that we must move 'from the specifically Christian faith experience to a concept of God, which claims universal validity.'[58] The cross reveals a God who can encounter death and still be God, for whom death becomes a 'God-phenomenon' and is used by God to define God's own being.[59] Jüngel finds that the Apostle Paul follows the centurion's confession in also interpreting Jesus' cry of forsakenness *positively*, since he proclaims that Jesus became a curse *for us*, and we may conclude that 'Jesus' Godforsakenness is now seen as God's most authentic work.[60]

### c. God as human

This positive interpretation of Jesus' cry as 'God's most authentic work' inspires Jüngel's development of the 'humanity' of God as his prime description for the divine life, an idea adopted from Karl Barth. God's humanity is not something secondary behind God's eternity, but rather the very event of the deity of God,[61] for God's divinity is made actual in his humanity.[62] The kenosis ('emptying out') implied in the incarnation and supremely in the Godforsakenness of Jesus is at the same time a plerosis ('filling up') in the being of God. Jüngel's understanding of the humanity of God is such that not only can God encounter Godforsakenness and death, but also Godforsakenness expresses the essence of divinity.

At the heart of this divine humanity is the suffering of God.[63] In becoming human to the point of forsakenness God shares with humankind the misery of death and suffers the Godforsakenness which arises from the identification with, and the bearing of, the godlessness of the world.[64] Therefore God suffers both human opposition to God and also God's own opposition against rebellion to God, which Barth had expressed as God suffering God's own 'No' against sinful humanity.[65] That God identified with the dead Jesus and endured Godforsakenness means that there must be some passivity in the inner life of God, which corresponds to Jesus' passion. This Barth had spoken of as obedience. Because such obedience from eternity is not strange to God, 'God is *able* to suffer and die as man'.[66] Jüngel goes further and speaks of the difference between divine and human suffering:

> Man's suffering is finite. God, however, is not the kind of God who does not suffer at all. He is the God who has a capacity for *infinite* suffering and it is because of his love that he suffers infinitely . . . . To speak to

man of the reconciliation which God has brought about means that his eyes should be opened to the fact that man's godlessness and guilt leave their marks upon God himself.[67]

This is clearly a challenge to traditional metaphysics,[68] but from the cross we learn that 'God can do this.'[69] that is, Jesus' Godforsakenness is the revelation of the being of God. Jüngel has made clear that his aim has been to redefine traditional divine attributes such as omnipotence, so that creative omnipotence proves itself to be *divine* power precisely in its capacity for powerlessness even to the point of death on the cross.[70] In suffering and powerlessness God is most authentically God. Now, it has been pointed out by both John Thompson and Paul Fiddes that Barth's account of divine suffering is carefully nuanced and retains a distinction between the 'immanent Trinity' (or the triune God in the divine inner being) and the 'economic Trinity' (or the triune God at work in the world). Thus Fiddes concludes that Barth 'could have spoken of God's immanent being as being defined by exposure to suffering and "nothingness", but he has not done so', suggesting further that Jüngel, in his paraphrase of Barth, 'slides over' this very fact, that Barth locates God's suffering only in the economic Trinity.[71] We will explore later how Jüngel does in fact go beyond Barth both in stressing the identity of the immanent and economic Trinity and locating suffering at the very heart of God to the point that it is a new experience for God.

Any coherent account of divine suffering which does not reduce God to the world process must be based on the foundation of God's freedom. We noted in an earlier chapter how Moltmann struggles at this very point to evade the Hegelian overtones of necessity, and previously in this chapter how Jüngel succeeds in speaking of the death of God while still upholding God's coherence as God; despite the influence of Hegel on Jüngel, he makes clear that God is not constrained by external necessity. In doing so, Jüngel also moves towards an understanding of divine vulnerability. In his short article, 'The Truth of Life', the interruption of the divine life in the death of Jesus is contrasted with the continual interruption we experience in human life. Human life *only* exists in the interruption of its continuity by the occurrence of truth, experienced most profoundly in the death of someone close. God, on the other hand, *'allows* the continuity of his own life to be interrupted through the death of Jesus Christ.'[72] This implication of divine freedom finds its echoes in other places. God 'allows himself to be broken up by the possibilities of non-being.'[73]

Jüngel, however, is not always consistent in this respect and such language stands in a certain tension with the understanding of divine suffering which he derives from his Barthian heritage, namely suffering as God's being-in-act. According to this way of thinking, 'from the very first . . . God's passion is to be understood as the divine *action*',[74] which seems a little at odds with the passive state of being 'interrupted' by others. Although such a tension is never resolved, we will consider later the way Jüngel, somewhat hesitantly, moves beyond Barth by introducing a measure of openness in which others contribute to God. Then we shall see the way in which such a notion of vulnerability can be further enhanced.

### d. God's presence in absence

Holding together the reality of Jesus' forsakenness with the assertion that somehow God is involved in the cross has always been the difficult task for the exegete and theologian. If the cross is God's most authentic work it means that 'in its final consequences even in the situation of Godforsakenness we are dealing with God'.[75] We must thus seek an explanation of how God is present in the Godforsakenness of Jesus. That the disciples realized that 'God has not forgotten this man who had been executed as a criminal'[76] offers a very generalized response, and the explanation of God in terms of non-necessity and mystery crosses the boundary of metaphysics into a new understanding of the whole relationship between God and creation. But Jüngel's most persistent answer is to describe the cross, in language reminiscent of Sölle, as the 'presence of the absent One.'[77] Jesus' cry is for the right God, who is 'concealed, absent. But once absent is not now nothing, but rather the hidden God.'[78] Yet, while for Sölle this is a mythological expression for human experience, for Jüngel it is a metaphorical description of *God's* suffering presence.

Jüngel has here a twofold aim: first, he wants to avoid the complete separation between God and death as found in the theistic tradition and exemplified by Tertullian's interpretation of Jesus' cry, which proposed that God did abandon the Jesus on the cross, though only his *humanity*;[79] second, he rejects the complete immanentism which dissolves God into the world process, as found chiefly in Hegel. In seeking to move beyond the alternatives of absence *or* presence, which in the metaphysical tradition are irreconcilable opposites,[80] presence *in* absence is Jüngel's attempt to think through God's self-affirmation in union with God's self-surrender, to state that absence is the freely chosen mode of God's presence,[81] and 'so to specify the mode of divine presence that the cross is not its negation but its actuality.'[82] How presence can be mediated by absence in this way is not easily explained, and Jüngel's whole approach to his understanding of God's presence on the cross has been described as 'frustratingly brief and unanalysed.'[83] Jüngel turns to the analogy between Jesus' death and resurrection – Jesus was absent through his death, yet present in his absence through the resurrection – to show how God could be present and absent in the whole life and death of Jesus.[84]

Yet there are two particular problems with Jüngel's presentation. The first is the use of 'absence' on the one hand, and either 'hiddenness' or 'withdrawal' on the other, as if they were simply synonymous.[85] Jüngel, for example, describes Jesus' death as both withdrawal and absence and defines withdrawal as 'a mode of existence in which absence and presence are closely related.'[86] Jüngel derives his thinking here mainly from Luther's classic exposition of the revealed and hidden God, drawing also on Barth and Bonhoeffer, yet each time in a way that does not clearly distinguish between God's hiddenness and absence. Jüngel, for example, takes Luther's famous contrast between the 'revealed God' (*deus revelatus*) and the 'concealed God' (*deus absconditus*), the latter title meaning God's invisibility was God's concrete hiddenness on the cross; Jüngel, however, takes the contrast to refer to God's presence in absence.[87] Jüngel also recognizes that Bonhoeffer's famous statement 'God lets himself be pushed out of the world onto the cross' has, in addition to its import for salvation, profound insight into the character of the divine being.[88] For Jüngel this means that absence is not simply the opposite of presence, but God is present as the one who is absent in the world. But again, 'absence' is Jüngel's own interpretation of Bonhoeffer's verb *herausdrägen* ('pushed out'), in the context of the modern feeling of the non-necessity of God. For Bonhoeffer, God can no longer be seen in the world as a necessary working hypothesis but only in the powerlessness of the cross, an idea which resonates loudly with Jüngel. Yet for God to be squeezed out onto the cross does not make God absent from the world altogether, but rather hidden, and not where the world would expect to find God.

The second problem returns to the centurion's confession and the difficult interpretation of *houtōs exepneusen* ('he died thus'). The centurion's declaration of divinity, and so the presence of God in the cross, was in response to Jesus' death. Jüngel's insistence on the presence of God mediated through absence (understood as simply equivalent to hiddenness) evades the question of how the truth of such revelation can be assured. If God's presence is through absence, on what basis can we assert that this absence is really God's *presence* rather than in truth the total absence of God? Luther resolved the dilemma by asserting that God was *hidden* on the cross to the eyes of reason, which could only accept a projection of human desire, but open only to the eyes of faith. Jüngel himself offers no conclusive answer.

Such language as 'presence in absence', despite its vital intention, is ultimately unsatisfactory, for it does not make it clear how God can be present in Godforsakenness. Luther's sense of hiddenness – we stand before a God who is present in weakness and suffering rather than in the traditional modes of power and control – offers rich possibilities, provided hiddenness can be explained as a means of revelation, but the dialectical talk of God's absence tends to confusion. It can even militate against Jüngel's stated intention of understanding that God is present as God in the Godforsakenness of Jesus. A better explanation is provided by the doctrine of the Trinity.

*e. God as Trinity*

Contrary to the conclusion that the death of Jesus calls into question the very being of God, the centurion's confession declared God to be present in the cross by attesting to the divinity of the forsaken Jesus. For this to be the case, Jüngel argues, a Trinitarian statement of the problem is required.[89] If the cross and resurrection are going to be more than a cyclic myth of death and rebirth, so that the death of Jesus can be the death of

God in such a way that God lives, then there must be some differentiation within the being of God. Such differentiation is implied by Jüngel's foundational emphasis, that on the cross God identified with the Godforsaken Jesus. Identification implies a relationship between Jesus and God in which the being of God is not exhausted. Jesus is declared to be the Son of God, but not the totality of God. God was in Jesus but also still God in and for God's self. If God as Father gives up God as Son to death on the cross, yet still remains united as God in Spirit, then the cross is the revelation not of a *simplex esse* (being in simplicity),[90] but of a complex God with inner Trinitarian relationships.

> The God who identifies himself with the dead Jesus encounters himself in the death of Jesus in such a way that he participates in Jesus' Godforsakenness.[91]

Ultimately, it is not the councils of the Church but the forsaken cry of Jesus that reveals God to be Trinity, for 'the shortest expression of the Trinity is the divine act of the cross.'[92] Jüngel seeks 'an explicit constituting of the Trinitarian concept of God through the Crucified One.'[93] In fact, he insists that this self-differentiation can only be understood adequately in the context of the Godforsakenness in Jesus' death.[94] We speak of inner relationships within God, because we see these revealed in God's identification with Jesus, which happened supremely in Jesus' Godforsaken death. The loss of the Father by the Son and so, conversely, the loss of the Son by the Father while united in the Spirit[95] must be at the very heart of these divine relationships. Enduring the forsakenness of the Son is not just possible for God, but at the very heart of God's being.[96]

Jüngel has been criticized, for example by John Webster and Alister McGrath,[97] for slipping between the description of God's *identification* with Jesus on the cross and God *being identical* with Jesus. While it is true that Jüngel never clarifies his own exact intention, identification and identity seem to be both used deliberately. Jüngel speaks of God's identity with Jesus on too many occasions for it to be an unintended slip[98] 'identity', in fact, merits its own significant listing in the index of *God as the Mystery of the World* – and often identification and identity are clearly linked together. Jüngel's point, then, is that God's identification with

Jesus is in fact a matter of being identical with the Crucified. This has important ramifications.

First, it strengthens Jüngel's Trinitarian conclusions.[99] If God is identical to Jesus then this 'forces' a real differentiation in God. God is identical with Jesus, but not all of God can be identical. Thus Jüngel can say that God is identical with Jesus, but also that it is the Son who is identical with this dead man.[100] Second, it strengthens Jüngel's Christology. Whereas identification alone might suggest a merely functional Christology, recognizing that identification means identity leads to Jüngel assuming a strong ontological connection between God and Jesus. Third, while the language of identification is more common, Jüngel frequently connects the stress on identity with God's experience of suffering and death.[101] It is because of God's identity with the man Jesus that 'one has begun to think God and perishability together'[102] and 'talk of the death of God gains a more profound meaning.'[103] This ontological Christology provides a firmer basis on which Jüngel can affirm the real encounter between God and death. The weakness, however, of equating identification with identity, and even when not expressly stated this always seems to be Jüngel's understanding, is that it limits God's identification with the rest of his creation, because for Jüngel identification has become a category of being. Such a Christological concentration, however, is in line with Jüngel's wider theology.

Jüngel is resolved to demonstrate that it is *truly* possible to think and speak of God because we are responding to God's self-revelation in Jesus' Godforsaken cry. On the same basis he also seeks to show that it is possible to think and speak *truly* of God. However much it may appear strange to our natural inclination, Jesus' death does indeed reveal the heart of the divine life, and Jesus' Godforsakenness is God's most authentic work. Jesus' cry reveals God as God truly is. Once again Goethe's dictum, 'no one is against God except God himself' (*nemo contra deum, nisi deus ipse*), appears as part of Jüngel's argument that 'the God who reveals himself to us is really *God himself*.[104] In his book *The Doctrine of the Trinity* Jüngel responds to the contemporary debate regarding the being of God between Herbert Braun and Helmut Gollwitzer. What had united these two theologians in their radical differences was their willingness to accept the distinction between God *pro se* ('for himself') and *pro nobis* ('for us'). Jüngel transcends this particular impasse by a detailed presentation of Barth's work in which Barth had already carefully argued for a correspondence between God *pro se* and *pro nobis*, so that 'revelation is the self-interpretation of God.'[105] Barth had argued that this self-interpretation of God is based on the self-relatedness of God. God *reveals* God on the cross as Father, Son and Spirit because God truly *is* Father, Son and Spirit.[106] Jüngel's answer to Braun's doubts and Gollwitzer's theistic theology is the same: the history of the man Jesus constitutes nothing less than the inner life of God.[107]

In a passage which goes to the heart of the matter and which also shows his love of complexity and word play, Jüngel insists that God's independence in God's own self can only be grounded in God's subsistence, by which he means God's incarnation in Jesus:

> Whoever . . . wishes to maintain and think about God's independence cannot avoid the task of thinking of God's independence [*Selbständigkeit*] out of God's subsistence [*Selbstand*].[108]

Although Jüngel resolves this dispute by drawing on Barth, he also makes his own contribution. Whereas Barth always maintained some distinction between the immanent and economic Trinity within their correspondence, Jüngel, while still upholding a 'gap of grace', adopts Karl Rahner's thesis that the immanent Trinity *is* the economic Trinity.[109] This enables Jüngel to speak of forsakenness at the very heart of God.

### f. Disruption without conflict

It is this doctrine of the Trinity rather than the more abstract idea of 'presence in absence' which enables Jüngel to speak of both divine presence in the cross and the reality of the Godforsakenness of Jesus. What occurred between Jesus and his God was a disruption in the divine life, 'the most extreme estrangement from himself which God experiences in the sacramental objectivity of the man Jesus who died on the cross.'[110] Jesus' cry therefore points to a reality in the divine life, rather than only a feeling of abandonment by God, without evacuating divinity from the cross.

Again, Jüngel follows Barth quite closely here, insisting that there can never be a sense of conflict or contradiction within God, for God is always true to God's self, suffering and experiencing estrangement without falling into conflict.[111] Colin Gunton, for example, offers a favourable interpretation of Jüngel, suggesting that both he and Barth come close to presenting contradiction in God without crossing the boundary into it, in contrast to Moltmann who clearly does.[112] There is a need for a subtle balance and dialectic between two views of the cross: on the one hand, it is the revelation of God as God truly is, so that it is an event of self-definition and not self-distortion,[113] while on the other hand it is as an experience of estrangement, as witnessed by Jesus' cry. To hold to such a dialectic is clearly Jüngel's aim, although the repeated quotation of Goethe and the suggestion that God allows his own being to be 'broken up' push this balance to the limit, which intrinsically raises the question of new experiences for God.

### g. God as Suffering Love

Building on what we have said so far, that God encounters death in Jesus, and that God's identification with the Godforsaken Jesus reveals God's self-differentiation which we know as the Trinity, Jüngel affirms that God is not just loving, but 'the radiant event of love itself', or in Trinitarian terms God is lover, beloved and bond of love between them.[114] Love is 'the unity of life and death in favour of life' or, in another oft-repeated phrase, God as love is 'a still greater selflessness within a very great self-relatedness.'[115] This particular definition of love approaches Jesus' Godforsakenness from two sides. First, God is *for us*, for God is a still greater selflessness, so Jesus' Godforsakenness is for our benefit. The statement 'God is love' can only be made on the basis that the Father 'separates himself from his Son';[116] 'God reveals himself as love in that he allows his own eternal life to be interrupted by the death of Jesus.'[117] Jesus' Godforsakenness reveals a God who is love and who loves us, so that the estrangement within God 'comes to the *benefit* of humanity as the most extreme sacramental determination of God's being as object.'[118] Second, in giving God's self away for us in Jesus' Godforsakenness, God is at the same time *true to God*, that is in the midst of this greater selflessness, God is still self-related. In God's own being, therefore, revelation and forsakenness are held together.

> [God] not only loves himself but loves another one and *thus* is and remains himself. God has himself only in that he gives himself away. But in giving himself away he has himself . . . . God in the midst of this most painful separation does not cease to be the *one and living* God, but rather is supremely God as such.[119]

That God is love means that Godforsakenness, which is 'God's most authentic work', is for our benefit since God is *for us* when God is truly *for God*. The common designations, 'agape' and 'eros', so often contrasted are here combined in a unified understanding of love, so that the more we give ourselves away (agape) the more we find ourselves (eros).[120] Such love which exists in giving itself away is necessarily suffering love. 'God allowed the continuity of his own eternal life to be interrupted so as to prove himself to be love.'[121]

It is at this point, however, that Jüngel comes dangerously close to Hegelianism. He asserts that 'the identifying statement "God is love" can be made *only* on the basis of the fact that God as loving one sends this his beloved Son into the world, which means to a certain death; that the loving one separates himself from his Son.'[122] Such a statement can easily be interpreted in Hegelian fashion, that separation and death not only reveal God as love, but also are necessary for God to be love. But a comparison with Barth clarifies the issue. Whereas Barth insisted on God's self-sufficiency, which was his basis for securing God's opening of the divine to us as an act of sheer grace,[123] Jüngel works with a dialectic of self–lessness and self-relatedness, or agape and eros; this, we can see, is in line with stressing the unity of the immanent and economic Trinity. Instead of positing a loving God *pro se* behind, and as the basis for, a loving God *pro nobis*, Jüngel proposes that God is truly God in self-renunciation, acting always out of freedom. 'God's self-surrender [*selbstpreisgabe*] is not God's self-abandonment [*selbstaufgabe*].'[124] In other words, while Barth retained the reservation that 'it could have been otherwise' in God's choice of partnership with humanity, Jüngel sees no need for it.[125] God is love, and so God's self-giving to us is an essential element of God's free choice to be God.[126]

### 3. Jesus' forsakenness as the life of God

Jüngel's interpretation of Jesus' cry as *phōnēi theou* ('voice of God') means that Jesus' Godforsaken death uniquely reveals the very heart of God. The cross reveals God as love, but God could not have become love only at the event of Jesus' death, otherwise love would be a self-distortion of God. If on the cross God is love and the cross reveals God as God truly is, then God's nature must always have been love. In an exceptional way on the cross the historical manifests the eternal.[127] Yet, this language of uniqueness has frequently hinted at more: that the death of Jesus, as well as revealing the nature of God, is actually significant for the inner life of God itself, that the life of God happens in Jesus' forsakenness:

> What happened on the cross of Jesus is an event which in its uniqueness discloses the depths of deity. The special eschatological event of the identification of God with the man Jesus is at the same time the inner-most mystery of the divine being.[128]

*a. The theological significance of the death of God*

In his essay entitled 'Of the Death of the Living God' Jüngel aims to think through to the end, theologically, the death of God. In so doing, he bases his thought on Luther who, in contrast to Zwingli, believed that God's being was touched by the cross, and on the Lutheran Hegel, who had shown that the death of God was not insignificant for the being of God. The death of God is therefore crucial, not just soteriologically, but also *theo*logically. Jüngel expresses this in various ways. Jüngel introduces his essay by affirming that Christian belief in the living God is inseparably tied up with the death of Jesus, so that this is 'the *crucial event* not only for our talk about God; this death event is much more the *crucial event* of the divine life itself.'[129] In seeking to assert that the cross is not the self-distortion of God, he counters that rather 'God *defined* himself as love on the cross of Jesus'[130] and, therefore, 'if God has defined himself as God in the death of Jesus, then death has ontological relevance for the being of God.'[131] In addition to self-revelation and self-definition, in some of his strongest language, Jüngel asserts that 'God himself *took place* in Jesus' Godforsakenness and death. What the passion story narrates is the actual *conceptualization* of the doctrine of the Trinity.'[132] It is difficult to express with certainty exactly what Jüngel intends by these varying phrases and whether they are essentially synonymous, but what is clear is that Jüngel suggests that Jesus' Godforsakenness actually affected the divine life.

At this point Jüngel, somewhat tentatively, is stepping out beyond the theology of Karl Barth into new territory. In his paraphrase of Barth, Jüngel presents Barth's view that God's passion 'is to be understood as God's *action*'; thus, for Barth, it is not enough to say that God is immutable (though this is true in one sense), because God *moves himself*.[133] With regard to ideas of God's changing and suffering, the emphasis is on God's own action. This finds an echo in Jüngel's description of God 'defining himself' and of God 'taking place' in Jesus' Godforsaken death. Yet Jüngel goes further than this. We have already noted that Jüngel makes some room for the action of creation on God, in God's 'allowing himself to be broken up by the possibilities of non-being'[134] and he expresses this most strongly by the image of the collision between God and death.

> God has exposed himself to the Act-of-Being of death which is alien to him. In the event of the death of Jesus, the being of God and the being of death so strike one against the other, that the being of one jeopardizes its own being against the being of the other.[135]

Accepting that Jüngel has developed Barth's theology here, can such thought be defended? In other words, can the Godforsakenness of Jesus affect the inner life of God without implying the possible end of the deity of God or making the created world necessary for God? The best answer, as we noted in our chapter on Moltmann,[136] is provided by a voluntary divine vulnerability, which Jüngel introduces but does not develop to its full potential. We are not simply faced, as some critics think,[137] with the stark alternatives that *either* God is revealed in the cross, *or* that the cross as a human act determines God. The way of willing vulnerability is a middle path between the two, in which there is an openness to suffering, and suffering is experienced as something which befalls the one who suffers. Such a notion when applied to God retains divine freedom, for it is God who chooses to open the divine life. It also gives full significance to creation as God's other, actively affecting God, but within the limits implicit in a balance between God's freedom and openness.

Jüngel provides the foundation for this approach with his dialectic of dissimilarity within similarity. God's *decision* to go into the far country is not strange for God, for obedience from eternity is not strange to the being of God;[138] indeed Jüngel expressly follows Barth in stating it is 'God's primal decision realized in our history.'[139] Yet in the far country, in the historical incarnation, God endures *what* is strange to God.[140] In vulnerability God is always true to God: there can be no possibility of death's being final for God because this would act against God's eternal nature, in a way that a new experience of forsakenness does not. God is not determined by creation but is open to the new experiences which creation gives. In one sense it is possible then to talk with Colin Gunton of 'some version of the immutability of God',[141] for God is always true to God. But for Gunton this implies that, as far as God's *being* is concerned, the cross can only be the revelation of God.

In ongoing theological conversation, there will always be a struggle to combine talk of divine immutability with divine vulnerability. Although he has been criticized for putting God's self-existence (*aseity*) into question,[142] Jüngel's abiding problem is that he actually lays too great a stress on divine rather than human agency. This certainly excludes the impinging of external necessity upon God, but it also reduces the significance of the activity of created beings. Here, as John Webster suggests, Jüngel's anthropology owes more to Luther's stress on 'justification by faith' than to Barth; it is derived from a prior understanding of justification in which humankind remains passive before the grace of God.[143] There is indeed a subtle balance implicit in any account of God's vulnerability – between divine freedom, in which there is no place for external necessity, and an openness to creation, which allows creation the freedom genuinely to contribute to the divine life. Jüngel constantly struggles to apportion a significant role to humanity in relationship with God, and so ultimately and unfortunately is only able to present a limited measure of divine vulnerability.

### b. A new experience of Godforsakenness

Jüngel proposes, first of all, that Jesus' Godforsakenness is a new experience of suffering for God. In moving beyond theism and atheism Jüngel departs from the metaphysical concept of God as 'absolutely pure act' (*actus purissimus*), which meant there could be nothing new for God, the clear implication being that in this new approach new things are possible for God. The distinctiveness of the cross is that through God's identification with Jesus, the death of Jesus becomes the death of God, in such a way that God encounters this alien death, although, of course, death did not hold its own.[144] Therefore, God endures a negation within God's self which creates room in God's being for other being, that is, for us.[145] To be sure, Jüngel does not think that the cross is the first time that God encounters negation and nothingness. On the basis of the cross a proper theology of creation can be built in which from the beginning God is revealed as 'creative being in the struggle with the annihilating nothingness of nothing'.[146] However, the unique salvific aspect of the cross – room is created in God for us – is tied into a unique theological interpretation, in which God experiences a unique interruption, estrangement and Godforsakenness.

Here the universal and particular should combine, for the death of Jesus shows that God's life is *capable* of suffering death and is also the unique occasion when death falls upon it for our sake.[147] We referred earlier to Jüngel's presentation of God's suffering, involving both the human contradiction of God and God's contradiction of man. It is this experience of sin, of creation slipping back or falling away from the good which is new for God. In fact, Paul Fiddes argues that if there is to be any sense in which God's experience of suffering and death are to be in any way connected to ours then death must be, in a phrase Fiddes borrows and develops from Jüngel himself, 'most alien and yet most God's own'.[148] If God is to suffer and experience death then this must introduce something strange to God. The problem for Jüngel is that while he affirms that God's self-giving involves hazarding the Godhead and taking the threat of negation seriously, he does not specify whether this happens at the cross alone or in eternity, and he offers little explanation of how a continual encounter with nothingness is connected to the unique experience of the cross.

### c. A new experience of God-relatedness

Not only is the cross the place of God's new experience of suffering, but Jüngel also points towards something new there within the divine relationships of the Trinity.

> The death of Jesus Christ, which forced a differentiation between God and God, has been properly understood only when one experiences, on the basis of the resurrection of Jesus Christ, that the divine modes of being, Father and Son, which in this death separated into such a great differentiation than which nothing greater can be imagined, now so differentiated relate to each other anew in the Holy Spirit.[149]

Now, such a term as 'forced' actually sits uncomfortably with Jüngel's stress on divine freedom from all external necessity, but it does suggest that the differentiation that is integral to an understanding of God's involvement in Jesus' death results in a new experience within God. This would mean that because of the separation within God due to the cross, Father, Son and Holy Spirit relate together in a new way. Whereas there are from eternity Trinitarian distinctions in unity within the Godhead, the separation due to Godforsakenness and the corresponding unity within separation appears as a new experience for God. In this section of *God as the Mystery of the World* Jüngel does stress that this is a relationship which is eternally ever-new, but it is closely linked to the differentiation of Father and Son on the cross and the new relationship made possible through the resurrection.

Jüngel does not suggest that Father, Son and Spirit *begin* a new relationship arising from the Christ event, but that there are new experiences for God *within* the eternal Trinitarian relationships arising from God's encounter with creation in the cross.[150] Jüngel echoes this sentiment elsewhere: this interruption of the divine life leads to the enhancement of God's life and ours,[151] and God as love 'heightens and expands his own being'.[152] It is notable again how much Jüngel's stress is on divine action. It is God who enhances his own life, as well as ours through the interruption; it is God who heightens and expands his own being. As we have argued above, a greater stress on God's willing vulnerability would safeguard God's freedom while bestowing a greater active role to humanity.

### 4. Jesus' forsakenness and a forsaken world

The motif of human passivity before God influences the wider practical implications arising from Jesus' cry of forsakenness. Jesus' cry is a word of God, and a word from God that interrupts and addresses humankind, not only revealing the true nature of God, but also calling forth a practical response from those addressed. Yet, whereas Moltmann and Sölle have always been at the forefront of political theology, Jüngel deliberately avoids taking this path. He provides a foundation for a strong stress on praxis, since he is concerned for the world for God's sake and argues for the universal truth of the Christian faith instead of it being localized in the Church, but he never actually provides such practical theology himself. He has been critical of those engaged in 'political theology', chiefly Moltmann and Johannes-Baptist Metz, for not being concrete enough,[153] but his own anthropology based on a passive view of justification seems a major hindrance to a political theology of his own.

Because Jüngel's theological concern has always been with God's action, there is little place in his work for the role of a person as a political agent. Even in *Christ, Justice and Peace*, which looks at the specifically practical and political issue of the Barmen declaration of the churches at the time of the rise of Hitler to power, Jüngel's own comments actually play down political activity. He speaks of the Church possessing *criteria* for that which is to be established in the earthly state as justice and peace,[154] and having a critical role, reminding the state of God's kingdom and righteousness,[155] but he does not specify any particular practical action. George Newlands, for example, admits 'it is easy to read Jüngel as simply another example of a Eurocentric intellectualism that is irrelevant to praxis'.[156]

There is an implicit admission of such criticisms in the preface to *God as the Mystery of the World*, in which Jüngel defends the need for

careful theological thinking to precede political action. He is concerned
that political thought must derive solely from doctrinal theology and not
the other way round, so that all political thought is built on solid founda-
tions, and he is critical of those who have leapt into action without proper
thought. Newlands describes as an 'invaluable factor' the balance which
Jüngel offers to those who have so concentrated on praxis that they have
lost the substantive centre of the Gospel.[157] But when Jüngel expresses his
fear that even he has not been slow enough in his thinking, he seems in
danger of loving theory for its own sake.[158]

Yet that is not the whole story. Tracing his theological project back to
his own experiences, chiefly in East Germany, Jüngel learnt about oppression and suppression and the Godforsakenness of the world.[159] He is
convinced that political, non-violent action to work against unjust systems is permitted and even commanded. But what he missed most in
'realized socialism' and found in the Church was the truth, and what he
has sought in theology is this truth. Thus his concern is always for carefully expressed theory. He believes that 'those who have eyes to read will
discover . . . more than enough political and social relevance of the
Christian faith in the Crucified God'.[160] Yet surely Jesus' forsaken cry
must address the reality of any socio-political situation to a far greater
degree than Jüngel's implicit relevance allows. Truth must be concrete.

## Notes to Chapter 8

[1] Eberhard Jüngel, *God as the Mystery of the World: On the Foundation of
the Theology of the Crucified One in the Dispute between Theism and Atheism*,
trans. Darrell L Guder, (Edinburgh: T. & T. Clark, 1983), p. 4.

[2] See Jüngel, 'God as a Word in Our Language', in F. Herzog (ed.) *Theology
of the Liberating Word* (Nashville: Abingdon, 1971), pp. 27-9.

[3] Jüngel, *God's Being is in Becoming. The Doctrine of the Trinity*, trans.
Horton Harris (Edinburgh; Scottish Academic Press, 1978), p. xi.

[4] *God as the Mystery of the World*, p. 362.

[5] Ibid., p. 51.

[6] Ibid., p. vii.

[7] Jüngel, 'God as a Word in Our Language', p. 29. Jüngel's epistemological
approach combines the existential hermeneutics of Heidegger, in that language is
the place where God comes, with the evangelical hermeneutics, at the forefront

of his Lutheran heritage and Barthian influence, that our thinking of God is only in response to God's address to us in his Word.

[8] Jüngel, *God as the Mystery of the World*, p. 11.

[9] Barth, *Church Dogmatics*, II/1, p. 4

[10] Jüngel, *The Doctrine of the Trinity*, pp. 11, 45; cf. 'God as a Word in Our Language', pp. 30, 34, 37. Similarly, 'God becomes objective in his Word', *The Doctrine of the Trinity*, p. 45.

[11] Jüngel, *The Doctrine of the Trinity*, p. 14, n. 43

[12] Jüngel, 'God as a Word in Our Language', p. 41.

[13] Jüngel, *God as the Mystery of the World*, p. 383.

[14] Ibid.

[15] See John Webster, *Eberhard Jüngel* (Cambridge: CUP, 1986), pp. 26-8.

[16] Eberhard Jüngel, 'Das Verhältnis von 'ökonomischer' und 'immanenter' Trinität', *Zeitschrift für Theologie und Kirche* 72 (1975), p. 353.

[17] Jüngel, *Death. The Riddle and the Mystery*, trans. I. and U..Nicol (Edinburgh: St Andrews, 1975), p. 96.

[18] Ibid., p. 105.

[19] Ibid., p. 96.

[20] Ibid., p. 105.

[21] Ibid.

[22] Ibid.

[23] Jüngel, *God as the Mystery of the World*, p. 51.

[24] Ibid., p. 361.

[25] For discussion, see above pp. 30-4.

[26] Jüngel, *God as the Mystery of the World*, p. 362.

[27] Ibid., p. 361.

[28] Ibid.

[29] Ibid., p. 357.

[30] See John Thompson, 'Jüngel on Barth', in John Webster (ed.), *The Possibilities of Theology* (Edinburgh: T. & T. Clark, 1994), pp. 171-2.

[31] Jüngel, *God as the Mystery of the World*, p. x. 'For responsible Christian usage of the word 'God', the Crucified One is virtually the real definition of what is meant by the word 'God'', ibid. p. 13. The qualifying 'virtually' is somewhat intriguing.

[32] Jüngel, *The Doctrine of the Trinity*, p. xv.

[33] Jüngel, 'Vom Tod des Lebendigen Gottes', p. 118, quoted from Paul Fiddes' unpublished translation.

[34] Jüngel, *God as the Mystery of the World*, p. 13.

[35] Ibid., p. 362.

[36] Thompson, 'Jüngel on Barth', p. 170.

[37] Thompson is concerned, as we hinted above, that identification is not a strong enough term because it establishes too great a distinction between Jesus' life and ministry and his death and resurrection. For our purpose, it is clear that Jüngel sees divinity expressed in Godforsakenness on the cross.

[38] See Webster, *Eberhard Jüngel*, p. 88.

[39] Thompson, 'Jüngel on Barth', p. 170.

[40] So Colin Gunton, 'The Being and Attributes of God' in Webster (ed.) *The Possibilities of Theology*, p. 9, concludes that although coming close Jüngel manages to avoid the trap of necessitarianism. Thompson, 'Jüngel on Barth', pp. 175-6, makes a similar assessment.

[41] Jüngel, *God as the Mystery of the World*, p. 363.

[42] e.g. Barth, *Church Dogmatics*, IV/1, pp. 194-204.

[43] Jüngel, *God as the Mystery of the World*, p. 102.

[44] Jüngel, 'Toward the Heart of the Matter', *Christian Century* (1991), p. 230.

[45] Someone like Sölle, who rejects both classical theism and the title atheism and who uses the 'death of God' in a significantly different way challenges Jüngel's rigid distinctions.

[46] Jüngel, 'Vom Tod des Lebendigen Gottes', p. 106.

[47] Jüngel, *God as the Mystery of the World*, p. 303.

[48] Jüngel, *Death*, p. 96.

[49] See, for example, Jüngel, *God as the Mystery of the World*, p. x.

[50] Ibid., p. 214.

[51] Ibid., p. 209.

[52] Ibid., p. 203.

[53] Ibid., p. 213.

[54] Ibid., p. 217. The problem is further complicated by the difficulty of translating 'Vergänglicheit', which literally means 'passing away'. Paul Fiddes, for example, 'Review of Webster, *Eberhard Jüngel*', *Journal of Theological Studies* 38 (1987), p. 276, criticizes Webster for always using the translation 'transience' rather than 'perishing' because it loses the concept of struggle with non-being. David Ford, 'Hosting a Dialogue', in Webster (ed.), *The Possibilities of Theology*, p. 37, concludes that 'perishing' is not very satisfactory, but also that 'transience' or 'transitoriness' are perhaps too weak.

[55] Jüngel, 'Vom Tod des Lebendigen Gottes' pp. 119-120.

[56] Jüngel, *God as the Mystery of the World*, p. 299.

[57] Jüngel, 'Vom Tod des Lebendigen Gottes', p. 119, quoted from Paul Fiddes' unpublished translation.

[58] Jüngel, *God as the Mystery of the World*, p. viii; cf. *Death*, p. 95: 'It would be no exaggeration to say that apart from the death of Jesus there would have been . . . no genuinely Christian understanding of the word 'God''. Paul Molnar, 'The Function of the Immanent Trinity in the Theology of Karl Barth', *Scottish Journal of Theology 42* (1989), p. 390, argues somewhat unconvincingly, that experience and the general theological context are more significant for Jüngel's understanding of God.

[59] Jüngel, 'Vom Tod des Lebendigen Gottes', p. 123.

[60] Jüngel, *God as the Mystery of the World*, p. 362.

[61] Ibid., p. 372.

[62] Ibid., p. 37; cf. Jüngel, *The Doctrine of the Trinity*, p. 72.

[63] Some modern writers, for example, McGrath, *The Making of Modern German Christology*, and Leo O'Donovan, 'The Mystery of God as a History of Love', *Theological Studies* 42 (1981), pp. 251-71, see Jüngel essentially as a theopaschite theologian. Webster, on the other hand, seeking to offer a broader picture of Jüngel as a theologian, plays down this particular aspect.

[64] Jüngel, *God as the Mystery of the World*, p. 367.

[65] Jüngel, *The Doctrine of the Trinity*, p. 83. See Barth, *Church Dogmatics*, IV/1, pp. 175f., 186f.

[66] Jüngel, *The Doctrine of the Trinity*, p. 86.

[67] Jüngel, *Death*, pp. 112-3. Moltmann, *God for a Secular Society*, p. 188, also links reconciliation and remembrance.

[68] Jüngel, *The Doctrine of the Trinity*, p. 84.

[69] Barth, *Church Dogmatics* IV/1 p. 187; Jüngel, *The Doctrine of the Trinity*, p. 85.

[70] Jüngel, 'Toward the Heart of the Matter', p. 232.

[71] Fiddes, *The Creative Suffering of God*, pp. 118-9; see Thompson, 'Jüngel on Barth', p. 149.

[72] Jüngel, 'The Truth of Life. Observations on Truth as the Interruption of the Continuity of Life' in R. W. A. McKinney (ed.), *Creation, Christ and Culture* (Edinburgh: T. & T. Clark, 1976), pp. 235-6, italics mine. This overall contrast is not diminished by Jüngel also stating that 'man is human precisely in that he allows himself to be interrupted', ibid. p. 235. This may contain an implicit call to human vulnerability in contrast to the Cartesian self-certainty.

[73] Jüngel, 'Wertlose Warheit', in S. Schelz (ed.) *Die Tyrannie der Werte*, (Hamburg: Lutherisches Verlaghaus, 1979), p. 67, quoted and translated by

Webster, *Eberhard Jüngel*, p. 66. Divine freedom is again closely linked to Jüngel's description of God as the unity of life and death for the sake of life.

74 See Jüngel, *The Doctrine of the Trinity*, p. 85, citing Barth, *Church Dogmatics*, IV/1, p. 254.

75 Jüngel, *God as the Mystery of the World*, p. 346.

76 Jüngel, *Death*, p. 96.

77 Jüngel, *God as the Mystery of the World*, p. 349.

78 Ibid., p. 51.

79 See ibid., p. 65, n. 27.

80 Ibid., pp. 54-5.

81 Ibid., p. 300.

82 So Webster, *Eberhard Jüngel*, p. 68, summarizes Jüngel's purpose.

83 Ibid.

84 Jüngel, *God as the Mystery of the World*, p. 349.

85 Webster, *Eberhard Jüngel*, pp. 67-8, uses absence and hiddenness as if they were interchangeable.

86 Jüngel, *Death*, pp. 106-7.

87 Jüngel, *The Freedom of a Christian. Luther's Significance for Contemporary Theology*, trans. R. A. Harrisville (Minneapolis: Ausburg, 1988), p. 32: 'For me, Luther's significance for contemporary theology consists not least in the fact that he did not oppose this premise . . . an understanding of the Bible which construed its texts as references to an absent God, but as events in which God as the *absent one* is *present*'.

88 Bonhoeffer, *Letters and Papers from Prison*, p. 311. For Jüngel's treatment see his *God as the Mystery of the World*, pp. 57-63.

89 Jüngel, *The Doctrine of the Trinity*, p. xiv.

90 Jüngel, 'Vom Tod des Lebendigen Gottes', p. 116.

91 Jüngel, *God as the Mystery of the World*, p. 368.

92 Jüngel, 'Das Verhältnis von 'ökonomischer' und 'immanenter' Trinität' p. 356.

93 Ibid..

94 Jüngel, *God as the Mystery of the World*, p. 365. It is significant that Jüngel's most detailed work on Jesus' cry in *God as the Mystery of the World* occurs in the section 'Jesus Christ as the Vestige of the Trinity'.

95 Ibid., p. 374.

96 See Fiddes, *The Creative Suffering of God*, p. 123.

97 Webster, *Eberhard Jüngel*, p. 34, n. 54 suggests that 'identification and identity are not always clearly distinguished'; McGrath, *The Making of Modern*

*German Christology*, p. 195 is unsure whether, in Jüngel, God is identical to Jesus or only identifies with him. Yet in the book's second edition, (Leicester: Apollos, 1994), p. 213, McGrath drops any mention of identity and speaks only of identification.

98 Jüngel, *God as the Mystery of the World*, pp. 190, 193, 209, 280, 297, 314, 329, 334, 363, 373, 379, 385, 388; *The Doctrine of the Trinity*, p. 87; *Death*, p. 108; see also Jüngel, 'Das Sein Jesu Christi als Ereignis der Versöhnung Gottes mit einer gottlosen Welt', *Evangelische Theologie* 38 (1978). p. 11 and Jüngel, 'Metaphorische Warheit' in P. Ricoeur & E. Jüngel, *Metapher* (*Evangelische Theologie, Sonderheft*, 1974), p. 45.

99 Jüngel, *God as the Mystery of the World*, pp. 329, 363 links identification, identity and the self-differentiation within God.

100 Ibid., pp. 385, 388.

101 See Jüngel, *The Doctrine of the Trinity*, p. 87; *Death*, p. 108.

102 Jüngel, *God as the Mystery of the World*, p. 193.

103 Ibid., p. 209.

104 Ibid., p. 346.

105 Barth, *Church Dogmatics* I/1, p. 311.

106 Jüngel, *The Doctrine of the Trinity*, p. 30.

107 Thus Webster, *Eberhard Jüngel*, p. 18, summarizes Jüngel's purpose in his *The Doctrine of the Trinity*.

108 Jüngel, *The Doctrine of the Trinity*, p. 92

109 Webster's summary, *Eberhard Jüngel*, p. 17, that the thrust of Barth's theology was to make God 'prose' *identical* with God 'pro nobis' seems somewhat odd, especially when also quoting directly Barth's statements on correspondence.

110 Jüngel, *The Doctrine of the Trinity*, p. 53.

111 See Jüngel's exposition of Barth in *The Doctrine of the Trinity*, p. 84.

112 Gunton, 'The Being and Attributes of God', p. 15.

113 Jüngel, *God as the Mystery of the World*, pp. 221, 364.

114 Ibid., p. 327.

115 Ibid., pp. 317, 328, 369, 374.

116 Ibid., p. 327.

117 Jüngel, 'The Truth of Life', p. 236.

118 Jüngel, *The Doctrine of the Trinity*, p. 53.

119 Jüngel, *God as the Mystery of the World*, p. 328.

120 Ibid., pp. 317-320.

121 Jüngel, 'The Truth of Life', p. 326.

122 Jüngel, *God as the Mystery of the World*, p. 327.

123 Barth, *Church Dogmatics* I/1, p. 40

124 Jüngel, 'Säkularisierung – Theologische Anmerkungen zum Begriff einer weltlichen Welt', in K. Herbert (ed.) *Christliche Freiheit im Dienst am Menschen* (Frankfurt: Otto Lembeck, 1972), p. 57, quoted in Webster, *Eberhard Jüngel*, p. 66.

125 See Fiddes, *Creative Suffering*, pp. 118-9.

126 Webster, *Eberhard Jüngel*, pp. 71-72 is favourable to Jüngel's formulation; Thompson, 'Jüngel on Barth', pp. 175-6, on the other hand, is concerned that self–lessness is greater than self-relatedness, and that it implies some kind of change in God. He does admit though that Jüngel only comes 'dangerously close' to making incarnation and cross necessary for God.

127 Jüngel, *The Doctrine of the Trinity*, p. 83.

128 Jüngel, *God as the Mystery of the World*, p. 220.

129 Jüngel, 'Vom Tod des Lebendigen Gottes' p. 106, quoted from Paul Fiddes' unpublished translation (italics mine).

130 Jüngel, *God as the Mystery of the World*, p. 200 (italics mine).

131 Jüngel, 'Vom Tod des Lebendigen Gottes', p. 119, quoted from Paul Fiddes' unpublished translation.

132 Jüngel, *God as the Mystery of the World*, p. 370 (italics mine).

133 Barth, *Church Dogmatics* II/1 p. 370.

134 Jüngel, 'Wertlose Warheit. ' p. 67, quoted and translated by Webster, *Eberhard Jüngel*, p. 66. Colin Gunton, in 'The Being and Attributes of God', pp. 19-20, concludes that for Jüngel the cross reveals what is true eternally of the immutable being of God, rather than being determinative of the being of God; however, he is probably reading Jüngel in too Barthian a way. John Thompson, in 'Jüngel on Barth', p. 175, finds that Jüngel proposes an increase and change in God, in a similar way to Hans Urs von Balthasar.

135 Jüngel, 'Vom Tod des Lebendigen Gottes', p. 120, quoted from Paul Fiddes' unpublished translation.

136 See above, p. 90-1.

137 For example, Colin Gunton, in 'The Being and Attributes of God', pp. 19-20, appears to assume that these are the only alternatives, and concludes that for Jüngel the cross reveals what is true eternally of the immutable being of God, rather than being determinative of the being of God; however, he is once again probably reading Jüngel in too Barthian a way. John Thompson, in 'Jüngel on Barth', p. 175, finds that Jüngel proposes an increase and change in God, in a similar way to Hans Urs von Balthasar.

138 Jüngel, *The Doctrine of the Trinity*, p. 86.

[139] Ibid., p. 3.

[140] Ibid.

[141] Gunton, 'The Being and Attributes of God', p. 19.

[142] Webster, *Eberhard Jüngel*, p. 65, refers to Oeing-Hanhoff's criticisms.

[143] Webster, 'Justification, Analogy and Action', in Webster (ed.) *The Possibilities of Theology*, p. 120; Geoffrey Wainwright's essay 'Church and Sacrament(s)', in the same collection, also argues that Jüngel plays down human action by a constant stress on divine action.

[144] Jüngel, *God as the Mystery of the World*, pp. 218-9.

[145] Jüngel, 'Vom Tod des Lebendigen Gottes', p. 120.

[146] Jüngel, *God as the Mystery of the World*, p. 218.

[147] Jüngel, 'Vom Tod des Lebendigen Gottes', p. 121.

[148] Fiddes, *The Creative Suffering of God*, pp. 205-214.

[149] Jüngel, *God as the Mystery of the World*, p. 374.

[150] Gunton, 'The Being and Attributes of God', p. 20, quotes one of a number of references to the 'eternally new' divine relationship, italicizing 'eternally'. However, Jüngel himself only places emphasis on 'new'. Gunton seems to be reading his own concerns into Jüngel here.

[151] Jüngel, 'The Truth of Life', p. 236.

[152] Jüngel, *God as the Mystery of the World*, p. 369. Thompson's very concern, 'Jüngel on Barth', p. 175, that such a statement suggests change in God, agrees with this interpretation.

[153] Jüngel, 'Toward the Heart of the Matter', p. 229.

[154] Jüngel, *Christ, Justice and Peace* (Edinburgh: T. & T. Clark, 1992), p. 71.

[155] Ibid., p. 53; see Webster, 'Justification, Analogy and Action', pp. 130-138 and Jüngel, 'Toward the Heart of the Matter', pp. 232-3, where Jüngel's conclusion seems to be that human action does not bring in the kingdom of God.

[156] George Newlands, 'The Love of God and the Future of Theology', in Webster (ed.), *The Possibilities of Theology*, p. 201.

[157] Ibid.

[158] Jüngel, *God as the Mystery of the World*, p. xi; cf. Jüngel's preemptive comment at the end of his *The Doctrine of the Trinity*, p. 106, n. 159: 'over against those who complain that this book has been scarcely intelligible . . . I regret my inability to formulate the problem to be treated even more subtly'.

[159] See, Jüngel, 'Toward the Heart of the Matter', pp. 144-57.

[160] Jüngel, *God as the Mystery of the World*, p. xi.

# 9
# Hans Urs von Balthasar: Renewing the Tradition

In Jesus' cry of forsakenness the hiddenness of God is revealed. This is at the centre of Hans Urs von Balthasar's interpretation of Barth's stress on the humanity of God, and is a theme that lies at the very heart of von Balthasar's life. Founding the secular institute of the Community of St John together with Adrienne von Speyr, von Balthasar maintained the traditional vows of poverty, chastity and obedience, although in such a way that they were no longer made manifest through a religious order. Rather, the consecrated life was hidden by the secular profession, in the same way that Johannine theology speaks of the hidden and dying seed which produces much fruit.[1] Such a move, which hastened his departure from the Jesuit Order, also reflects von Balthasar's central methodology, innovation within the tradition.

As may be expected of a Catholic theologian, the ecclesial tradition, especially of the Church Fathers, is of considerable importance. Of von Balthasar's many projects, the translating, interpreting and publishing of patristic texts form a significant part. Yet von Balthasar's aim is not simply to bequeath the tradition to others but to develop it and, on occasions, quite boldly to reinterpret it in a new context, as seen in his utilizing of Barth's neo-orthodoxy. Similarly the secular institute retains much from the established orders of the Church, but branches out from the tradition in new and creative ways.

## 1. Abandonment in the biblical witness

Of our four theologians von Balthasar appears to be the most dependent on the scriptural witness, judging by the extent of his biblical references. Yet he is not a specialist New Testament scholar and his approach is often tangential to the methods of modern biblical scholarship. Instead, as Aidan Nichols notes, von Balthasar prefers a contemplative reading of scripture, which alone can do justice to the glory of God therein

contained,[2] which von Balthasar himself characterizes as a 'kneeling not
a sitting theology'.[3] This results in both an absence of discussion concerning some scholarly questions and also a penchant for a more
allegorical style of interpretation, with Origen heralded as the great patristic interpreter.[4] It follows that generally von Balthasar favours John's
Gospel, with its motif of glory, and finds in the Johannine writings, with
their rich veins of symbolic possibilities, the summit of New Testament
expression.[5]

### *a. Historicity*

Given von Balthasar's interest in John, it is significant that in his discussion on the cross he actually begins with Mark's Gospel.

> Primacy must go to the cry of abandonment – in Mark the single word
> from the cross – and only relativized to the position of 'fourth word' by
> an arbitrary decision about ordering in a harmonization of the Gospel.[6]

Von Balthasar reaches this verdict because, of all the words from the
cross, the Marcan cry of forsakenness best expresses the inner meaning of
the passion events themselves. Jesus' cry is not out of place or unexpected, but the climax of all that the Gospel describes. The whole of
Jesus' life is orientated towards the cross, and the cross sums up a whole
life lived in self-abandonment.[7] Within this, Gethsemane stands out as a
turning point, where, forsaken by the sleeping disciples,[8] Jesus also experiences 'an isolation vis-à-vis the God who distances himself, but who has
not yet disappeared,'[9] and which will grow into the total abandonment of
the cross. Von Balthasar adds theological weight to this Biblical interpretation through the intimate connection between the incarnation and
passion. Rejecting the extremes of either an accidental passion added on
to a purposed incarnation, or a merely functional incarnation simply
enabling the passion, von Balthasar understands the whole of Jesus' life
and death as a unity, which comes to its focal point in his Godforsaken
cry.[10] In agreement with our earlier biblical research, Jesus' cry is the climax of the Gospel story. Jesus' life – and also, in line with his dependence

on scripture, of von Balthasar's own theology[11] – is orientated towards the cry of abandonment; it is '*the* great word on the cross'.[12]

On this foundation von Balthasar initiates a frustratingly brief discussion on the relationship between this cry and the rest of the biblical witness. Von Balthasar clearly accepts the historical authenticity of the cry, although the various and often complicated historical questions are condensed into one sweeping conclusion that 'the authenticity is shown by the misunderstanding of those who stand near'.[13] There is no consideration, for example, of the relationship between the cry of forsakenness and the later inarticulate cry, although they are often intertwined, especially in von Balthasar's interpretation of the silence of the cross.[14] The historicity of Jesus' cry does not, in fact, seem a crucial consideration for von Balthasar, since the events themselves convey this very meaning. The Gospels, after all, are not purely historical documents, but seek to convey the inner meaning of the passion.[15] Yet von Balthasar is quick to uphold the reality of Jesus' experience. It is neither to be considered as myth,[16] nor 'be rendered innocuous'[17] by an interpretation based on the happy ending of Psalm 22, for the 'word directs us to the unique point which is Jesus . . . and insists on being interpreted within its own limits'.[18] Von Balthasar does compare Jesus' cry with previous experiences in the Old Testament, notably the prophet's distress in Isaiah 21:3-4,[19] as well as later mystical experiences of the dark night of the soul,[20] but in such a way that the uniqueness of Jesus' cry stands out, providing a Christological interpretative framework for all other comparable encounters with God.

On the other hand, von Balthasar does take more time to consider the relationship between Jesus' cry and the other 'words of the cross'.[21] While von Balthasar is inconsistent in his historical assessments of the other Gospels, at times being favourably disposed to their historicity, yet at one point concluding that 'the other words from the cross must be for the greater part interpretations of the situation' by the church,[22] the Marcan narrative always takes centre stage. The passion accounts of Luke and even the favoured John are therefore interpreted in the light of Jesus' abandonment. The Johannine 'I thirst' is important for it 'expresses abandonment in another, no less impressive way: the source of living water, springing up to eternal life, of which all are invited to drink has audibly drained away and itself become thirsty ground'.[23] A deeper and compatible meaning is also drawn from the giving of Mary to John. In the same way that the Father withdraws from Jesus on the cross, so Jesus withdraws from his mother, giving her a sense of solidarity with him in his death.[24] Then in typical style and within a Johannine framework of thought, the tearing of the curtain and the tearing of Jesus' side are placed alongside to give mutual insight, von Balthasar seeing in both a parable of a further tearing of the heart of God.[25]

Similarly, von Balthasar's priority is to draw out the theological complementarity between Mark and Luke, despite significant variant details, notably the replacing of Psalm 22:1 with Psalm 31:6. Von Balthasar finds in the Lucan *paratithemai* (place/ entrust) an emphasizing of the meaning of the Marcan *exepneusen* (breathe out/ die), which in turn finds a greater stress still in the Johannine *paredōken* (hand over), rather than a contradiction of Jesus' forsaken cry. Theologically, at least, Mark and Luke offer a fuller picture of the abandonment of the cross for 'at the decisive moment Luke replaces the ultimate *paradosis* by the Father, namely, the Son's cry of abandonment on the cross, with the ultimate *paradosis* by the Son, who gives over his spirit into the hands of the Father'.[26] Although von Balthasar treats some complicated textual issues quite simply and his historical assessment of the other words of the cross is inconsistent, it is clear that, for him, Jesus' cry of forsakenness is historical, foundational and to be interpreted in its own right. It also becomes the somewhat allegorical interpretative key for the other Gospels.

### b. Handing over

The climactic cry is thus intimately connected to the rest of the passion, and one important link is provided by the repeated use of the verb *paradidōmi*, which on one occasion von Balthasar actually translates as 'abandons'.[27] He also quotes Popkes' conclusion that 'he who is thus handed over is, in the truest sense of the word, abandoned by God', stressing the essential dimension of judgement and wrath.[28] In fact, von Balthasar draws heavily on Wiard Popkes' lengthy discussion of the biblical usage of the word, in both its Old Testament background and its later New Testament development, in a discussion which is essentially repeated in both *Mysterium Paschale* and *The Glory of the Lord*.[29] In the Gospels Jesus is always the passive subject of handing over, supremely by God but also by Judas, which follows on from the Old Testament pattern of human executors of the divine will who are nevertheless responsible for their own actions. This passivity is balanced in other parts of the New Testament by the active gift that Jesus makes of himself. Von Balthasar admits that the whole handing over of Jesus remains a mystery, and that 'the concurrently operative elements cannot be strait-jacketed into any comprehensible system,'[30] but suggests that the only possible basis for comprehension must be Trinitarian. The Father hands over the Son out of love and the Son gives himself for us, displaying the Father's unconditional love.[31]

Within this Trinitarian understanding von Balthasar repeatedly stresses the dominant theme of the active handing over of the Son by the Father – the human handing over can only play a subordinate role[32] – which has 'the ineluctable character of an act of judgement' even if ultimately out of love. Thus, both in *Mysterium Paschale* and *The Glory of the Lord*,[33] von Balthasar reproduces the same extended quotation from Popkes, which has become notorious in some quarters through its use by Moltmann. Von Balthasar wrote before Moltmann's *The Crucified God*, through which the whole issue was brought to a wider audience, but similarly quotes Popkes positively in the flow of his argument.[34] Von Balthasar seeks a reciprocal understanding of the cross such that the handing over by the Father is balanced by the handing over by the Son, but there are times when the action of the Father, expressed as judgement, predominates. In this sense von Balthasar is liable to the same criticism of a sadistic Father which Sölle heaped on Moltmann.

In outline, von Balthasar's understanding of Jesus' cry has many similarities to the exegesis I presented in earlier chapters: Jesus' cry as the climax of the Gospel, and the need for Jesus' cry to be interpreted in its own right and not on the basis of Psalm 22. What is disappointing in von Balthasar's writing is the lack of further exegesis of the text. Although von Balthasar quotes scripture frequently, here, at least, he has not grappled with the difficulties that are an intrinsic part of this text. Furthermore, his interpretation of the text opens himself to problems later. His tendency to harmonize the Gospel accounts may be reflected in the tension we will find in von Balthasar's desire both to uphold the impassibility of God, but still place negativity within the divine life. And his dependence on a theology of surrender in which the Father acts on the Son is never fully resolved or satisfactorily explained as being compatible with the divine Trinitarian love.[35]

## 2. Abandonment as silence

*a. The silence of the Son*

One of von Balthasar's unique and most original contributions to our understanding of the cry of forsakenness is his exploration of the silence of Jesus. 'In the "great cry" in the "darkness" he sinks into the realm of the dead from out of which no word of his any longer makes itself heard'.[36] Jesus' cry - '*the* great word from the cross' - is the culmination of a predominant and 'ever-deepening silence'.[37] This begins at conception – the nine months in the womb being a time of silence for the 'Word made flesh' – and continues into his life. At his trial, Jesus' silence may have brought astonishment and scorn, but fulfilled Isaiah's picture of the lamb which does not open its mouth, and this leads on towards the abandonment, the inarticulate cry and the silence between Friday and Sunday.  •
'The paradoxical eloquence of the silent Word', so clearly expressed in the Marcan account of the cross and the silence of the grave, 'particularly haunts von Balthasar's imagination'.[38]

Still further reflection on this central aspect of Jesus' death develops into a motif of silence which is used to interpret the whole of Jesus' life. 'The act of the Word's becoming man means an act of becoming silent,'[39] leading to 'a word as not-word, a word that abandons itself and dissolves itself'.[40] The theme of silence, then, is used as an expression of the very essence of Jesus' existence. The Gospels, of course, record much that Jesus said, and, in the case of Luke and John, even on the cross, but the very act of the Word becoming flesh[41] means a silencing of the Word. More than just a notable feature of Jesus' life, silence expresses what may more commonly be described as the hiddenness of the Word in the person of Jesus.[42]

Von Balthasar identifies this as what is decisively and uniquely Christian. God's voice through the old covenant 'had become continuously louder,'[43] but, although in many ways Jesus is presented in terms of Old Testament expectations, von Balthasar insists that there can be no simple promise and fulfilment pattern, because Jesus' death and resurrection break this apart, transcending all the Old Testament allusions.[44] Instead of the words of promise we find the death of Christ which 'is no longer a word; it is silence, the silence and death of God as the fulfilment of the speaking, promising, living God'.[45] The key New Testament passage is the kenotic hymn in Philippians 2:6-11. Von Balthasar's exposition centres on the contrast that is made, not between the divine and the human, but between the divine form and the form of a slave, which von Balthasar insists must actually be a formlessness. The Word enters into a formless and therefore wordless existence in the flesh, evidenced by the self-abandonment of Jesus. The silence of the Word in the life and, supremely, death of Jesus is a veiling of the Son's divine form in the incarnation, such that the Son's divinity is hidden in his humanity. There is glory in this hiddenness, but a glory, as expressed in the Fourth Gospel, which embraces death. From this we can understand von Balthasar's concern for a Christologically orientated aesthetics. In death Jesus Christ is formless, in contrast to the forms and images of the Old Testament, but Christian faith has proclaimed that this formless one actually bestows form on all living things.[46]

## b. The silence of the Father

In the main, von Balthasar uses this theme of silence to explain the life of Jesus, the Word made flesh, but there are occasions when von Balthasar also points to the silence of the Father, although he has not explored and developed this in a systematic way. In Gethsemane Jesus experiences isolation. He calls on the Father with 'pleading tenderness . . . yet no communication with the Father follows,'[47] except the angel in Luke's account. As the action moves to the cross, Jesus dies not a natural death, but the particular death of one abandoned by the Father. This was no mere feeling, as if the reality were in fact quite different, but a real and all-consuming forsakenness. Here von Balthasar certainly breaks from the

inherited Catholic tradition, which insisted on the continual beatific vision
of Jesus. The cross 'must not be rendered innocuous as though the
Crucified, in undisturbed union with God, had prayed the Psalms and died
in the peace of God'.[48] It must be admitted that von Balthasar is not
always entirely consistent here, such as endorsing Vincent Taylor's conclusion that on the cross there is the most amazing distance between fact
and feeling,[49] but overall, for von Balthasar the cry of abandonment is a
moment of separation and silence.[50] It is slightly surprising that von
Balthasar himself has not made more of this feature of the silence of the
cross, especially given his strong interpretation of abandonment. In fact,
the motif of the silence of the Father towards the Son, as well as that of
the Son towards the world, could very helpfully be drawn on to illustrate
the inner-Trinitarian relationships at the heart of abandonment.

### c. Revelation in silence

Yet neither the silent Word nor the silent Father, expressed in the abandonment of Jesus, are entirely mute. Where the Word falls silent, and here
von Balthasar specifically refers to Mark 15:34 and the connected inarticulate cry, 'the true message is proclaimed loudly: the message of the heart
of God, broken open'.[51] Therefore 'we have to understand precisely his
[the Logos] non-speaking as his final revelation'.[52] Here the imagery of
forsakenness and silence cohere, for the silence of forsakenness opens up
a space for the Father's own self-expression. In the wordlessness of death
this event of God, this breaking open of the last realities of God's heart,
pictured in John's description of the piercing of Jesus' side and the flow-
ing of blood and water, is made visible. Thus 'in death, that which
remains unutterable in life becomes speech'.[53] The Word, reduced to
silence receives the greatest transparency to the Father,[54] the Father
'expresses himself in him in a way without precedent'[55] and so in the
silent abandonment of Jesus God attains the most authentic revelation and
glorification.[56] In the words of Luther, God discloses Godself *sub con-
trario*, in the very act of self-concealment.[57] Out of the silence emerges a
new word, and a new form of beauty, beginning with the resurrection.
Jesus is the 'form' of God, revealed in the formlessness of the cross.

Von Balthasar develops the twin themes of hiddenness and revelation further, for the Word of God has become 'wordless and ever more word-less'[58] in the re-verbalization by Gospel, kerygma and theology. This condensed sentence suggests that in both the very words of the New Testament and later theology there remains an essential silence, that is the Word is hidden because it is expressed only through human words, but that the very human words which convey the divine wordlessness, also become a new word of revelation. In giving space for human expression, albeit inspired by the Spirit, God is both hidden and revealed in and through human words. Jesus' cry, therefore, has a continuing significance, for the silence of forsakenness allows space for human speech and in this the Word of God is revealed.

This 'wordless re-verbalization' offers some interesting parallels with Barth's exposition of divine revelation, in the way that he relates the twofold nature of God as *Deus Revelatus* and *Deus Absconditus* ('God revealed and concealed') to the threefold nature of the Word – living as Christ, written in the New Testament and preached.[59] Drawing on von Balthasar's thought, we might speak, as he does not explicitly, of a three-fold 'silent vulnerability' of God, allowing God's divinity to be expressed by Jesus, by the Bible and by the ministry of Word and Sacrament. What is clear from von Balthasar's own work is the overriding ecclesiastical nature of his thought, for this new word is centred upon the New Testament, the dogmatic theology of the Church and the Eucharist.[60] It is supremely the church in which the Word is both hidden and revealed.

### 3. Abandonment as an experience of hell

The cry of abandonment and its accompanying wordless shout bring to a climax the Gospel theme of silence. Yet, with Jesus' forsaken cry as its basis, von Balthasar explores how this silence continues and how both abandonment and silence are deepened between Jesus' death and resur-rection. For the 'descent into hell' is a 'journey in pure wordlessness, for after all the incarnate Word of God is dead'.[61] The Gospels, von Balthasar admits, are themselves silent on the issue – the only reverent possibility[62] – but this silence gives von Balthasar space to explore his theology of Holy Saturday,[63] the second distinctively unique feature of von

Balthasar's theology, and one greatly dependent upon the mystical experiences of Adrienne von Speyr.[64]

### a. Passivity

In distinction from the Reformers, who condensed all Jesus' experience of hell onto the cross,[65] von Balthasar attempts to distinguish carefully between the events of Friday and Saturday in Holy Week, between the active nature of the cross and the passive experience of being dead and buried, while retaining one overall experience of abandonment.[66] Von Balthasar does not suggest a second distinct experience on Saturday, as if somehow Jesus' death was not sufficient,[67] but explores how the abandonment in Jesus' cry continues when hell gapes open.[68] Such an approach seems to take seriously the temporal aspect of the cross and resurrection, for if the abandonment of the cross is resolved in the resurrection, we must reflect on what may have happened between the abandonment of the dying Jesus and the resurrection of the dead Jesus. It also takes with complete seriousness the full reality of Jesus' experience of abandonment on the cross. The hiatus, the break in events, represented by the cross is the gap between God and the sinner, and Jesus does not leap it as if it were insignificant, but goes through the utter reality of death to the other side. If Jesus' work is said to be a triumph, then it is realized only through the cry of Godforsakenness in the darkness.[69]

Such reflection leads von Balthasar to offer a distinctly new interpretation of the traditional 'descended into hell' of the creed and of the passage in 1 Peter 3:18-20, 4:6 upon which it is based. Rejecting as mythological any active understanding of Jesus' descent to hell, as if he underwent a struggle to release hell's captives like some classical demigod,[70] von Balthasar explains this 'descent' as something entirely passive. He prefers the title 'Going to the Dead', because, although it is still in the active voice it is less active than the traditional Descent.[71] Jesus' preaching to the dead (1 Peter 4:6) is a passive solidarity, in which the eloquent silence requires no words, but is an efficacious outworking of what was accomplished in the temporality of history.[72] By offering such a reinterpretation of the traditional doctrine von Balthasar has salvation in mind, concerned that Jesus be in total solidarity with the sinner and bear the total penalty of sin, and also seeking to interpret a doctrine which some have completely rejected in such a way that it can be understood and affirmed in the modern world.[73] Jesus' passive solidarity with the dead on Holy Saturday is therefore both theologically necessary and culturally relevant.

Yet, as we have already noted in other instances, an aspect of von Balthasar's unsystematic style is a tendency for a dominant idea to be seemingly contradicted in other places. Von Balthasar himself condenses Jesus' experiences of dying and being dead together when he speaks of the *cross* of Christ as being at the very last extremity of hell.[74] On the other hand, he does, on occasion, distinguish rather too sharply between the experiences of cross and grave. On the cross the Father is 'merely . . . veiled and lost to view', whereas in hell, the Son is 'forced to enter into that which is opposite to the Father, into the pure essence of sin . . . into that which is condemned by God, in which God cannot be found'.[75] This clearly does undermine the depth and sufficiency of the cross, undercut what von Balthasar has said elsewhere, and open him to criticism.[76] Although this passage is found in one of his later publications, von Balthasar gives no other suggestion that he is making a major change in his thinking, and the main thrust of his theology still seems to be only an active-passive distinction within a unified experience of abandonment.

*b. Separation*

Although the whole theology of Holy Saturday has resulted in much discussion, the key question from our perspective is the state of the relationship between the Father and Son, which the Son's solidarity with the dead presupposes. This in turn revolves around the kind of passive experience which going to the dead entailed. Von Balthasar begins by describing Jesus' 'descent' into Sheol as something which all experience, both the just and the wicked, thus ensuring that Jesus is in solidarity with all.[77] The Old Testament theology of Sheol was a loss of relationship with the living God, which Jesus also endured in solidarity with sinners. Yet, because of the unique relationship between Father and Son, Godforsakenness took the Son 'far beyond Sheol and Gehenna';[78] to be inclusive of all, Jesus' death needed to be exclusive and unique in its expiatory value.[79] The righteous, who had died before Christ, had died in hope, awaiting redemption, and therefore this light of hope shone even in Sheol. The uniqueness of Christ's death was that he alone experienced the full 'pains of the damned' (*poena damni*), which until that point had only been provisional.[80] It is Christ who 'sets the limits of the extension of damnation',[81] for only he was 'able to measure the depths of that abyss'.[82] Von Balthasar describes this experience of Sheol, which 'no redemptive light had brightened',[83] as a vision of the second death,[84] an experience of 'sin as such', abstracted from the human being and contemplated in its bare reality.[85] In distinct contrast to Augustine, Jesus did not view a heavily populated hell, or even a heavily populated purgatory, but the pure substantiality of hell, that is in sin itself.[86]

Once again there is a frustrating lack of clarity in von Balthasar's description of the experience of Holy Saturday. First, he conveys the results of Jesus' going to the dead with a wide range of expressions, mainly drawn from traditional and Biblical language, such as 'second death, '*poena damni*', 'sin as such'. These evocative expressions are clearly metaphorical, and in employing them von Balthasar can be bold in his descriptions. What is never clarified is the nature of the metaphysical reality to which such metaphorical expressions point. In what sense can we understand Jesus' pure vision of sin, abstracted from human lives?

Second, von Balthasar struggles with his quantifying of the extent of Jesus' solidarity with humankind in relation to Jesus' experience of 'hell'. On the one hand, von Balthasar seems uncertain whether Jesus' experience on Holy Saturday should be described as 'hell' at all. If hell is Christologically orientated and a function of the Christ event, then can Jesus' own experience be described in this way? 'It makes no sense to call this suffering 'hell,' for in Jesus there is no kind of hatred of God'.[87] Thus von Balthasar himself rejects Luther's identification of Jesus with the 'No' of sin.[88] At this point, von Balthasar has just insisted that the human 'No' to God is only spoken *within* the 'Yes' of the Son, and although real is 'merely a twisted knot within the Son's pouring forth',[89] thereby perhaps reducing the depth of the human 'No' itself. Yet, on the other hand, von Balthasar does describe Holy Saturday as an experience of hell, such that Jesus endures 'the suffering of the damned who cannot be damned any further, that is to say . . . as far as the punishment of hell,'[90] embracing that which is utterly opposed to God. In a footnote in his second volume of the *Theologik*, one of his last major works, von Balthasar actually 'confesses' to a compromise in *Mysterium Paschale* by referring only to Jesus' 'solidarity with the dead', instead of adopting the more daring doctrine of von Speyr, that Jesus also 'had to be tasting the condemnation and fate of the eternally damned in his descent into hell'.[91]

What *is* clear is that the real separation between Father and Son, which was initially portrayed by the silence of the Word and the silence of the Father, is further emphasized by a theology of Holy Saturday. In the grave the abandonment, and silence, of the cross is continued and deepened so that it becomes definitively timeless.[92] This is not to eternalize Jesus' experience of hell – von Balthasar attempts to distinguish between different kinds of timelessness of heaven, hell and Jesus' Godforsakenness[93] – but to stress the reality of Jesus' abandonment, for in the darkness of Saturday the light of Sunday was not even experienced as a possibility. There was no certainty of resurrection, but only the indefinite solidarity with the dead in Godforsakenness.

*c. Salvation*

Von Balthasar's exposition of Jesus' descent into Hell has important implications for salvation. First, von Balthasar places great stress on the dramatic nature of the cross. Rejecting the idea of salvation through revelation that he finds exemplified in Rahner,[94] von Balthasar explains the action between God and humankind as being such that an objective change in their relationship occurs. By bearing sin on the cross, the sin is separated from the sinner who can then stand in a new relationship with God. There is a real change of place between sinless Son and sinful humanity.[95] The dramatic nature of the event involves the Father and Son resolving divine anger against sin and removing divine wrath towards humanity within their relationship, to the point of the abandonment of the Son. Although von Balthasar also decisively rejects the extreme of penal substitution advocated by some of the Reformers,[96] the particular dramatic account he gives does mean that 'a certain negativity is inserted into the inner-Trinitarian relationships'.[97] The abandonment of Jesus thus has implications for the Trinitarian life of God.

Second, in considering the effectiveness of this substitution, von Balthasar raises the possibility of a universal salvation. If ruin and death are taken up into the covenant through the incarnation and passion of the Son, eternal life takes on Godforsakenness and death, so that now death and Godforsakenness become places of encounter with God.[98] While attempting to uphold the necessary tension between divine and human freedom, von Balthasar hopes for a future reconciliation of all, on the grounds that those who forsake God find themselves confronted by the One forsaken by God, so bringing renewed hope in the darkest place.[99] The Son's experience of hell on Holy Saturday provides the hope that all others will be spared such an abandonment. The combination of the Godforsakenness entailed in the Son's going to the dead with the potential damnation of some of creation raises in von Balthasar's mind serious questions about the nature of God, who would then both endure the separation of the Son and also face the potential tragedy of the loss of what has been created. Rejecting outright any notion that salvation and damnation bring equal glory to God, can the loss of both the Son and a part of creation leave God unmoved?[100] Ultimately, to avoid this tragedy for God, von Balthasar must accept a universalist position. We must further reflect on von Balthasar's conception of the relationship between the abandonment of Jesus and the inner life of God.

## 4. Abandonment at the heart of God

*a. Revelation*

Von Balthasar has always taken Jesus' cry of forsakenness with great seriousness and seeks to interpret it within the wider context of the cross. But this must not lead to an interpretation based simply on Jesus' human nature, for 'after all, is it not a revelation of the 'heart' of God?'[101] Considering the descent into hell as the final point of kenosis (or self-emptying), and this kenosis as the expression of inner-Trinitarian life, Aidan Nichols concludes that for von Balthasar 'the Christ of Holy Saturday is the consummate icon of what God is like'.[102] In similar fashion to Moltmann and Jüngel, and echoing Mark's careful juxtaposition of Jesus' cry and the centurion's declaration of divinity, Jesus' abandonment is the greatest revelation of God. 'The Son's cry of dereliction on the cross . . . is the loftiest assertion in the knowledge of God, because as night it is truth's ultimate confirmation'.[103] It is Jesus, and supremely in his passion, who is the one truly human being who contains the totality of God's revelation. This may well require a change in our own concept of God, such that Jesus' abandonment and death are not excluded from our understanding of God's eternal nature. Karl Barth is particularly influential here, and is quoted at length on a number of occasions. Von Balthasar gives Barth the final words on the theological understanding of God's kenosis, for 'by acting as he did He proves to us precisely that he is capable of this, that to do such a thing lies absolutely within His nature'.[104] The abandonment of Jesus is thus the revelation of the inner life of God.

The God who can be revealed in the abandonment of Jesus must first and foremost be Trinitarian. 'For it is precisely in the kenosis of Christ (and nowhere else) that the inner majesty of God's love appears, of God who is 'love' and therefore a Trinity'.[105] The whole of the Christ event can only be properly understood from a Trinitarian perspective, the delivering up of Jesus can only be maintained in a Trinitarian fashion,[106] and the abandonment and separation on the cross have as their presupposition the eternal relationships between Father, Son and Spirit.[107] This drama of salvation thus reveals both a dramatic and glorious God, not static and lifeless, but embracing an ultimate diversity and liveliness within the unity of the divine life, and it is the sheer splendour of the divine love which is revealed in the events of the cross. 'Indeed God proves to be so living, so mobile, that he can reveal his life precisely in death, his Trinitarian communality even in abandonment'.[108] Von Balthasar draws on the traditional personal language of 'processions', 'relations' and 'missions' in God to capture this renewed dynamic expression.

The Father's nature is to hold on to nothing for himself, but to give everything to his Son. The Son, who is of the same essence as the Father, responds by holding on to nothing for himself, but offers everything back to the Father, in the Holy Spirit, for self-giving is the ultimate characterization of the inner divine life. Although von Balthasar explicitly rejects the division into two separate gods, evident in early Christian heresies,[109] there are occasions when von Balthasar so stresses the distinctions between the portrayal of God in Old and New Testaments that he can speak of two *images* of God.[110] The fundamental nature of God in the Old Testament was to 'hold on' to his glory, whereas the self-emptying of Jesus reveals self-abandonment to be the essence of divinity, something 'inconceivable in the Old Testament',[111] which in turn demands the replacing of one ideal by another. Von Balthasar is aware that the death of Jesus is not obviously the revelation of God. In fact, Jesus' cry might be an 'impenetrable veil which shows a cruel God' who abandons the Son.[112] It must be that in this ultimate concealment God is most revealed in love for the world. In Barth's words, 'the abasement of God is his supreme honour, since it confirms and demonstrates nothing other than his divine being'.[113]

### b. Correspondence

Not only does the cross reveal God as God is, but it also closely corresponds to God – the event of Jesus [is] the definite, superabundant consequence of the event of God himself[114] – although in such a way that the inner life of God always has priority. The doctrine of the Trinity can be unfolded on the basis of the cross, because the Trinity is the ever-present presupposition of the cross.[115] We have already seen how Jesus' 'descent into hell' builds upon the kenosis of the incarnation and how this in turn reveals self-abandonment at the heart of God. 'The exteriorization of God (in the incarnation) has its ontic possibility in the eternal exteriorization of God – that is his tripersonal self-gift,'[116] for 'the ultimate presupposition of the kenosis is the "selflessness" of the Persons in the inner-Trinitarian life of love'.[117]

Von Balthasar does write of God's history with the world, but always insists that this corresponds to God's prior eternal history within the Trinity, for the inner Trinitarian 'event' is the basis for the economy of the incarnation. God is self-sufficient in God's inner-Trinitarian life,[118] and so in opposition to Karl Rahner von Balthasar argues for a meaningful distinction between the Immanent Trinity (God in God's self) and the Economic Trinity (God at work in the world);[119] God freely chooses to create and relate to the world. Thus von Balthasar criticizes Moltmann, and the whole Hegelian method, for there, he believes, God is merged into the world process rather than being involved from a position of transcendence.[120] Von Balthasar insists that there must be a basis *in the Trinity itself* for the analogical application to God of such mysterious attributes as pain and suffering.[121]

On this basis of correspondence, von Balthasar then argues that abandonment is not something alien to God, but rather profoundly appropriate to the divine life,[122] for the abandonment of Jesus on the cross must also correspond to the inner divine life. There is no necessity by which God has to lose God's self to be able to attain God's self, in the Hegelian sense;[123] rather everything comes from the divine freedom which chooses the Incarnation as a glorious expression of the vitality of God's inner life.[124] God's essence does not *become* universally kenotic, but the divine power is so ordered as to make room for the incarnation and cross.[125] In order to maintain this correspondence between God's inner life and the events of the passion, von Balthasar speaks of an 'infinite distance' within the Trinity, kept open and bridged by the Holy Spirit, which allows for the possibility of abandonment as a divine event of God's self-revelation.

> This 'infinite distance' which recapitulates[126] the sinner's mode of alienation from God, will remain forever the highest revelation known to the world of the diastasis (within the eternal being of God) between the Father and Son in the Holy Spirit.[127]

The separation between Father and Son involved in Jesus' abandonment corresponds to and derives from this infinite distance between Father and Son – Godforsakenness is a mode of the Son's bond with the Father[128] – a distance that is only fully revealed in forsakenness of Jesus on the cross. 'If Jesus can be forsaken by the Father, the conditions of this 'forsaking' must lie within the Trinity, in the absolute distance/distinction between the Hypostasis who surrendered the Godhead and the Hypostasis who received it'.[129] This distance within the Godhead includes and grounds all other distances and separations in the finite world, including the distance of sin.[130] This 'infinite distance' relates the issue of Jesus' abandonment to the whole relationship of the economic to the immanent and of the temporal to the eternal. Although von Balthasar comments on this in many places,[131] there are certainly occasions when the eternal is so dominant that the temporal seems only a pale reflection.[132] The alienation

God experiences in creation is only part of a journey already and always accomplished in the Trinity, so in the incarnation the Son 'traverses the realms of forsakenness that as God, he has already (and always) traversed'.[133] The positive advantage of this for von Balthasar is that it allows Jesus' cry on the cross to be a divine experience but in such a way that God is not changed, because the very abandonment of Jesus has its roots in the being of God. All negative things can be traced back to the positive in God.[134]

If the cross thus corresponds to God, it leads von Balthasar to suggest what appear to be highly unusual, though positive, divine attributes. There is in God a positive 'Godlessness' arising out of the distance of self-giving, and this is the basis for the corresponding negative 'Godlessness' due to sin. Equally, von Balthasar speaks of a 'living death' which is the basis for our experience of death as an end, and the darkness of God which is an aspect of divine light.[135] This does not mean, of course, that there is sin and evil within God; but negatives which in our existence arise from evil correspond to, and derive from, the positive infinite distance in God.[136]

### c. Change

In his exploration of the correspondence between the cross and the Trinity the question of divine immutability, the unchangeability of God, is von Balthasar's constant concern.[137] He is seeking a third way, a middle path between the two extremes of a 'mythological divine suffering' which he finds expounded by Moltmann and process theology, and a traditional theology which located the kenosis entirely within the human nature of Jesus, leaving the divine without any real relationship with the world.[138] Although von Balthasar is clear about the types of theology he rejects, he is not entirely fair to Moltmann, for his theology is more nuanced than simply being an example of Hegelianism or process thought as von Balthasar sometimes suggests.[139] Von Balthasar himself has admitted that, with some clarification, his position on the forsakenness of the world being taken up into God comes close to Moltmann.

Von Balthasar expresses his own aim most clearly in the short preface to the second edition of *Mysterium Paschale*, in 1981.[140] In this book he sets out to rethink the doctrine of divine immutability, which in some writers had often resulted in a very static view of God,[141] while also rejecting the mythological idea of mutability, which is in danger of reducing God to the process of the world. Neither, ultimately, is sufficient a description for the God who is always ever-greater than our human description, or does justice to the dramatic nature of 'threeness' or the essential changelessness of 'oneness'.[142] Von Balthasar does not want to reject the idea of immutability completely, or reduce it to the conception of covenant fidelity, but he does want to see it renewed so that an immutability of being can also hold within it the idea of the vitality and liveliness of God. It is to this end that von Balthasar insists that incarnation and passion are not strange for God, but represent in time the eternal self-giving of God.

> God, then has no need to 'change' when he makes a reality of the wonders of his charity, wonders which include the Incarnation and more particularly, the Passion of Christ . . . All the contingent 'abasements' of God in the economy of salvation are forever included and outstripped in the eternal event of Love.[143]

But equally, in a way somewhat reminiscent of Jüngel, von Balthasar recognizes that the incarnation and passion represent a real encounter of God with the world, in which God assumes what is radically contrary to the divine.[144] If one takes seriously the historical kenosis which leads to the incarnation and passion one allows an event *into* a God who is beyond change.[145] There remains then this tension in von Balthasar's thought between the cross as something entirely appropriate for God and not strange – the incarnation does not change the relationship between Father and Son[146] – yet also in some way being a kind of 'new' experience. This tension leads to what appear to be contradictory statements about the relationship of change and suffering to God, a situation further complicated by the nature of the language which von Balthasar uses. Von Balthasar tackles metaphysical topics with language that is consistently poetic and metaphorical,[147] written in a musical style that strongly resists systematization.[148] Metaphor is an important and necessary feature of theological discourse and certainly recognizes the limits of human language to express the divine mystery, but also demands a careful assessment of exactly how von Balthasar understands God to relate to the world.

Von Balthasar consistently rejects any understanding of God's mutability which concludes that God is changed by an external cause and which can be measured in temporal or spatial categories. Immutability cannot be simply limited to having an unchanging covenant faithfulness, but looks through this to a quality of divinity as such.[149] Working back from the cross, any experience of suffering that arises from within the world is excluded from God.[150] But von Balthasar wants to move beyond a static immutability, and to see change as a perfection of immutability which allows liveliness and variety within God; this leads to bold assertions, that although suffering that comes from within the world is excluded from God, something happens in God to justify suffering and God's sharing in it.[151] There are occasions when von Balthasar is cautious, venturing that there is *something* in God that can develop into suffering;[152] there are occasions when he is clearly employing poetic imagery, such as that in the death of Jesus we see 'the heart of God pierced open';[153] but there are also moments when von Balthasar clearly portrays a mutuality between God and the world such that God is both affected and enriched by the incarnation to the point that bearing unbearable sin causes God to suffer.[154] In general terms von Balthasar looks for an interplay between God and the world in which God is affected, but remains changeless in his immutability. Therefore von Balthasar rejects the fashionable talk of the pain of God, as slipping into a mythological mutability, but he still searches for something in God that can develop into suffering.[155]

Von Balthasar's suggestion that God is somehow affected without being changed is based again on the relationship between the immanent (God in God's own self) and the economic (God as active in the world) that we encountered in connection with the 'infinite distance' within God. The immanent Trinity is marked by complete self-giving and receptivity and von Balthasar 'stammers'[156] to develop an insight from Jean Galot, that the reciprocal surrender within the Trinity, although not painful itself, is the foundation for God's relationship with the world with all its pain.[157] Thus it is an aspect of the positive liveliness of God which is the basis for something like divine suffering. Von Balthasar adopts a very similar approach to the proposed enrichment of the being of God by creation. The world is not something totally separate from God, but rather is created within the Trinity. The Father does not look outwards to create, but looks inward to the Son.[158] The participation of the world within the Trinity thus becomes an eternal gift from the Persons within the Trinity to each other.[159] God is enriched by creation, so creation is not superfluous, but since this enrichment is the gift between Father, Son and Spirit it is not something external which changes God.

But what does von Balthasar actually mean when he speaks so persuasively of God both being affected and enriched by creation and able to experience something like divine suffering? Does Jesus' abandonment on the cross change God? Von Balthasar offers a clear 'No'.[160] Von Balthasar is willing to use radical metaphorical language. The abandonment of Jesus adds to and enriches the divine life, for it is one aspect in which 'the world acquires an inward share in the divine exchange of life'.[161] The incarnation brings a new current into the divine life which draws in our human love and in the resurrection, a 'new joy arises after the renunciation involved in separation'.[162] But such metaphorical language does not imply any metaphysical change in God. Does Jesus' abandonment on the cross cause God to suffer? Von Balthasar is less clear on this issue, but finally the answer also has to be 'No'. The 'something like suffering' in God, which von Balthasar proposes, may be the basis for human pain, but anything with a real analogy to what we experience as suffering is ultimately excluded from God.

### 5. Real forsakenness and vulnerability?

Following through the concept of Godforsakenness which he derives from Jesus' cry, von Balthasar arrives at a concept of God marked by the tension of upholding something of the traditional concept of immutability while seeking to relate God to a suffering world in a new way. Gerard O'Hanlon, in his comprehensive study of von Balthasar's doctrine of immutability concludes that von Balthasar says both yes *and* no to change and suffering in God, and insists that he has a nuanced and 'razor-edged'[163] approach to the subject. O'Hanlon himself appreciates von Balthasar's subtle new approach to divine immutability, and while suggesting it must still be viewed as a hypothesis, it is clearly one O'Hanlon is seeking to develop. Yet, despite O'Hanlon's positive assessment, in the face of real questions, there do seem to be persistent difficulties in von Balthasar's whole approach, which will in turn have consequences for the pastoral application of von Balthasar's thinking.

First, it is unclear how the entirely positive 'infinite distance' within the Trinitarian self-giving of God can completely explain the suffering of sin, and more particularly the abandonment of Jesus. Either it downplays the negative, so that abandonment is not really a problem, or it eternalizes the negative in the divine life. This is the nub of the problem. Von Balthasar wants to portray the divine life as able to embrace negativity without being constituted by it in some Hegelian way; rather he envisages that, within the eternal liveliness of God, negativity does not cause God to suffer or change. The human 'No' is first rendered possible and then swallowed up by the 'Yes' of the Son. But it does not seem possible to hold both together, even in a subtle razor-edged approach. If negativity is part of the divine life, then an immutable God can embrace it. But if negativity is the result of sin, then even an 'infinite' distance within God is so different in nature from what is utterly opposed to God that embracing such negativity must lead to suffering and change.

At times von Balthasar seems to downplay that which is negative in the world, by his stress on the all-embracing separation within God. The infinite distance is not only the basis for the separation on the cross, but goes beyond it. The 'Godlessness' of love in the Trinity undergirds, renders possible and goes beyond the godlessness within the world, such that the Son as 'other' from the Father, grounds and surpasses all we mean by separation, pain and alienation in the world.[164] The economic is latent in the immanent 'without adding a foreign element to them as such. The only foreign element is sin, which is burned up within these relations which are fire'.[165] But by playing down sin von Balthasar undercuts the very stress on Jesus' abandonment for which he has passionately argued.

At other times, von Balthasar suggests that there is some kind of negativity within God, as the basis for God's encounter with sin on the cross, and this leads him to use language which suggests an inner divine conflict. We have noted above von Balthasar's integration of Popkes' discussion of the verb *paradidōmi* ('to hand over') and its associated stress on the abandoning Father. Von Balthasar does seek a Trinitarian explanation in which the handing over of the Son by the Father is balanced by the Son's own self-abandonment, the divine 'must' (*dei*) combined with Jesus' sovereign freedom,[166] and so he specifically rejects the Reformation emphasis on judgement and punishment; for von Balthasar, Jesus subjectively experiences the cross as punishment without its objectively being so.[167] For all this, however, the Father remains the real protagonist. Jesus has the sins of the world 'loaded onto him by God'; more than that, what Jesus bears is not as significant as the fact that it is God who has loaded it onto him. It is the fact that it is *God* who prescribes what is utterly opposed to God that awakens absolute dread in Jesus.[168]

Von Balthasar concludes that 'only a conflict between God in heaven and God the representative on earth can explain'[169] the abandonment and contradiction of the cross. In later work there does seem to be a softening of this position and an uncertainty as to the nature of the relationship between Father and Son on the cross. In his *Theo-Drama* von Balthasar now writes that the Father *appears* to load sin onto the Son[170] and that the Father did not will men to crucify Jesus.[171] Yet von Balthasar still persists in pursuing a positive negativity in God. In a somewhat mysterious passage that is heavily indebted to Adrienne von Speyr, von Balthasar describes the Trinitarian relationship in terms of the Father showing the Son the mystery of the Father's darkness. Such a darkness which necessitated the turning away of the Father from the Son, and which the Son experienced in wordlessness, is both an expression of divine anger against sin and of the 'super-light' of divine freedom. By conceiving darkness in such dialectical terms von Balthasar can conclude that, in the same way, suffering is a mode of joy and separation is a mode of union; so even dereliction is a mode of the eternal communion between Father, Son and Spirit.[172]

I suggest that exploring the passive silence of the Father instead of an active 'loading on of sins' by the Father would offer a potentially more fruitful approach to the relationship between Father and Son. Although von Balthasar stresses the real and immutable unity within God in the midst of forsakenness, so that he claims there is no contradiction within

God,[173] his prioritizing of eternal realities does seem to leave him with some kind of contradiction.

A second major criticism of von Balthasar's approach is that it seems doubtful whether he gives enough significance to creation. By insisting so strongly on the priority of the eternal over the temporal von Balthasar is able to speak of creation affecting God, but only as part of the eternal Trinitarian relationships. Von Balthasar seeks to explain the distinctness of creation from God within the context of its being within the divine life, but the impression remains that creation is only the playing out of eternal decisions and not something in a free relationship with God. Although von Balthasar stresses that human freedom is real and needs no other ground,[174] this is undermined by the repeated insistence that the human drama of 'No' to God can only be played out in the midst of the 'Yes' of the divine drama. 'It is the case of the play within the play: our play 'plays' within his play'.[175] Von Balthasar criticizes Barth for having everything happen in eternity, yet is subject to his own criticism. Despite all that is said to the contrary, there is the distinct impression that von Balthasar portrays a divine drama alone, and not one that is fully dramatic in terms of the divine-human relationship.

Von Balthasar quite rightly seeks to maintain a right distinction between God and the world as the basis for a real relationship between them. He makes clear his dissatisfaction both with the theological tradition he has inherited and modern attempts to go beyond it, but ultimately much uncertainty remains about his own proposition. Von Balthasar speaks of God's vulnerability,[176] but it is actually doubtful whether that exists to any real degree. It is precisely this, as we have said before and will explore more fully in the next chapter, which could offer von Balthasar a firmer basis for the divine-human relationship.

A third criticism is a pastoral matter. Von Balthasar's reluctance to ascribe a real experience of suffering to God undermines the sense of solidarity that God has with us, a spiritual issue of some importance for von Balthasar. Even evoking a principle of similarity within a greater dissimilarity, a wedge is driven between God's experience of the world and ours. This is confirmed by the way in which von Balthasar relates this mysterious 'something akin to suffering' to the eternal joy of God. Referring positively to Jacques Maritain's suggestion that there is a real analogy between our pain and God's pain, such that divine pain is a mode of perfection, von Balthasar notes how Maritain then gives examples of how great maturity cannot be obtained without suffering. Joy and pain are in fact inexorably linked together so that pain 'imparts an incomparably and precious nobility'.[177] In God then this divine 'pain' is forever taken up within the perfection of divine joy.

Such an understanding leaves God remote from the experiences of millions of people for whom suffering is the major reality in their lives, with rather less joy. We must ask whether von Balthasar's whole theology of divine immutability, and especially his suggestion of some mysterious perfection in God 'akin' to human suffering, is actually a razor-edged approach to a most difficult subject, or whether it loses any real sense of meaning in its very dependence on mystery. Furthermore, von Balthasar does not seem to take the full horror of suffering seriously enough. Von Balthasar's theology may speak to those who experience suffering which they can 'work on' and which will be productive, to use Sölle's distinction. Such suffering may impart a 'precious nobility', as Maritain suggested,[178] and such sufferers may recognize the mixture of suffering and joy. But this approach suggests that even the most barbaric experiences must be linked to heavenly joy. Von Balthasar quite clearly suggests that suffering is necessary for future blessedness[179] and that suffering should 'train us for the great act of self-surrender that concludes our life' rather than prompt us to improve the intolerable conditions of the world.[180] 'Might it not be that all the blood spilled in vain has something to do, after all with the precious blood with which we have been bought and washed'.[181] Von Balthasar's passionate metaphorical language promises much, but in metaphysical reality the downplaying of creation and sin trivializes the suffering of individuals, and the immutability of God erects a barrier between human pain and the life of God.[182] Without the protest inherent in the cross, suffering becomes justified as part of the system, even the system of salvation.

> If it is true that the suffering of the Crucified One can transform even worldly pain unintelligible to itself, into a co-redemptive suffering, then the most unbelievable, most cruel tortures, passions, concentration

camps . . . can be seen in close proximity to the Cross, to that utter night, interpreted by the unfathomable cry of why?[183]

Von Balthasar has certainly grappled with divine ontology, with the mystery of the divine being, but the picture of God he produces fails both Jesus' cry and the cries of many others. In von Balthasar's understanding, God fails fully to share the pain of suffering with us or to protest against the evil from which suffering springs. We will go on to look for the divine transformation of sin and suffering, but this must arise out of these twin concepts of presence and protest.

## Notes to Chapter 9

[1] John O'Donnell, *Hans Urs Von Balthasar* (London: Geoffrey Chapman), p. 1, n. 3; Edward Oakes, T*he Pattern of Redemption* (New York: Continuum, 1997), p. 3

[2] See Introduction to Hans Urs von Balthasar, *Mysterium Paschale* (Edinburgh: T. & T. Clark, 1990), p. 6.

[3] Oakes, p. 7, quoting Jakob Laubach's essay 'Hans Urs von Balthasar' in Leonard Reinisch (ed.), *Theologians of our Time* (Notre Dame: University of Notre Dame, 1964), p. 146-7.

[4] See Hans Urs von Balthasar, *The Glory of the Lord,* Volume VII (Edinburgh: T. & T. Clark, 1989), pp. 107-9, 155.

[5] Aidan Nichols, *The Word has Been Abroad* (Edinburgh: T. & T. Clark, 1998), p. 211.

[6] Von Balthasar, *Mysterium Paschale*, p. 125.

[7] Von Balthasar, *The Glory of the Lord*, VII, pp. 148, 212, 216.

[8] Von Balthasar, *Mysterium Paschale*, p. 72.

[9] Ibid., p. 100.

[10] This stress on the unbreakable link between incarnation and passion also ensures that Jesus' life and death are revelatory as well as soteriological. *Mysterium Paschale*, p. 14.

[11] Von Balthasar, *The Glory of the Lord,* VII, p. 202. In some of von Balthasar's later works, especially the last two volumes of *Theo-Drama*, the theme of forsakenness is very strong.

[12] Von Balthasar, *The Glory of the Lord,* VII, p. 226.

[13] Ibid. It is noteworthy that such a comment is actually lacking in the earlier *Mysterium Paschale,* which von Balthasar refers back to in *The Glory of the Lord,* VII, p. 203, n. 2., p. 229, n.6, for a fuller treatment of the subject.

[14] Von Balthasar, *Mysterium Paschale,* p. 72.

[15] Von Balthasar, *The Glory of the Lord,* VII, pp. 203-4.

[16] Von Balthasar, *Mysterium Paschale,* p. 122; *The Glory of the Lord,* VII, p. 204. It is interesting that, writing shortly after Sölle's *Christ the Representative,* von Balthasar both rejects a mythological interpretation and positively speaks of the 'Death of God', the title of Chapter 2 of *Mysterium Paschale,* without any reference to the radical 'Death of God' tradition. In von Balthasar, *Theo-Drama,* V (San Francisco: Ignatius, 1988-98), pp. 213-4, von Balthasar notes Nietzsche's fundamental reinterpretation of 'The death of God', but will not discuss it. He refers to Jüngel on a number of occasions, but sadly offers no engagement with his thinking.

[17] Von Balthasar, *Mysterium Paschale,* p. 122.

[18] Ibid., p. 125.

[19] Von Balthasar, *The Glory of the Lord,* VII, pp. 209-10.

[20] Von Balthasar, *Mysterium Paschale,* pp. 76-8.

[21] Von Balthasar sees Matthew's difference from Mark, in the presentation of very similar material, to be his stress on the apocalyptic nature of the passion. The tearing of the curtain inscribed with a representation of the cosmos signifies the end of the world, rather than simply the end of the law and cultus as in Mark. See *Mysterium Paschale,* p. 127.

[22] Von Balthasar, *The Glory of the Lord,* VII, p. 210. Von Balthasar later suggests that the Johannine 'I thirst' is historically probable, ibid., p. 226, while in his earlier book, *Mysterium Paschale,* p.126, he claimed this word was 'historically well-founded' because it explained the offering of a drink, and the word to Mary had a historic probability.

[23] Von Balthasar, *Mysterium Paschale,* pp. 125-6.

[24] Ibid., p. 126. This is an important Gospel incident that anchors, for von Balthasar, further Mariological development. The Lazarus incident is also interpreted, ibid., p. 135, christologically as indicating God-abandonment.

[25] Von Balthasar, *The Glory of the Lord,* VII, pp. 85-6.

[26] Von Balthasar, *Mysterium Paschale,* p. 109. John Saward, *The Mysteries of March: Hans Urs von Balthasar on the Incarnation and Easter* (London: Collins, 1990), pp. 46-7, presents a simple synthesis of Mark and Luke in a way von Balthasar does not.

[27] Von Balthasar, *The Glory of the Lord,* VII, p. 224.

[28] Von Balthasar, *Mysterium Paschale*, p. 108; see *The Glory of the Lord*, VII, p. 224.

[29] See von Balthasar, *Mysterium Paschale*, pp. 107-112, *The Glory of the Lord*, VII, pp. 223-225.

[30] Von Balthasar, *Mysterium Paschale*, p. 110.

[31] Ibid., p. 111.

[32] Ibid., p. 112.

[33] Ibid., pp. 111-112; *The Glory of the Lord*, VII, p. 225, n. 27.

[34] It may well be that Moltmann discovered this passage from Popkes by reading von Balthasar.

[35] Saward, *The Mysteries of March*, pp. 50-51, for example, relates von Balthasar's use of *'paradidōmi'*, but fails to tackle the problems such language involves.

[36] Von Balthasar, *Mysterium Paschale*, p. 72.

[37] Von Balthasar, *The Glory of the Lord*, VII, p. 225.

[38] Saward, *The Mysteries of March*, p. 34.

[39] Von Balthasar, *The Glory of the Lord*, VII, p. 143.

[40] Ibid., p. 142.

[41] Ibid., p. 142. Flesh does not speak, and even if flesh stands for humanity, speaking is only one of human activities. Ibid., p. 142.

[42] Ibid., pp. 218-9. Once again it is the thought of Mark and John which is integrated together, for the theme of hiddenness is particularly developed in their Gospels.

[43] Ibid., p. 85, quoting Nicholas of Cusa, *Excitationum*, lib. 3 (Paris, 1514), fol. 41a.

[44] Von Balthasar, *The Glory of the Lord*, VII, p. 202.

[45] Ibid., p. 81.

[46] See, ibid., pp. 84-5. Von Balthasar also finds in the 'wordless sighing' of the Spirit (Romans 8:26) a relationship with God beyond words in the same way that words are left behind Christ in his dying cry. Ibid., pp. 514-5.

[47] Von Balthasar, *Mysterium Paschale*, p. 100.

[48] Ibid., p. 122; cf. *Theo-Drama*, IV, p. 333: 'The Trinity does not hover 'unmoved' above the events of the cross – the view that Christ is somehow 'above' his abandonment by God and continues to enjoy the beatific vision'; and 'Ist der Gekreuzigte selig?' in *Communio* (1987), p. 108 (translated by Saward, *The Mysteries of March*, p.56): 'Any theology which says that Christ on the cross suffered only in the 'lower' part of the soul, while the 'peak of his [created] spirit' continued to enjoy the beatific vision, breaks the top off the drama of

redemption. It does not see that the Son as a whole, takes on himself the situation of the sinful world that has turned away from God . . . The Trinity is capable of more than pious theologians imagine'. See also *Theo-Drama*, V, pp. 254, 259, 263, 501.

[49] Von Balthasar, *Theo-Drama*, IV, p. 336.

[50] Von Balthasar, *Mysterium Paschale*, pp. 51-2. John O'Donnell's conclusion that Jesus was able to find God 'even in the darkest moment of the Father's *apparent* absence on the cross', *Hans Urs von Balthasar*, p. 156 (italics mine), does not accurately convey von Balthasar's thought and is also at odds with his own presentation of von Balthasar's theology of Holy Saturday, in which Jesus is separated from the Father and the light is extinguished.

[51] Von Balthasar, *The Glory of the Lord*, VII, p. 86.

[52] Von Balthasar, *Mysterium Paschale*, p. 79.

[53] Von Balthasar, *The Glory of the Lord*, VII, p. 86.

[54] Ibid., p. 211.

[55] Ibid.

[56] Von Balthasar, *Mysterium Paschale*, p. 14.

[57] Ibid., p. 52.

[58] Von Balthasar, *The Glory of the Lord*, VII, p. 152.

[59] Karl Barth, *Church Dogmatics*, trans. G. W. Bromiley and T. F. Torrance, (Edinburgh: T. & T. Clark, 1936-75), I/1, pp. 321, 330.

[60] Von Balthasar, *The Glory of the Lord*, VII, pp. 148-59.

[61] Von Balthasar, *Theo-Drama*, V, p. 267.

[62] Von Balthasar, *Mysterium Paschale*, p. 148. Raymond Brown, *The Death of the Messiah: From Gethsemane to the Grave*, Vol II, (London: Geoffrey Chapman, 1994), pp. 1286-7, criticizes von Balthasar's theology because, while being a 'magnificent concept', it is not centred on what the canonical evangelists assign to this day. In fact it is paradoxically different from Matthew, the only Gospel to record any details of the events of the Sabbath, which stresses that sin continues in the form of the Jewish leaders seeking a guard for the tomb, and more in line with the Gospel of Peter which contains a heavenly voice asking the risen Christ if he has preached to the dead. Yet Brown has missed von Balthasar's point, which is that none of the Gospels say anything about *Jesus* between death and resurrection, and the activity of the Jewish leaders seems to have little bearing on a theology of Jesus' 'descent into Hell'. In fact, in contrast to Brown, it could be argued that the continuation of sin points to Jesus' solidarity with sinners in his death.

63 Oakes, *The Pattern of Redemption*, pp. 238-9, suggests that von Balthasar extrapolates a theology from the logic of the events in similar fashion to the Church's theology of Mary.

64 Von Balthasar has insisted that it would be wrong to separate his theology from that of Adrienne von Speyr's. See O'Donnell's discussion in *Hans Urs von Balthasar*, p. 74. In the later books of *Theo-Drama* and *Theologik*, references to von Speyr abound.

65 Von Balthasar, *Mysterium Paschale*, pp. 169-70.

66 Ibid., p. 148.

67 Ibid., p, 164.

68 Von Balthasar, *The Glory of the Lord*, VII, p. 202.

69 Von Balthasar, *Mysterium Paschale*, p. 49.

70 Von Balthasar, *Mysterium Paschale*, pp. 151-2, 156, 173; *The Glory of the Lord*, VII, p. 230.

71 Thus the balancing titles of *Mysterium Paschale*, 'Going to the Cross', 'Going to the Dead' and 'Going to the Father'.

72 Von Balthasar, *Mysterium Paschale*, p. 151. Oakes, *The Pattern of Redemption*, p. 241, considers an active descent of the risen Christ to be the authorial intention in this passage and suggests that von Balthasar would not want to deny the considerable Scriptural warrant for icons of the resplendent Christ in hell. Such an interpretation of von Balthasar is open to question. Whereas *The Glory of the Lord*, VII, p. 230, simply gives a brief statement of this passive interpretation, the longer discussion in *Mysterium Paschale*, is much clearer. Although the vague suggestion that within a theology of solidarity the mythological traits can be given their due place, p. 151, offers some support to Oakes, von Balthasar's assertion that he 'excludes from the outset all mythological motifs in Christ's going to the dead', p. 152, seems to rule out all other interpretations of this text.

73 Von Balthasar, *Mysterium Paschale*, pp. 151-2.

74 Von Balthasar, *Theo-Drama*, V, p. 193: 'Thus it seems that the cross of Christ, laden with every sinful refusal of man, must stand at the very last extremity of hell; indeed it must stand beyond hell, where the Son is forsaken by the Father in a way that only he can know'.

75 Ibid., p. 267. It is interesting that this is partly a quotation from Adrienne von Speyr, *The Birth of the Church* (*Johannes*, Vol. 4. San Francisco: Ignatius Press, 1994), p. 212, although, as we have seen, von Balthasar would insist that no inference can be drawn from this.

[76] Rossé, *The Cry of Jesus on the Cross*, trans. Stephen Wentworth Arndt, (New York: Paulist Press, 1987), pp. 94-5, criticizes von Balthasar's passive account of Holy Saturday on this very point, making the cross insufficient, and for missing out the resurrection in the interpretation of 1 Peter 3-4. Yet Rossé's comments are not based on this passage, for he only quotes *Mysterium Paschale* and *The Glory of the Lord,* VII. He wants to place the experience of hell on the cross and in so doing has missed the whole thrust of von Balthasar's theology.

[77] Von Balthasar, *Mysterium Paschale*, pp. 161-5.

[78] Von Balthasar, *Theo-Drama,* V, p. 256.

[79] Von Balthasar, *Mysterium Paschale*, p. 168; *The Glory of the Lord*, VII, p. 231. In both places von Balthasar develops Paul Althaus' thought.

[80] Von Balthasar, *The Glory of the Lord*, VII, pp. 232-3.

[81] Von Balthasar, *Mysterium Paschale*, p. 167.

[82] Ibid., p. 168.

[83] Ibid., p. 172.

[84] Ibid., p. 168.

[85] Ibid., pp. 172-3; *The Glory of the Lord*, VII, p. 233.

[86] Von Balthasar, *Mysterium Paschale*, p. 173.

[87] Hans Urs von Balthasar, *Du Krönst das Jahrmit deiner Huld: Radiopredigten* (Einsiedeln: Johannes Verlag, 1982), p. 75, translated in Saward, *The Mysteries of March*, p. 44.

[88] Von Balthasar, *Theo-Drama*, IV, pp. 336.

[89] Ibid., p. 330.

[90] Von Balthasar, *The Glory of the Lord*, VII, p. 232. Von Balthasar is himself quoting Nicholas of Cusa.

[91] Thus Oakes' summarizes, in *The Pattern of Redemption*, p. 282; cf. von Balthasar, *Theologik*, II (Einsiedeln: Johannes Verlag, 1983-7), p. 315, n. 1.

[92] Von Balthasar, *The Glory of the Lord*, VII, pp. 225, 334; *Theo-Drama*, IV, pp. 336-7.

[93] Von Balthasar, *Theo-Drama*, V, pp. 305-11.

[94] Von Balthasar, *Theo-Drama*, IV, pp. 273-84.

[95] Ibid., p. 241; see *Theo-Drama*, V, pp. 266-7.

[96] Von Balthasar, *Theo-Drama*, IV, pp. 273-84.

[97] Gerard O'Hanlon, *The Immutability of God in the Theology of Hans von Balthasar* (Cambridge: CUP, 1990), p. 42.

[98] Von Balthasar, *The Glory of the Lord*, VII, p. 39.

[99] Von Balthasar, *Theo-Drama*, V, pp. 312-4.

[100] Ibid., p. 213.

[101] Ibid., p. 215.

[102] Von Balthasar, *Mysterium Paschale*, p. 7.

[103] Von Balthasar, *Theo-Drama*, V, p. 262, quoting Adrienne von Speyr, *Der Mensch von Gott* (Einsiedeln: Johannes Verlag, 1966), pp. 33-4; See also *Mysterium Paschale*, p. 14. 'In this happening . . . God himself, in the moment of the world's very perdition, attains his most authentic revelation and glorification'.

[104] Barth, *Church Dogmatics*, IV/1, p. 185; quoted in von Balthasar, *Mysterium Paschale*, p. 81; See von Balthasar, *The Glory of the Lord*, VII, p. 215.

[105] Hans Urs von Balthasar, *Love Alone: The Way of Revelation: A Theological Perspective*, trans. Rodeline Albrecht and Maureen Sullivan, (London: Burns and Oates, 1969), p. 71. See also Hans Urs von Balthasar, *Der dreifache Kranz* (Einsiedeln: Johannes Verlag, 1977), p. 64 quoted in *The von Balthasar Reader*, trans. Robert J. Daly and Fred Lawrence, (Edinburgh: T. & T. Clark, 1982), p. 148, *Theo-Drama*, V, p. 260 and von Balthasar, *Du Krönst das Jahrmit*, p. 75, translated by Saward, *The Mysteries of March*, p. 54: 'Many theologians nowadays rightly say: it is precisely on the cross that this difference is revealed; precisely there that the mystery of the divine Trinity is disclosed'.

[106] Von Balthasar, *The Glory of the Lord*, VII, p. 225.

[107] Von Balthasar adds that the revelation of the Trinity prepared for in the garden and in abandonment only comes fully to light in the resurrection of Jesus by the Father. *Mysterium Paschale*, pp. 212-3.

[108] Hans Urs von Balthasar, *Pneuma und Institution: Skizzen zur Theologie*, IV, (Einsiedeln: Johannes Verlag, 1974), 402, in *The von Balthasar Reader*, p. 151.

[109] Hans Urs von Balthasar, *The Glory of the Lord: A Theological Aesthetics*, Vol. I, trans. Erasmo Leiva-Merikakis, (Edinburgh: T. & T. Clark, 1982), p. 656.

[110] Von Balthasar, *Mysterium Paschale*, pp. 27-8.

[111] Von Balthasar, *The Glory of the Lord*, VII, p. 147.

[112] Von Balthasar, *Theo-Drama*, V, p. 494.

[113] Barth, *Church Dogmatics*, IV/1, p. 134, quoted in von Balthasar, *Mysterium Paschale*, p. 81. The translation is by Aidan Nichols as it appears in *Mysterium Paschale*.

[114] Von Balthasar, *Mysterium Paschale*, p. 204.

[115] Von Balthasar, *Theo-Drama*, IV, p. 319.

[116] Von Balthasar, *Mysterium Paschale*, p. 28. In *Theo-Drama*, V, p. 243, von Balthasar quotes a passage from H. Schürmann, *Jesus Ureigner Tod* (Herder,

1975), pp. 146ff, which, written later than *Mysterium Paschale*, is very similar to the above quotation.

[117] Von Balthasar, *Mysterium Paschale*, p. 35.

[118] Von Balthasar, *The Glory of the Lord*, VII, p. 17; *Theo-Drama*, III, p. 287.

[119] Von Balthasar, *Theo-Drama*, IV, pp. 320-1.

[120] Ibid., p. 322. von Balthasar would agree with Moltmann if he said that God was revealed *for the world* only in the opposite; see *Theo-Drama*, V, p. 228.

[121] Von Balthasar, *Theo-Drama*, V, p. 234.

[122] Von Balthasar, *Theo-Drama*, III, p. 226.

[123] See von Balthasar, *Theo-Drama*, II, p. 256: 'In generating the Son the Father does not 'lose' himself to someone else in order thereby to 'regain' himself; for he is *always* himself by giving himself. The Son, too, is always himself by allowing himself to be generated and by allowing the Father to do with him as he pleases. The Spirit is always himself by understanding his 'I' as the 'we' of the Father and Son, by being 'exporiated' for the sake of what is most proper to them. (Without grasping this there is no escape from the machinery of Hegelian dialectic.)' See also *The Glory of the Lord*, VII, pp. 213-4, *Theo-Drama*, V, p. 508 and p. 264, where von Balthasar, quoting von Speyr, says that the temporal can be inscribed on the eternal, which is not Hegelian, but could be misunderstood in a Hegelian way. Unfortunately, von Balthasar does not explain why it is *not* Hegelian.

[124] Von Balthasar, *Theo-Drama*, V, p. 251.

[125] Von Balthasar, *Mysterium Paschale*, p. 29.

[126] 'Recapitulates' is an inaccurate translation of the German 'in sich hineinholt', suggesting that the sinners' mode of alienation is *prior* to the infinite distance, a thought not contained in the German and the opposite of Balthasar's entire theology. Literally Balthasar writes that the infinite distance *holds in itself* the sinners' mode of alienation.

[127] Von Balthasar, *Theo-Drama*, III, p. 228.

[128] Von Balthasar, *Theo-Drama*, V, pp. 257, 268.

[129] Von Balthasar, *Theo-Drama*, IV, p. 333.

[130] Ibid., pp. 323, 325.

[131] See O'Hanlon, *The Immutability of God*, pp. 88-109 for a full discussion.

[132] Von Balthasar, *Theo-Drama*, V, p. 509.

[133] Ibid., p. 502.

[134] Ibid. p. 517.

[135] Ibid., p. 265.

[136] Von Balthasar, *Theo-Drama*, IV, pp. 324, 328; *Theo-Drama*, V, pp. 562-3.

137 John Thompson, *Modern Trinitarian Perspectives* (Oxford: OUP, 1994), p. 57.

138 Von Balthasar moves from the Chalcedon basis of Christology which he takes as a starting point, *The Glory of the Lord*, VII, p. 13, to stress that something happened to God, *Theo-Drama*, IV, p. 324. See Oakes, *The Pattern of Redemption*, p. 230-1 and O'Hanlon, *The Immutability of God*, p. 43.

139 Von Balthasar, *Theo-Drama*, V, p. 229. It is also interesting that Rahner, *Karl Rahner in Dialogue: Conversations and Interviews* (New York: Crossroads, 1986), p. 126, singles out von Balthasar, von Speyr and Moltmann as examples of gnostic theology of the death of God. Perhaps it is a closeness with Moltmann which has led von Balthasar to indicate so sharply what he perceives to be the differences.

140 Von Balthasar, *Mysterium Paschale*, pp. vii-viii; cf. *Theo-Drama*, IV, p. 333.

141 Von Balthasar has a much more positive appreciation of the patristic tradition than, for example, Moltmann, *Theo-Drama*, V, p. 221, n. 33. He insists that 'apatheia' was not taken over from Greek philosophy uncritically, that Origen is not so isolated and names Aquinas as a principle exponent of a static God.

142 See Oakes, *The Pattern of Redemption*, p. 283 and O'Hanlon, *The Immutability of God*, p. 112.

143 Von Balthasar, *Mysterium Paschale*, p. ix.

144 Ibid., p. 52.

145 Ibid., p. 30.

146 Von Balthasar, *Theo-Drama*, V, p. 514.

147 O'Donnell, *Hans Urs von Balthasar*, p. 70; O'Hanlon, *The Immutability of God*, pp. 137-42.

148 Oakes, *The Pattern of Redemption*, pp. 133-5.

149 Von Balthasar, *Theo-Drama*, V, p. 222.

150 Von Balthasar, *Theo-Drama*, IV, p. 324.

151 Ibid.

152 Ibid., p. 327-8

153 Von Balthasar, *The Glory of the Lord*, VII, p. 86.

154 Von Balthasar, *Theo-Drama*, IV, p. 329.

155 Ibid., p. 328.

156 Oakes, *The Pattern of Redemption*, p. 287. Von Balthasar himself describes Philippians 2 as stammering out the mystery, *Mysterium Paschale*, p. 26.

157 Von Balthasar, *Theo-Drama*, V, p. 240-1.

[158] Ibid., pp. 247, 510.

[159] Ibid., pp. 507, 509, 521.

[160] Ibid., p. 513.

[161] Ibid., p. 521.

[162] Ibid., p. 518.

[163] O'Hanlon, *The Immutability of God*, p. 174. Von Balthasar himself admits, Theo-Drama, II, p. 49, that there is only a hair's breadth separating the real suffering of the God-man and the non-suffering of God.

[164] Von Balthasar, *Theo-Drama*, IV, pp. 324-5.

[165] Von Balthasar, *Theo-Drama*, V, p. 268.

[166] Von Balthasar, *Mysterium Paschale*, p. 18-9.

[167] Von Balthasar, *Theo-Drama*, IV, p. 338. There is no sense in which we can say that God the Father 'punishes' the suffering Son in our place. Von Balthasar, *Du krönst*, p. 76, translated by Saward, *The Mysteries of March*, p. 41.

[168] Von Balthasar, *The Glory of the Lord*, VII, p. 209.

[169] Von Balthasar, *Der dreifache Kranz*, pp. 45-7, in *The von Balthasar Reader*, p. 147.

[170] Von Balthasar, *Theo-Drama*, IV, p. 335.

[171] Von Balthasar, *Theo-Drama*, V, p. 251.

[172] Von Balthasar, *Theo-Drama*, V, pp. 267-8.

[173] See von Balthasar, *Theo-Drama*, V, 261-2, 265, 518.

[174] Von Balthasar, *Theo-Drama*, IV, p. 328.

[175] Von Balthasar, *Theo-Drama*, I, p. 20.

[176] For example, von Balthasar, *Theo-Drama*, IV, p. 329.

[177] Von Balthasar, *Theo-Drama*, V, pp. 240-42.

[178] J. Maritain, 'Quelques réflexions sur le savoir théologique' in E. R. Korn (ed.), *Approches sans Entrares* (Fayard, 1973), p. 307; cit. von Balthasar, *Theo-Drama*, V, p. 242.

[179] Von Balthasar, *Theo-Drama*, V, p. 256.

[180] Ibid., p. 499.

[181] Ibid.

[182] O'Hanlon's assessment, 'Theological Dramatics', in Bede McGregor and Thomas Norris (eds.) *The Beauty of Christ: An Introduction to the Theology of Hans Urs von Balthasar*, (Edinburgh: T. & T. Clark, 1994), p. 109, is correct when he says that ' from one who is so conscious of the reality of evil, there is a curious lack of engagement with the great modern structural evils'.

[183] Ibid., p. 501.

# Part III
# The Pastoral Experience

# 10
# Vulnerability: Overcoming Conflict

Jesus' Godforsaken cry has had a radical effect on recent understanding of the revelation of God, reorientating theological analysis of its occasion and content. The decisive turning point, in fact, occurred in the previous generation as Barth pioneered a reversal of the patristic tradition which had recognized the humanity of Christ in the cross and his divinity in the resurrection. In a development which had an immense impact on those who followed,[1] Barth saw that it was rather the cross itself which revealed Jesus' divine nature and that it was in such weakness, humiliation and Godforsakenness that God was supremely God.[2] While this was certainly highly influential for the direction of theology in the second half of the twentieth century and a significant overturning of the tradition, Barth is actually returning to Mark's original insight. Our earlier biblical study has shown that first, Jesus' abandonment on the cross is to be taken with the utmost seriousness, and, second, that it is precisely here, in Jesus' Godforsaken death, that God is supremely revealed.

Our four authors have tackled the Gospel text in different ways: Moltmann grapples most with the historical-critical problems, but we have seen that there are still some fundamental issues left unresolved. Sölle demythologizes the text, thus side-stepping critical considerations, but struggles to provide a biblical foundation for her theology. Jüngel begins to tackle the exegetical questions, but dogmatic certainties over-shadow any thorough investigation. Von Balthasar comes closest to grasping the climactic nature of Jesus' cry, but again the failure to continue with more detailed exegesis is disappointing. Despite these quite fundamental differences, all four authors have still sought to explore in their own way this basic Marcan insight, that Jesus' Godforsaken death reveals the heart of God.

A number of key descriptions of the being of God have emerged in the work of these theologians: God as love, God as suffering (although with certain caveats in von Balthasar), God as Trinity (although here Sölle is an exception). A further concept, nascent in all four authors but nowhere fully developed, is that of the vulnerability of God. Although this is linked to the notion of suffering, vulnerability must be recognized as something distinct. Its two twin axioms, as I have stated them above,[3] are an *openness* to being wounded, so that suffering is a real possibility but not a logical necessity, and an understanding that suffering is something which *happens* to us. This takes us to the very heart of Jesus' forsakenness and thus the nature of God, linking and undergirding all that has been revealed of the divine life. Exploring this further will build on Mark's dramatic and theological climax, help correct some of the difficulties we have encountered and take us deeper into the mystery of God.

## 1. Active suffering

The theme of vulnerability most strongly resonates with the work of Dorothee Sölle, who is the most theologically dependent on the humanity of Jesus on the cross. Yet we have seen that in her early work Sölle equated vulnerability with the helplessness of God, making God to be entirely passive and so trapped in the suffering of the world. Real suffering certainly requires an element of passivity as something that genuinely befalls us, yet divine suffering must also be understood within the framework of God's active freedom. Vulnerability does not imply that suffering is in any sense forced upon God, which is an unavoidable consequence of Sölle's view of helplessness, but that it is God's nature to always choose the path of love in which the possibility of suffering befalling God is a real, and even likely, possibility.[4] Sölle herself moves towards such an understanding in her later books. Vulnerability actively places God on the side of the victims, sharing in their suffering, in a morally acceptable way, so that God genuinely suffers yet always as the result of divine freedom.

Moltmann's description of 'active suffering' moves towards this interpretation of vulnerability, but this phrase in Moltmann's own work is never fully explained or established and is consistently undercut by the rejection of an element of passivity in God's encounter with the world. The suggestion that God always remains the 'Master of pain',[5] or worse, that God is the actual author of divine suffering, brings into doubt Moltmann's very conception of a suffering God. God's experience of suffering, if it is to be understandable and relevant, must be in some ways analogous to our own, in a way that von Balthasar, in particular, rejects.

That is, there must be some element of passivity involved in God's experience. But, if it is to be divine suffering then it must also be different from our experiences, not forced upon God helplessly, as is often the case with human suffering, but freely accepted. It is this very balance between similarity and difference, midway between Sölle and Moltmann, that is provided for in the concept of willing vulnerability. This assures that God's suffering is truly suffering and truly divine.

## 2. Encountering negativity

Jesus' cry immediately draws attention to the seeming incongruity at the heart of the cross. God is revealed in the midst of suffering, death and where God is declared to be absent. God, therefore, encounters negativity, that which is opposed to God. In order to affirm what appears, in the light of tradition, to be such a startling proposal, Moltmann, von Balthasar and Jüngel all draw on the creative tension which emerges from Barth that the cross is both strange, yet not strange for God. God is always true to God, but God encounters what is strange, even what is radically opposite, in the cross. If the cross is *totally* strange to God then it is hard to conceive either how there can be any relationship between God and Jesus' Godforsakenness or how God can remain God in the experience of death. On the other hand, if there is *nothing* strange about divine revelation in Godforsakenness then it either raises questions about the reality of Jesus' experience or suggests some eternal Godforsakenness in the divine life. But this process of thinking about God and negativity has proved difficult for Moltmann due to the dark shadow of Hegelianism and, despite Moltmann's intention, the necessity of negativity is never removed. It is equally difficult for von Balthasar, whose desire to uphold a form of immutability, even if somewhat differentiated from the scholastic tradition, forces a negativity in the eternal being of God.

Willing vulnerability offers a way of understanding God's genuine openness to the world, in which God experiences what is new, strange and even opposite to the divine life, as the result of divine freedom and while always remaining true to God's self. It is experiencing what is strange which is not strange for God because it is in the very act of being open to others that God is being true to God. Vulnerability, therefore, allows God to be affected and changed by the cross, and by the whole of God's relationship with creation, without reducing God into the world process, as von Balthasar feared; it also meets the concern (expressed, for instance, by Colin Gunton)[6] that if the cross were in any sense determinative for God some future event might be the real death of God. It is this sense of vulnerability which seems to be implied by Jüngel's conception of God as the unity of life and death in favour of life.[7] Such a description celebrates the overcoming of negativity in the life of God but only through the experiencing and suffering of that very negativity. We must not turn Mark's insight into a kenotic theology in which God *became* vulnerable on the cross, as is sometimes more popularly supposed,[8] but we should insist that God can be revealed in Godforsakenness because God is essentially vulnerable. Such a notion of vulnerability provides for a real encounter between God and creation but within the limits that God remains true to God.

This vulnerability revealed in Jesus' Godforsaken cry can then be traced back to the very heart of God's trinitarian life. Building on Jüngel's insight that there must be a degree of passivity in the inner life of God which corresponds to the passion of Jesus,[9] we might say that vulnerability is revealed in Jesus' cry because it is the hallmark of God's trinitarian life. Father, Son and Spirit exist in love and openness. If the ancient doctrine of perichoresis is to be understood within a relational rather than substantial notion of the Trinity then it requires a total openness between the divine persons. This same intra-divine openness exists between God and creation and is experienced by God as vulnerability, as is most clearly seen in Jesus' forsakenness. Although we have seen that Moltmann's distinction between the Father's experience of death and the Son's experience of dying is problematic, it does point us towards the mutuality that is an integral part of the cross. The Son loses the Father and the Father also loses the Son. This can only happen if vulnerability is an essential divine attribute. Yet Moltmann's biggest problem is the language of 'God against God' which down plays this very mutuality.

## 3. Overcoming conflict

The desire to take Jesus' cry seriously and not resort to an interpretation based on Jesus only feeling abandoned, has in differing ways led to images and language of divine conflict. Moltmann's language of 'God against God' encapsulated within a dialectic that still bears Hegelian influence has been rightly criticized by Sölle for either being sadistic, in that the Father sends suffering on the Son, or masochistic, in that God is the cause of God's own suffering. Equally, von Balthasar's 'infinite distance' which contains the possibility and conditions of sin also places the origin of suffering firmly within the Godhead, so that temporal history becomes simply an outworking of eternal realities. This divine conflict is the consequence of von Balthasar's desire to uphold the reality of Jesus' cry without allowing any meaningful metaphysical change or suffering to be attributed to God. Willing vulnerability, on the other hand, seeks a consistent understanding of divine being, uniting the immanent and economic aspects of God, fulfilling Jüngel's desire to distinguish properly between God and the world, but allowing for a real mutuality between them. This sense of willing vulnerability overcomes the persistent sense in Moltmann that God is the author of suffering and removes any lingering aspects of an eternal conflict found in von Balthasar, without, crucially, reducing God into the world process. It allows for the application of contingent suffering to God, whilst expressly ruling out necessary and metaphysical suffering.

By removing this sense of eternal conflict, vulnerability focuses our attention instead on the aspect of the cross in time. Even then it could be misleading to talk of a temporal *conflict*, as if Father and Son were at odds on the cross; better would be to speak of a temporal *disruption* caused by God's encounter with sin. As our representative before God Jesus experiences God's 'No' against humankind. That the passion, according to von Balthasar, 'awakes absolute dread in Jesus'[10] rightly describes this temporal encounter that leads to the abandonment between Father and Son which is resolved in the resurrection. Yet it is noteworthy that it is von Balthasar and Moltmann, who have both used Popkes' research on the New Testament use of *paradidōmi*, who both struggle with implications of eternal conflict. Popkes' original intention was to draw attention to the varied usage of *paradidōmi* in the New Testament, particularly the interplay between human agents, such as Judas, and a divine agent, God. The handing over of Jesus by Judas, the Chief Priests and Pilate is clearly meant literally. However, the handing over of Jesus by God must be understood in a metaphorical way. Neither Moltmann nor von Balthasar consider this difference and simply adopt the language of God against God, suggesting an active and quite literal abandonment. But we could speak of a nevertheless real, yet passive abandonment of Jesus by God, which could be described as a 'handing over', which has similarities yet differences to the literal abandonment by human agents, but which avoids the language and necessity of a trinitarian conflict. It is this passive abandonment which is so evocatively captured in the motif of silence, which von Balthasar develops, but not to its full potential.

The Father abandons the Son in as much as at this crucial and climactic time the Father is silent. This encompasses the Father's non-intervention to save the Son, but goes beyond it, for the Father not only does nothing, but is also silent. This takes Jesus' cry with utter seriousness and in no way plays down its significance. Silence is real and can be both painful and terrifying, and in the Gospel narratives is in total contrast to all that Jesus has known. In this light, such a passive silence makes perfect sense of the New Testament assertion that the Father 'handed over' the Son, and is in line with an interpretation of Jesus' cry quite familiar to the early Church.[11] Yet, while asserting a real disruption in the divine life – this is a unique experience for Jesus and for God – any sense of an eternal divine conflict is ruled out. The silence of the Father is then the real abandonment that Jesus experiences on the cross.

Such silence can be terrifying, but von Balthasar has helpfully pointed out that silence also allows space. First, it allows space for revelation. In the same way that Jesus' silence before Pilate expresses his own vulnerability, so the silence of the cross, and indeed of the grave, allows space for God's vulnerability to be revealed in the waiting. If vulnerability is at the heart of God, then in the humanity and death of Jesus God's divinity is gloriously revealed. Yet to human eyes, which look for power as a sign of divinity, the cross can only be seen as a failure, and it is in this sense that we can speak of the veiling of God's divinity. Mark's conclusion that divinity is revealed in the death of Jesus can never be perceived other than with the eyes of faith. Such revelation in silence, as von Balthasar helpfully suggests, is not restricted to the historic event of the cross, for it is in the hiddenness of God in the vulnerable ministry of word and sacrament that God continues to be revealed.

Second, it allows space for love. Moltmann and von Balthasar have constantly struggled because they have embraced a theological system that has, in different ways eternalized the abandonment of the cross. We have argued that the silence of the Father recognizes the real, but temporal nature, of Jesus' abandonment. But does it make sense to be able to talk of even a temporal disruption in the life of God? If we work with an understanding of the Trinity as some kind of divine 'substance', then such a disruption in the 'threeness' of God does call into question the unity of God's 'oneness'. But if God is described in relational terms, then silence can affect and disrupt these relationships without breaking them apart. Considering the human experience of forsakenness, Sölle concludes, drawing on a phrase from Simone Weil, that the only response is to 'keep on loving in the void'.[12] Applying this human insight to the Trinity, we can say that the Father and Son go on loving in the void of the cross. Identifying with the human 'No' to God, Jesus hears in the silence the divine 'No' to sin, but does not give up on God. And allowing him to stand with sinners, the Father does not give up on the Son, but continues to look for him, and with him the whole of humankind. Jesus' cry was neither one of despair nor one of undisrupted trust. To speak of Father and Son 'loving in the void' looks to the future, but does not yet resolve the essential starkness of Jesus' cry, as does, for example, Boff's description of Jesus' 'absolute hope and trust in the nameless Mystery'.[13] Jesus' cry is a cry for God, a cry that seeks God in the silence, that still looks for God to speak. But in this silence as the Son identifies with the human 'No' so the Father too must look for the Son. The pain of the silence is deafening, but in the silence there is still space to love.

Third, the silence allows space for resurrection. The silence of the Word that reaches its climax on the cross and in the grave is broken by the Father speaking the resurrection and calling into being the new creation. The silence is real, but is not the end as the relationship between the Father and Son is restored.

## 4. Openness to creation

Jesus' cry as fully human and in solidarity with all those experiencing God's silence brings humanity to God in such a way that God is deeply affected and changed by the experience. This is at the heart of our presentation of vulnerability. Yet if the cross is in this way a genuinely new experience for God, then it both implies and necessitates God's openness to the world. We have seen, however, how Moltmann, Jüngel and von Balthasar all struggle to find any real sense of significance for creation in their overall theological systems. Von Balthasar's 'infinite distance' places too much emphasis on the divine rather than the human drama, and leads him to suggest that creation does enrich God, but only as something already within the Trinity.[14] Jüngel's stress on divine agency, together with a very passive anthropology based on his Lutheran understanding of justification, again plays down creation, and Moltmann, who in various ways seeks to draw the created world into a wider understanding of God, never fully achieves it. The concept of vulnerability is needed if creation is to be of significance for God, essential for a genuine understanding of divine suffering, and if creation is to have its own intrinsic worth, essential if it is to be viewed as God's good work and – in the case of humankind – made in God's image. Vulnerability establishes the right kind of relationship between God and creation.

Such vulnerability, first, adds to the significance of creation as the medium of God's self-revelation. Although we have criticized both Sölle and Jüngel for their particular dialectics of God's presence in absence, some way must be found to incorporate both God's revelation and God's veiling in the cross. We could say that God, in vulnerability, chooses creation through which to be revealed. Not that this gives creation an innate or natural power to point to God, but that God chooses to reveal God's self through such a medium that God is thereby hidden at the same time as being revealed. Creation is therefore of significance for God as the conveyor of divine revelation. Second, such a doctrine of vulnerability also allows for some aspects of the future to be left open, dependent upon creation's contribution. This does not put in question God's defeat of evil or the new creation as if they were dependent upon particular human responses, but does allow creation to contribute to the final form of the future. Jüngel and von Balthasar both create some space for this, envisaging that God's being is heightened and expanded in relationship with creation, although there is the persistent impression that this is really the result of God working on God. By contrast it is Moltmann's distinction between the Trinity of origin and Trinity of goal[15] which is most helpful and important here, because it genuinely allows for creation to make a difference.

Such a distinction between origin and goal does not imply that there are two different 'Gods' – there is obviously much that does not change, for God remains loving, giving and vulnerable – nor does it place in doubt the ultimate recreation of the world. Rather it develops the Barthian insight that God in the election of Jesus Christ chooses not to be God without us.[16] God chooses to link God's future inextricably with ours and since creation has intrinsic worth and significance for God the final form of the eschatological glorification depends upon both divine and human creativity. It is not possible to have two paths to the same end, for the particular path followed intrinsically effects the end that is reached. If the path which God chooses includes the co-creativity of creation then this will lead to the very particular future of the Trinity of goal. Despite von Balthasar's final insistence on a universal salvation in order finally to avoid tragedy for God, that in fact remains a very real possibility which we must face. If divine freedom and vulnerability creates space for genuine human freedom then the rejection of God by some can never be finally discounted. Eschatological joy must include space for divine tragedy and pain.

## 5. Conclusion

Taking Jesus' cry seriously, reveals vulnerability at the very heart of the triune God. But the cry is also the ultimate instance of this very vulnerability, for while God has always been opening the divine life to creation, never was this deeper or fuller than on the cross. Mark's starting point for understanding God was Jesus' Godforsaken death. If we too begin here then any concept of the divine being must be founded not on notions of the absoluteness of omnipotence, but on willing vulnerability. Such an ontology will have profound implications for the Church in its life and ministry. Moltmann recognized that when trinitarianism was reduced to monotheism this produced a God conceived in terms of power and control and was mirrored in the attitude and actions of leaders in Church and State.[17] Yet, on the other hand trinitarianism can become a triumvirate of power. What is needed is a vulnerable trinitarianism. The vulnerability revealed in Jesus' cry might then be continued in the life of the Church. Structures, services, leadership and mission will all need to be reassessed and redefined in the light of this revelation. Vulnerability will need to become a hallmark of the Christian disciple.

## Notes to Chapter 10

[1] Moltmann, Jüngel and von Balthasar all acknowledge their debt to Barth; Sölle, on the other hand, is generally critical, but is writing from a context in which Barth's influence is implicit.

[2] See, for example, Barth, *Church Dogmatics*, IV/1, pp. 186-8.

[3] See above, p. 164.

[4] This idea has already been expounded by Paul Fiddes, *The Creative Suffering of God*, pp. 61-2.

[5] Moltmann, *The Trinity and the Kingdom of God*, p. 23.

[6] See above, pp. 160, 174n.

[7] Jüngel, *God as the Mystery of the World*, p. x.

[8] See, for example, Tom Smail, *Once and for All* (London: Darton, Longman and Todd, 1998), p. 120.

[9] Jüngel, *The Doctrine of the Trinity*, pp. 85-6.

[10] Hans Urs von Balthasar, *The Glory of the Lord*, VII, p. 209. But von Balthasar's problem is that he insists that it is in fact God who prescribes what is utterly opposed to God which then awakens this dread.

[11] Theodoretus, PG 80, 1010, quoted by Rossé, *The Cry of Jesus on the Cross*, p. 77. See, above p. 14.

[12] Sölle, *Suffering*, p. 156.

[13] Boff, *Passion of Christ, Passion of the World*, trans. R. Barr (Maryknoll: Orbis, 1987), pp. 51-2. Fiddes' comments on Boff, in *Past Event, Present Salvation*, (London: Darton, Longman and Todd, 1989), pp. 193-4 are to be preferred to Tom Smail's, *Once and for All*, p. 136.

[14] Hans Urs von Balthasar, *Theo-Drama*, V, pp. 507, 509.

[15] Moltmann, *The Future of Creation*, trans. M. Kohl, (London: SCM, 1979), pp. 92-4.

[16] Barth, *Church Dogmatics*, IV/3.1, p. 119.

[17] Moltmann, *The Crucified God*, pp. 325-9; *The Trinity and the Kingdom of God*, pp. 131, 191-7.

# 11
# Love: Pursuing Atonement

In response to Jesus' cry of forsakenness the temple curtain is torn in two and the centurion confesses Jesus' divine sonship. Although Mark certainly offers no worked out metaphor for interpreting Jesus' death on the cross, let alone some theory of atonement, these carefully combined climactic images hint at the way in which Jesus' Godforsaken death not only reveals God's essential nature, but is also decisive for God's relationship with creation. In the context of the dispute over the temple the tearing of the curtain not only symbolizes God's judgement on the temple and its leaders but also highlights Jesus as the way to God. We may recall the suggestion that the description of the centurion as 'facing him' – *ex enantias autou* – may echo an idiomatic expression for entering the temple, and so standing in the presence of God.[1] By implication God is now to be approached, not through a sacrificial cult but through Jesus and his death.

This motif of approaching God is further emphasized by the forceful 'tearing' of the curtain, especially in the light of the important parallelism between Jesus' baptism and death. The striking similarities highlight the contrast implied in the change of tenses of the verb *skizō* between the two events. Whereas the 'tearing apart' of the heavens at the baptism of Jesus (1:10) is in the present tense, it is in the tense of a past completed action (aorist) with the tearing apart of the curtain (15:38), suggesting the finality of Jesus' death as a way to God. Further, that it is a Gentile soldier who alone recognizes Jesus' divinity emphasizes that this new way is open now to all. Such aspects of the Gospel narrative do not constitute a specific doctrine of salvation, but they certainly point to the wider theme of reconciliation with God.

For all four theologians, reflecting on Jesus' cry necessarily leads on to wide-ranging considerations about salvation, and the importance of Jesus' *Godforsaken* death for our understanding of atonement. The classic dilemma of the link between one decisive past event and our present experience of salvation leads to the universalizing of Jesus' Godforsakenness in a variety of ways. This evocative theme of forsakenness has led our authors to use a wide variety of metaphors to expound the significance of Jesus' cry. Such metaphorical language is useful, indeed essential, in describing an understanding of atonement, and communicates at a deep level. But we must be acutely aware of the kind of language we are using and constantly ask exactly what is being implied and imagined by such language. We might put the issue simply by asking 'what is changed by Jesus' experience of Godforsakenness?' On one occasion Moltmann cautions against answering Jesus' cry with a theory of atonement. The only possible answer to Jesus' cry is another experience, the resurrection.[2] Such a point is important, for the very starkness of Jesus' cry means there can be no simple and easy answer. But it is legitimate, as Moltmann himself does, to draw out the hints which Mark gives that Jesus' death recreates our relationship with God.

## 1. Solidarity

One important way that Jesus' Godforsaken death has been interpreted by all four authors is through the image of solidarity. Abandoned by his family and friends, rejected by his own people, let down by the legal system and finally forsaken by God Jesus stands with us and shares our suffering. Not that this was the first or only time that God had shared the sufferings of creation, but in this unique and decisive event God, in love, stood in solidarity with all who suffered. At this point Moltmann expands traditional atonement thinking by consistently speaking of the 'godless and godforsaken', so that the traditional Protestant doctrine of justification for sinners and the liberation stress on the poor can mutually enrich each other. The justifying God brings freedom both to those deprived of justice and to the unjust, freedom for those sinned against and sinners alike.[3] Although Moltmann and, to an even greater extent, Sölle, distinguish too sharply between sinners and sinned against, between the executioners and the victims, for in the complexities of life we are both, their insistence that sin and suffering must be thought of together is an important one. Jesus dies as an innocent victim at the hands of oppressors and so his cross of solidarity must speak to both problems.

Building on this image of solidarity, for Sölle the universalizing factor in Jesus' cry of forsakenness is its repeatability. In crying out Jesus stands in solidarity with us, but equally calls us to stand with him, to 'grow up' and break out and seek our salvation.[4] Although there is no place in Moltmann for the purely subjective approach of Sölle and he is one of those whom Sölle criticizes precisely for offering an exclusive interpretation of Jesus' cry, Moltmann does himself actually offer a similar universalizing understanding of Jesus' forsakenness. The knowledge that Christ has gone through everything that threatens us, that he surrenders himself for us to the abyss of abandonment frees us from fear and anxiety.[5] As those who are Godforsaken we can begin to accept ourselves when we see in the cross that God has accepted us.[6] One persistent problem we have already highlighted is that both Moltmann and von Balthasar undermine this sense of solidarity by somehow conceiving of God on both sides of the fence, as the one who suffers and also the one who sends the suffering. Taking this criticism into account, the concept of solidarity is still an important one, both in its own right and as the basis for any further understanding of atonement.

We can, however, deepen this motif of solidarity. We have seen that in Jesus' Godforsaken death God is changed through a new experience of human suffering that is equally divine. The God who has always reached out in love to a suffering world becomes most deeply in solidarity with creation in the cross of Jesus. Drawing again on Barth's image, the importance of Jesus' Godforsakenness is that, in Jesus, God journeys into the far country, into the depth of estrangement in order to offer us forgiveness and reconciliation. The cross is more than a revelation of God's eternal love, although that is of course one aspect. Rather, it is a unique act of solidarity with creation that draws our response. What then is changed by Jesus' Godforsakenness? Firstly, God is changed by this divine experience of human suffering, enabling God to have a greater depth of solidarity with us. Secondly, as God stands in solidarity with me, calling forth and creating a response, I am changed. Thirdly, then, my relationship with God is changed. God's seeking act of solidarity draws my response of repentance and I am reconciled to God.[7] There is atonement. What is more, with this image of solidarity there is a clear link between Jesus' Godforsaken death and our atonement with God.

## 2. Covenant

Although this explanation provides an objective basis for atonement, in
that God is changed by the particular event of Jesus' Godforsaken death,
it might be argued that the greater emphasis lies on our subjective
response. We notice that Moltmann, Jüngel and von Balthasar, while
using the motif of solidarity, also use language which seeks a greater
objective basis to atonement, in a way which is often linked with Jesus'
Godforsakenness. Sölle also, despite her fundamental stress on the example of Christ, goes beyond Jesus' solidarity with us and develops the
theme of Christ's representation, of God before us and of us before God.
Although she proceeds very carefully, stressing that unlike Barth she does
not see representation in terms of substitution,[8] there is still a limited
sense in which she understands Jesus acting on our behalf. Jesus, as our
representative, 'holds our place open'[9] so that God 'continues to count on
us, look for us, wait for us'.[10] This representation is only provisional, buy-
ing us time and calling us to action, but even in this limited way Jesus not
only stands with us, he also acts for us. Moltmann, Jüngel and von
Balthasar take this further and seek a stronger sense of Jesus' vicarious
sufferings, in which Christ dies 'for us'. Moltmann, for example, speaks
of God reconciling the world-in-contradiction by enduring the contradiction, not by contradicting the contradiction.[11] That is, it is divine suffering
which leads to atonement, based on the compassion of the Father, the
Godforsakenness of the Son and the exonerating power of the Spirit.[12]

Yet *how* does God's suffering provide atonement? Moltmann never
offers a full answer, but it is clear that here, as for von Balthasar too, the
universalizing element is a universal vicarious representation. Moltmann
explicitly seeks to go beyond only solidarity, although that is the fundamental basis, to an atonement Christology in which Christ died 'for us',
based on a relational approach. It is not that our sins have to be made
good, but that we as sinners need to be justified and given back to life.[13]
Moltmann attempts various explanations of how this is possible. In *The
Crucified God* he speaks of the cross 'containing' all suffering, but this is
clearly metaphorical language which cannot be taken literally.[14] More
recently he turns to the image of God in Christ as the 'victim among victims', transforming sin into his own suffering. It is victims who forgive

and can testify to reconciliation with the perpetrators.[15] But once again Moltmann is not able to go beyond or behind the metaphorical language. We are thus faced with one of the abiding mysteries of Christian theology: how can Jesus' Godforsaken death be of vicarious benefit to the whole of humankind?

Jüngel attempts to understand the vicarious nature of Jesus' life and death by moving away from moral considerations into the very nature of being. Justification is therefore not about forgiveness, but about the proper definition of humanity and the proper distinction between humankind and God. 'To be justified means: for one's own good to be distinguished from God'.[16] Jüngel links this to God's identification with Jesus in his Godforsaken death, establishing a new relationship in the relationlessness of death. 'In so far as Jesus Christ is true Man, the truth of our humanity resides in him. And so in his person, as true man united to God, Jesus Christ constitutes our proper humanity'.[17] Jüngel offers an objective explanation of Jesus' vicarious death because our humanity is derived from the humanity of Christ, properly defined in its relationship to God. But the problem with Jüngel's account, as John Webster points out, is the very limited definition of sin and absence of any sense of forgiveness and reconciliation.[18] Unlike Moltmann it fails to tackle the reality of life as it is experienced by many, both the victims and perpetrators.

It will already be apparent that although they use metaphorical language which points toward a greater objectivity, Moltmann, Jüngel and von Balthasar are unable to explain the exact nature of the images they use. We are faced with the real possibility that we are not able to go beyond these metaphorical images to explain how Jesus' Godforsaken death accomplishes atonement with God. If God's attitude to us is not changed, as is envisaged in *penal* substitution – a notion all our theologians reject – then what is changed by Jesus' Godforsaken death? Undoubtedly I share the struggle that Moltmann and others face, but perhaps one clue may be to explore the way in which the context of our relationship to God is changed. Due to Jesus sharing our Godforsakenness to the point of death and being raised to life again, the stage on which we play out our lives, including our relationship with God, is different. Such a notion links naturally with the concept of covenant. The eucharistic language of the early Church understood the cup as a symbol of the new covenant effected through Jesus' death, fulfilling the Old Testament promises of a restoration of the broken covenant. This new covenant establishes right relations with God, as both Moltmann and Jüngel desire, but also takes seriously sin and the need for forgiveness. In Jesus' Godforsakenness God experiences and shares in the fundamental human situation of estrangement, that is of the broken covenant. That Jesus, in standing with humankind, experiences the silence of the Father is a profound indication of the very brokenness of this covenant. Yet in this brokenness the covenant is renewed.

First, by standing with Godforsaken humanity God affirms God's own commitment to creation, not leaving it in estrangement but sharing its predicament to the very depths. Second, in the midst of this brokenness Jesus still looks for God, in the essence of his cry, affirming the right judgement of God on sin, making an event which P. T. Forsyth described as 'The Great Confessional'.[19] Third, God responds to the confession of Jesus from within the brokenness of sin by raising him from the dead and renewing the relationship. Building on the insight that the cross and resurrection offer new experiences to God, of genuinely human suffering and of relating anew, the establishing of the new covenant offers a recreation of the human relationship with God based on this new encounter of God with creation. Such language again barely gets beyond the metaphorical, but this theme of a changed context may help us to connect our atonement with Jesus' Godforsakenness.

### 3. Transformation

Moltmann, Jüngel and von Balthasar also use language which speaks even more emotively of the transformation of this context in which the divine-human relationship occurs. Because of Jesus' experience on the cross Godforsakenness and hell are now places of encounter with God, where God is present.[20] Hell, Moltmann insists, is objectively transformed. 'If hell was the place of Godforsakenness, ever since Christ's descent into hell it has been this no more'.[21] Jüngel uses similar language in speaking of God's encounter with death. 'God kills death', not by leaving it behind, but by taking it into life, so that it becomes a

God-phenomenon.[22] Death is changed, so that it is no longer being (*Wesen*) but now only nuisance (*Unwesen*).[23] Such language is highly evocative and many may perceive its immediate existential relevance, but such language, when applied to our experiences, is also clearly metaphorical. What does it mean for God to kill death, for hell to be transformed by Jesus' Godforsaken death and even for Godforsakenness now to be a place of encounter with God?

Jüngel suggests that while death has become a phenomenon of God it still awaits the believer as a phenomenon of the world, although a kind of dying is also experienced now, demythologized of its power.[24] In other words, interpreting these particular metaphors of transformation requires the right balance between the present and the future. The universalizing element in Jesus' Godforsakenness is the *final* transformation, at the last, of death, hell and Godforsakenness. This implies not only that Jesus' death points towards an eschatological future, but also that this very future happens in the midst of history *in* Jesus' death and resurrection. Moltmann is right in stating that the scandalous element in the resurrection is that it was a Godforsaken man who was raised,[25] but the New Testament adds that Jesus was raised as the first fruits of all humanity.[26] Therefore, Moltmann suggests that because all human conflict is 'in' God, all feuds have an end.[27] We must make clear that not all feuds are ended yet, but there will be an end to all feuds in the new creation. It is the future which is changed, but we can use such language also of the present, for the eschaton is proleptically present in the death and resurrection of Jesus.

Exploring further our earlier notion of a change in context may help give greater clarity to this eschatological dimension of atonement. If the setting of a play were to be changed, then the whole play that follows is itself different. Using this analogy we might say that if the context of our lives is changed then for us too the future is different. This may also be a way of strengthening the language of solidarity we discussed earlier. By experiencing Godforsakenness in Jesus, God is changed, not in attitude towards us, but in experience of human suffering. By raising Jesus from the dead God has acted in human history to begin the eschatological transformation. In this way both Jesus' Godforsaken death and his resurrection have forged a new context in which we live with a different relationship with God.

We must further remember that Sölle protests against such a future-orientated and objective concept of salvation because it leads to an apathetic and 'honey-sweet' Christianity.[28] If God is going to change things in the future, then, she claims, this mitigates against acting in the present to overcome the Godforsaken hells which are the present experience of some. Sölle is right in as much as an emphasis on grace has been and can always be misunderstood, resulting in the failure to engage in the present situation of the world. But this is not automatically the case. One aspect of this new context in which we live is the creation of the church, arising out of Jesus' Godforsaken death and resurrection. The church as an institution has of course been fallible, creating suffering rather than protesting against it. But if God has acted in advance of the end in Jesus to transform the world, then the church's mission, arising from that eschatological event, is to continue this same transformation. When understood out of Jesus' Godforsakenness, grace stimulates solidarity, protest and transformation.

## 4. Conclusion

Jesus' Godforsaken cry is an essential element within God's atoning work. It reveals God's total solidarity with us to the very depths of estrangement, an experience which changes both God and us. On this basis we might tentatively speak of the changing of the context of our lives, renewing the covenant and beginning the transformation to be completed in the eschatological future. In response to this work of God's love the church is called to become a community of reconciliation in which solidarity, covenant relationship and transformation are all actualized and experienced. It is not that God, who is active in the whole world through the Spirit, is therefore limited to working through the church. Rather the community of God's people is assigned a particular role within God's mission. The experience of Godforsakenness on the cross which God overcame in the resurrection is to be a means of continual transformation within the life of God's people.

## Notes to Chapter 11

[1] Harry L. Chronis, 'The Torn Veil: Cultus and Christology in Mark 15:37-9', pp. 109-10.

[2] Moltmann, *The Power of the Powerless*, pp. 118-19.

[3] Moltmann, *The Spirit of Life*, p. 128.

[4] Sölle, *Suffering*, pp. 82, 85, 147; Sölle, *The Inward Road and the Way Back*, p. 101.

[5] Moltmann, *Jesus Christ for Today's World*, p. 56.

[6] Moltmann, *The Crucified God*, p. 277.

[7] See Fiddes, *Past Event and Present Salvation*, especially chs. 7 and 8 for a detailed development of this theme of the cross as an event that creates change.

[8] Sölle, *Christ the Representative*, p. 89. Barth himself, however, does not envisage a *penal* substitution.

[9] Ibid., p. 104.

[10] Ibid., p. 103.

[11] Moltmann, *The Spirit of Life*, p. 136. Such language is also Barthian. See Barth, *Church Dogmatics*, IV/1, p.59.

[12] Moltmann, *The Spirit of Life*, p. 137.

[13] Ibid., p. 136; Moltmann, *Jesus Christ for Today's World*, p. 42.

[14] Moltmann, *The Crucified God*, pp. 246, 255, 257. See Fiddes, *The Creative Suffering of God*, pp. 6-12, for a critique of Moltmann in this area.

[15] Moltmann, *Jesus Christ for Today's World*, pp. 41-42.

[16] Jüngel, *The Freedom of a Christian*, p. 26, quoted in Webster, *Eberhard Jüngel: An Introduction*, p. 91.

[17] Webster, *Eberhard Jüngel*, p. 102.

[18] Ibid., p. 91.

[19] P. T. Forsyth, *The Work of Christ: Lectures to Young Ministers*, (London: Independent Press, 1938).

[20] See, for example, Moltmann, *The Crucified God*, pp. 195, 276; von Balthasar, *The Glory of the Lord*, VII, p. 39 and *Theo-Drama*, V, pp. 312-14.

[21] Moltmann, *Jesus Christ for Today's World*, p. 66.

[22] Jüngel, 'Vom Tod des Lebendigen Gottes', p. 123.

[23] Ibid., p. 120.

[24] Ibid., p. 124.

[25] Moltmann, *The Crucified God*, p. 175.

[26] 1 Corinthians 15:23

[27] Moltmann, *The Future of Creation*, p. 66.

[28] Sölle, *Suffering*, pp. 128-30.

# 12
# Justice: Seeking Theodicy

Jesus' cry of forsakenness has no independent existence from the particular historical situation in which Jesus died, but can only be understood from within that context. As has already been made clear, forsakenness by God is linked in the Gospel narrative to Jesus' increasing solitude, abandoned by friends, authorities and the judicial system. Jesus cries to God, suffering innocently in the face of injustice. Therefore any interpretation of Jesus' cry must have at its heart these issues of suffering and injustice. Moltmann, we saw, expanded the traditional scope of atonement and began with Jesus' solidarity with the Godless and Godforsaken, effectively combining salvation and theodicy. But reflecting further on the latter, we must ask what Jesus' cry says to the many others who share similar experiences. As our opening chapter suggested, for these German theologians, of the post-war generation, Auschwitz is a fundamental background, and in the case of Moltmann and Sölle an explicit and constant point of reference. Any interpretation of Jesus' cry must therefore be able to be addressed to those who cried out in the concentration camps of the twentieth century.

For this reason both Moltmann and Sölle reject even the possibility of a traditional theoretical theodicy. The 'answer' offered by Jesus' cry will be of a completely different order, offering a narrative account of God's love and justice rather than seeking to justify God's omnipotence, love and comprehensibility. It is as a narrative that Jesus' cry can be told along side Elie Wiesel's account of the boy hanging on the gallows. It was there, we recall, that Wiesel heard a man asking the question, 'Where is God now?'. Kenneth Surin recognizes that in many ways this has become a test case for any writing on suffering: 'The real test of any theodicy – perhaps the *only* test – is: how is it going to answer this man? Or, perhaps more fundamentally: *can* it answer this man?'[1] The question, 'Where is God?', which Wiesel hears in the midst of the utter ambiguity of his faith, is really a searching after God. Very recently, reflecting again on the events of his youth, Wiesel insists that 'it is possible to be angry with God and still maintain some remnants of faith. I am looking for an answer to

the question I asked Him 50 years ago: Why?'[2] So the question 'where?'
leads us to a particular approach to theodicy – one which offers no complete answers, but passionately searches for God. Where is God in the
midst of the pain and suffering of the world? In *The Way of Jesus Christ*
Moltmann discusses six possible answers to this theodicy question which
arise from the sufferings of Christ: where was God on the cross? The first
three answers, that God hides his face, that God merely permits Jesus'
death and that God wishes Jesus to die in this way, are all dismissed as
not even being answers. Reflection on the final three answers will help us
in our search for a true understanding of God and suffering.[3]

### 1. A cry of pain

Jesus' cry 'My God, why have you forsaken me?' is fundamentally a cry
of pain. Abandoned by his own people, as represented by the Jewish leaders, forsaken by his friends and followers, Jesus faces the agony of death
alone, even without the closeness of his God and Father. And *where* is
God in the pain of the cross? Moltmann insists that *God himself was in
Christ* and that the cross points to the depth of divine suffering. 'Jesus'
weakness was God's weakness too; Jesus' suffering was God's suffering;
Jesus' death also meant his death for God his Father.'[4] Jesus' cry of forsakenness moves the theodicy discussion forward from its theoretical
impasse, and finds instead God sharing in the suffering of the creation. In
the Godforsakenness of Jesus, God shows himself to be with and for the
Godless and Godforsaken.

All four authors in differing ways explore this fundamental reality of
divine suffering. Even von Balthasar, who desires to maintain some
aspects of impassibility, recognizes the pastoral need for asserting that
God is able to share in our experiences. It is out of such pastoral concern
that he struggles and perseveres with the concept of 'something like suffering' in God within a lively impassibility. Yet the pressing issue of
theodicy focuses our attention more sharply still on the need for a more
precise explanation of divine suffering.

It is important that we envisage God to suffer genuinely, and that
means for suffering to be something that happens to God. Here Wiesel's
story most creatively opens up the meaning of the Gospel narrative. If

there can be any answer to Wiesel's searching question then there must be *some* analogy between God's experience of death in Jesus' cross and the hanging of the boy in the concentration camp. Building on our earlier arguments, this does not make God's experience entirely the same as the hanged boy's, for God is not a helpless victim, but rather recognizes a measure of passivity in God's own experience. It is here that Moltmann, Jüngel and von Balthasar have all been shown to struggle, placing too much emphasis on the suffering of God as a divine *activity*.

It is important too that we envisage God's sufferings to be genuinely divine, the aspect with which Sölle struggles most, concerned that an account of the particular suffering of God may overshadow and even justify the myriad experiences of human suffering. Yet, if it is the narrative of the particular death of Jesus of Nazareth which will be our response to the issue of theodicy, then this must be both a unique suffering of God, but one that is also universal in its significance. We can affirm that God has always been the suffering God, both constantly entering imaginatively into human suffering and also experiencing rejection by God's own created and elected people. Arising out of these universal experiences God endures the unique estrangement of the cross, it being divine incarnate suffering in a way in which God's empathizing with human suffering in general is not. If God's particular suffering on the cross can thus be described as a new experience, then God must experience all consequent suffering differently. There will, of course, be a significant measure of continuity between God's experience of pain and suffering before and after the cross, but the particular Godforsaken death of Jesus is of universal significance because within the similarity it affords God a new human experience of suffering.

We must resist the temptation to explain the uniqueness of the cross in terms of the depth of suffering involved, as if Jesus suffered more than any other. Such a claim is both impossible to verify as well as devaluing human suffering as Sölle feared. What does cause the cross to stand out from all other suffering is that it is divine incarnate suffering. And it is this very exclusivity of the cross that leads to a new inclusivity that takes seriously all other instances of human suffering. If God is changed by the encounter on the cross, then God relates to all suffering anew, not

justifying it or even overshadowing it, but upholding the dignity of the
sufferer by sharing more deeply their experiences.

A fundamental and vital response to the question of human suffering,
therefore, will be the narrative of the cross in which Jesus' cry of pain
points us to the suffering God. But simply using the language of suffering
does not in itself suffice. An essential element in a narrative theodicy will
be a clear account of divine suffering, so that God's pain can truly meet
with our pain. Such a notion must be built upon our previous discussion
of vulnerability. It is when God is recognized to be essentially vulnerable
that God's experience can be analogous enough to human suffering to be
termed suffering itself, while still being genuinely divine. Such suffering,
which flows from God's vulnerability and love, is also an integral aspect
of God's justice. It is not possible to go behind this creation in which we
exist, and ask whether the world could have been created without suffering or without the same level of suffering which we experience. But,
given the world as it is, God shows what justice means by sharing in the
risk involved in granting creation a measure of freedom. This does not
offer an explanation for suffering but asserts that God reveals divine justice by God's ongoing and vulnerable involvement in creation's life.

## 2. A cry of protest

Jesus' cry of forsakenness is also a cry for God, that God should do what
is right, and in this sense it is a cry of protest against what is happening on
the cross. We find in Moltmann a double understanding of protest. On the
one hand, suffering itself can be a protest, for a mysticism of the cross is
'already implicitly a protest against misery'[5] and the 'consciousness of
sorrow is a protest against suffering'.[6] On the other hand, Christ is 'the
protesting God involved in human sorrow and suffering.'[7] This corresponds to a second answer that Moltmann gives to the theodicy question,
that God also '*protests against Jesus' death*' by raising him from the dead.
Through the resurrection, God confutes Jesus' betrayers, judges and executioners.'[8] Therefore both Father and Son are united by this sense of
protest, which does not simply accept suffering as part of God's
inscrutable will, but seeks some change and resolution. Too many traditional theodicies were based upon a concept of God as the guardian of the

status quo and sought to justify suffering as somehow part of God's plan. Jesus' cry to his Father and the response of the resurrection do not accept that suffering is simply to be endured. Jesus' cry protests against the very experience of forsakenness.

The resurrection of Jesus is a demonstration that the injustice and forsakenness experienced on the cross does not have the last word and points us forward to the future resurrection when there will be an end to suffering.[9] Resurrection on its own cannot offer an adequate theodicy, but provides an eschatology that underpins Moltmann's wider theology, prompted by the question of God's righteousness. The belief in a general resurrection arose not out of a desire for eternal life for the individual and for good fortune, but out of a concern for God's righteousness. In a world where there is clearly injustice, does death set a limit on God's righteousness? Clearly this cannot be the case; resurrection 'thus represents a hope for God, for the sake of God and his right.'[10] The resurrection of Jesus departs from Jewish apocalyptic because it introduces a new righteousness of grace. 'The new and scandalous element in the Christian message of Easter was not that some man or other was raised, before anyone else, but that the one who was raised was this condemned, executed and forsaken man.'[11] The resurrection of the forsaken Jesus points to the end of suffering for those who are forsaken and alone and protests against present suffering in favour of God's future.

The claim that the cry of forsakenness and the resurrection of the crucified Christ combine in a double act of protest needs careful teasing out if it is not to remain somewhat contradictory. Jesus' cry is a cry to God. If the cross is God's predestined will then it makes little sense for Jesus' cry to be one of protest against what God has done, or, for that matter, the resurrection to be a protest against the cross. If Jesus is protesting against what seems to be an act of the Father, then in trinitarian terms there is a protest of God against God and a disunity of will. Equally, however, if the cross is understood as the result of God's vulnerable opening of the divine life to creation (as I have been advocating), then what sense can there be in a cry or act of protest against God's own trinitarian choice? An essential element in a narrative theodicy will be tracing the delicate balance between divine and human activity in the cross.

This is something, as we have seen repeatedly now, that Moltmann is unable to achieve. Despite those occasional glimpses of an understanding of vulnerability, that God 'voluntarily opens himself up to the possibility of being affected by another',[12] Moltmann still writes that 'the suffering of love is God's supreme work on God himself'.[13] Here Sölle's criticisms of an unextricated theological sadism are most telling, although Moltmann protests that this is undermined by his wider theological system. It is at this point that von Balthasar is also at his weakest, not only for allowing suffering to originate with God, but consciously seeking a positive explanation for even the most terrible suffering. There is in von Balthasar a much greater sense of justification of the present than any kind of protest on behalf of the future.

The Son does not protest against the action of the Father, as if the Father actively hands over an unwilling Son. The Father equally cannot be conceived as protesting in the resurrection against the cross, if the cross is to be understood as the Father's own decision to hand over the Son. Rather, it is God's will for Jesus to be on the path of love.[14] The cross is therefore *in* the will of God, since it is the consequence of love encountering sin, but not as a specific event, the direct predestined will of God. As such then both Jesus' cry and resurrection are protests, but against what is wrong in creation, namely sin. The Gospel writers remind us that Jesus was crucified between two criminals and that he died rejected and forsaken by those around him, stressing his solidarity with us, becoming one with sinful humanity, and it is on this basis that the New Testament can also speak of Jesus becoming sin and enduring God's curse.[15] God draws close to creation but humankind responds with the cross, a loud human 'no' against God. Borrowing words from Karl Barth, we can say that as God's representative before us, Jesus endures our 'no' to God; as our representative before God Jesus endures God's 'No' to us. This is why we must insist on such a careful explanation of human and divine action in the cross and resurrection. We must reject any notion that God specifically chooses to suffer, either masochistically as an inner-trinitarian choice or sadistically as the Father's choice for the Son. Instead the Gospel narrative reveals a God who out of love chooses to share the life of creation and accept the consequences of such vulnerability, which means we must avoid the language of Moltmann and von Balthasar in particular, which undermines this aspect of divine protest in favour of a divine justification of suffering.

The uniqueness of the cross is that Jesus hears the 'No' of humankind to God in the very act of crucifixion and the 'No' of God in the silence of the Father. Within the silence Jesus cries out, looking for God, protesting against the disruption of God's creation. The uniqueness of the resurrection is that God says 'Yes' to God, the Father affirming the sacrificial love of the Son, and God says 'Yes' to humankind in raising Jesus as representative of all. The resurrection thus echoes the cry, protesting against the disruption and promising a new creation. The Son's cry which looks for the Father in the silence, is answered by the resurrection as the Father looks for the Son. Such is God's concern for justice that Father and Son are united in protest against all the sin and evil experienced in creation.

### 3. A cry that is heard

In an earlier discussion we observed that Jesus' cry should not be interpreted in the light of the ending of Psalm 22, thus weakening the sense of desolation in the cross. Jesus' cry points us to a real disruption in the life of the Trinity caused by God's opening up God's own life to be affected by sin. But this is not the end of the story. The Gospel narrative shows that Jesus' cry does not stand in isolation, ignored and forgotten, but was heard and elicits a response, first from the centurion and then in the resurrection. Even though there are still some uncertainties about the interpretation of *huios* (whether 'a son' or 'the Son'), the centurion's response clearly challenges the conclusion that this was the death of a man completely forsaken and alone without God. Rather, Jesus' cry was heard and draws a response from the centurion which affirms God's presence in the suffering of Jesus and a response from God which protests against suffering caused by human sin.

The final step, then, moving beyond presence and protest is that the cross and resurrection is a transforming act in which God is at work, overcoming evil and suffering. This leads us to Moltmann's third answer to the theodicy question, which is that '*through the resurrection God turns the cross on Golgotha to good* for the betrayers, the judges and the executioners, Jews and Gentiles. Those who destroyed the living Christ by crucifixion are saved from their own final destruction by the cross of the risen Christ'.[16]

Moltmann, therefore, introduces into his interpretation of the cross an eschatological element when there *will be* an 'overcoming of the history of man's sorrow and the fulfilment of his history of hope'.[17] This eschatological resolution is possible for Moltmann because God not only shares our suffering but makes it God's own.

> Only if all disaster, forsakenness by God, absolute death, the infinite curse of damnation and sinking into nothingness is in God himself, is community with God eternal salvation, infinite joy, indestructible election and divine life.[18]

Moltmann seeks to take suffering with the utmost seriousness, for all suffering and evil is incorporated into the eternal life of God. Yet the problem for which Moltmann has been criticized is that such a scheme is in danger of ontologizing evil, giving it eternal being and reality, rather than overcoming it. In the context of justice it is the critique from liberation theology which is the most telling. So Leonardo Boff concludes:

> God has not undergone the cross in order to eternalize it and deprive us all of hope. On the contrary, God has assumed it because God means to put an end to all the crosses of history.[19]

Moltmann certainly points us in the right direction, for we cannot conceive of God as some 'deus ex machina' who has no part in the drama but finally appears to put things right. God must share in the weakness and pain of creation and in that way overcome suffering and turn things to the good. We are left, therefore, with a dilemma. If God does suffer eternally, thereby taking human suffering seriously, there is the danger that evil is eternalized. If, on the other hand, God does not suffer eternally, the significance of human suffering is downplayed and Sölle's fears become real. Such a position is also more open to Dostoevsky's protest, through his character Ivan Karamazov,[20] that this human suffering somehow becomes required for the eschatological joy. Kenneth Surin suggests a radical reinterpretation of Moltmann's theology, drawing a distinction between the immanent and economic Trinity and restricting the event of the cross to the latter.[21] Yet, despite Surin's claims to the contrary, this must drastically reduce the possibility of conceiving the genuine suffering of God.[22]

A more fruitful possibility is offered by the Gospel image, this time drawn from John, of the wounds of the risen Christ. Our third essential element in a narrative theodicy is, therefore, that God remembers all our experiences of suffering. The agonies of the victims of Auschwitz are not devalued because they are wiped out by a divine eraser, but they are actually taken up by God and remembered. God has put an end to all the crosses of history, but has not forgotten them. Although, for us, memory may seem a very weak notion, the remembering of God, drawn from the reality of the risen Christ's wounds, is a most profound image.[23] For God to remember necessitates a reality which has to do with being. In other words, God continues to suffer. But evil and sin are not eternalized or ontologized, although God remembers the past and all the suffering that has been caused by evil and sin. God is victorious over evil and sin in the cross and resurrection and they have no part in the new creation, but God takes the whole of our lives so seriously that even though sin is conquered, the memory of the suffering it caused leads to the continual suffering of God.

This remembering by God also links with a further aspect of God's suffering, the possible tragedy for God due to the ultimate rejection of divine love by human beings, something von Balthasar was so concerned to avoid. There can surely be no new rejection of God in the eschatological future, as there will be no new sin and evil, but the failure of some to respond to God's love and to realize their full value as human beings will also lead to the continual suffering of God and the possibility that God's hopes will be thwarted. Both divine compassion and divine loss imply that the divine eschatological joy has space for a continuing suffering. This must then affect the kind of 'heaven' that we picture and we hope for. If there is some sense in which God suffers, will it be entirely suffering-free for us? A sense of justice means that we should expect God to put things right, and so human suffering must be resolved, and our understanding of God means that there is nothing that will cause us suffering.

But if our lives are to have the highest value, then can what is past simply be forgotten by us?

We should then be open to the thought that the kind of relationship between God and creation for which we have been arguing implies that our human eschatological joy must also have space for some kind of continuing suffering. Revelation 21:4 certainly promises a new order of things, but one in which human memory and human hopes must have some real part. This highlights the importance of the terms *re*creation and *re*surrection. It is this present world which the future *re*deems, and it is through sharing intimately in its pain that God holds out the possibility of resurrection, a resurrection which transforms the past but does not obliterate it. Resurrection is always costly for God and it is a cost, which Moltmann rightly asserts, that God bears eternally. Such is God's involvement in the risk of creation that God demonstrates justice by remembering all of creation's history.

## 4. Conclusion

Building on Moltmann's own propositions we have identified three essential elements in a narrative theodicy: a clear account of divine suffering as genuine suffering; a proper understanding of the divine and human roles in the cross which point to a forceful divine protest against sin; a suggestion of divine memory which takes human suffering with the greatest seriousness without ontologizing evil and sin. In the strictest sense even such a compassionate theodicy does not answer the question Wiesel heard as he stood before the gallows. In the most profound way the only response possible is silence. But silence always contains space and in that space, alongside this cry of agony, God's protesting suffering can be heard. Important also is the fact that God's suffering is not finished and complete but continues both as God remembers and as God embraces the freedom of creation.

It is certainly true that even such a narrative account of theodicy must be judged by its ability to motivate human involvement in the practical response to the cause of human suffering. That God shares our suffering calls for a genuine human solidarity with those who suffer today, a concept so passionately explored by both Moltmann and Sölle. The need for a vulnerable church in response to a vulnerable God becomes concretely manifest in such solidarity. That God protests against suffering, forbids any human justification of suffering in the name of economic progress, international law or the like. A protesting God calls forth a protesting and so prophetic church. It is right that the church has been at the heart of the recent Jubilee Campaign to cancel third world debt. That God remembers the suffering history of the world means we too must not forget the victims, even when their own suffering is ended. The opening of the permanent British memorial and exhibition to the Holocaust is not only a laudable human project, it is a reflection of the divine life. Where is God? Hopefully in the midst of God's people, suffering, protesting and remembering.

## Notes to Chapter 12

[1] Kenneth Surin, *Theology and the Problem of Evil*, p. 117.

[2] Wiesel, quoted in *The Daily Telegraph*, 31 July 2000. See Wiesel's description of the ambiguity in his *All Rivers Run to the Sea* (London: Harper Collins, 1997), p. 84. Moltmann too more recently has recognized the ambiguity, in his book *God for a Secular Society: The Public Relevance of Theology,* trans. M. Kohl (London: SCM, 1997), pp. 179-80.

[3] Moltmann, *The Way of Jesus Christ*, p. 177.

[4] Ibid.

[5] Moltmann, *The Crucified* God, p 50. The phrase is actually quoted from Marx.

[6] Ibid., p. 225.

[7] Ibid., p. 226.

[8] Moltmann, *The Way of Jesus Christ*, p. 177 (italics mine).

[9] Ibid., pp. 175-6.

[10] Ibid., p. 174.

[11] Ibid., p. 175.

[12] Moltmann, *The Crucified God*, p. 230.

[13] Moltmann, *The Trinity and the Kingdom of God*, p. 99.

[14] See above.

[15] 2 Corinthians 5:21, Galatians 3:13.

[16] Moltmann, *The Way of Jesus Christ*, pp. 177-8 (italics mine).

[17] Ibid., p. 278.

[18] Moltmann, *The Crucified God*, p. 246.

[19] Boff, *Passion of Christ, Passion of the world*, p. 144. See Surin, *Theology and the Problem of Evil*, p. 130, for similar criticisms.

[20] Fyodor Dostoevsky, *The Brothers Karamazov*, transl. D. Magarshack (Harmondsworth: Penguin, 1958), pp. 286-7.

[21] Surin, *Theology and the Problem of Evil*, pp. 131-32.

[22] Here, see Fiddes' discussion, in his *The Creative Suffering of God*, pp. 112-23.

[23] Compare Wiesel's comment, *All Rivers Run to the Sea*, p. 150: 'What would man be without his capacity to remember? Memory is a passion no less powerful or pervasive than love'.

## Afterword

From our human perspective it is indeed strange that God should condescend to become human and that God's Son should die on the cross. Yet we have sought to show that far from being strange there is something entirely appropriate about God's suffering on the cross. In addition to the more common attribute of love, the God revealed by Jesus Christ is essentially vulnerable and just. The cross is therefore the greatest revelation of the God who is most divine in becoming human and most true to God's self in self-giving, and the deepest and most profound instance of this eternal nature. In many ways there is something particularly 'modern' about this conception, in that in recent years it has become a firmly established understanding of divine ontology. But we have also sought to show that this was also Mark's original insight. Expressed in narrative rather than dogmatic terms the earliest Gospel reaches its climactic point in Jesus' cry of dereliction, the tearing of the temple curtain and the confession of the centurion. The Word became flesh to the depths of accepting a Godforsaken death. The flesh now becomes Word, for it is the suffering and silence of Jesus on the cross which communicates the depths of God's eternal love. The response of the church must be, first, to stand with the centurion at the foot of the cross so that it too might recognise the true nature of God. Second, then, the church must live in such a way that the divine qualities of love, vulnerability and justice become incarnate in its worship and mission. Were this to be the case, Jesus' Godforsaken death would be seen to be anything but the strange ways of God.

# Index of Biblical References

# Index of Names and Subjects